THOMPSON
HIS LIFE AND LOCOMOTIVES

For my grandfather Albert Edward Graves (1885-1980).

Edward Thompson's life was shaped by the traumas of two world wars, first as a soldier in the trenches, then as Chief Mechanical Engineer with the LNER. He was part of a remarkable generation, but inevitably one deeply scarred by their experiences. Both my grandfathers also served in these wars with great distinction. When writing about Thompson I felt led by their words and memories when trying to understand what fighting, dying and killing for one's king and country in the 1914-18 war really meant. Towards the end of his life, Albert recalled with great honesty his three years on the Western Front, being wounded four times, gassed, the effects of constant shell fire and the appalling living conditions. Such had been its impact that he summed it up with the words, 'I still live the experience each day and dream about it each night. The smell of death has never left me.' For those 'who weren't there' the impact of war is almost impossible to understand. Yet they were expected to return to the civilian world and take up the reins of their lives as though nothing had happened. It is, perhaps, of small wonder that they and this existence didn't sit happily together and for some, including Thompson, the re-adjustment proved a harsh and bruising experience.

THOMPSON
HIS LIFE AND LOCOMOTIVES

Tim Hillier-Graves

PEN & SWORD
TRANSPORT

AN IMPRINT OF PEN & SWORD BOOKS LTD.
YORKSHIRE – PHILADELPHIA

First published in Great Britain in 2021 by
Pen and Sword Transport

An imprint of
Pen & Sword Books Ltd
Yorkshire - Philadelphia

ISBN 978 1 52673 116 6

A CIP catalogue record for this book is
available from the British Library.

Typeset by SJmagic DESIGN SERVICES, India.
Printed and bound in India by Replika Press Pvt. Ltd.

Pen & Sword Books Ltd incorporates the Imprints of Pen & Sword
Books Archaeology, Atlas, Aviation, Battleground, Discovery, Family History,
History, Maritime, Military, Naval, Politics, Railways, Select, Transport,
True Crime, Fiction, Frontline Books, Leo Cooper, Praetorian Press,
Seaforth Publishing, Wharncliffe and White Owl.

For a complete list of Pen & Sword titles please contact
PEN & SWORD BOOKS LIMITED
47 Church Street, Barnsley, South Yorkshire, S70 2AS, England
E-mail: enquiries@pen-and-sword.co.uk
Website: www.pen-and-sword.co.uk

or

PEN AND SWORD BOOKS
1950 Lawrence Rd, Havertown, PA 19083, USA
E-mail: Uspen-and-sword@casematepublishers.com
Website: www.penandswordbooks.com

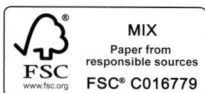

FSC
www.fsc.org

MIX
Paper from
responsible sources
FSC® C016779

CONTENTS

INTRODUCTION

The B1 4-6-0, thought by many to be Edward Thompson's most successful design. (*PR/RH*)

Over lunch in Salisbury, 100 yards from the novichok incident three days earlier, John Scott-Morgan, Pen and Sword's Commissioning Editor, and I discussed future projects. Being stoical Brits we, of course, took these things in our stride and ignored the many policeman and people shrouded in protective clothing hovering around and tucked into large plates of fish and chips. I had just finished a trilogy of books about the LMS, focussing on Turbomotive, the Princess Royals and Tom Coleman, the company's talented but long forgotten Chief Designer. We talked about the LNER and John suggested that Edward Thompson might be a worthy subject for me to pursue – his life and work being long overdue for re-assessment. My first reaction was 'not him!'; he tried to destroy Gresley's legacy and has, in many people's eyes, become a pariah for doing so. Our conversation then turned to attempts made to resurrect his reputation, most notably by Peter Grafton in his admirable biography of the man. But despite these brave efforts, poor Thompson remains an outcast of whom the worst is always thought or suspected.

Quick as a flash, and fearing for my sanity, I suggested writing about Gresley and then Peppercorn. So we struck a deal and a trilogy was born – all three men, a volume each, but interlinked to show cause and effect and bring into play the teams that supported their great endeavours along the way. And to round off the story, there will be a fourth volume that takes the story of the locomotives they led in developing up to the end of steam in Britain to see how they fared under BR.

Once this project had begun, it soon became apparent that all three men were rarely masters of their own destiny. So time, place, circumstances, and the random chance of fate had to be woven into this tale. It is here that many issues that coloured events and relationships had their origins and where explanations might lie. As my research deepened and explanations were forthcoming, I came to see all three men in a new light and my respect for them deepened. Yet what surprised me most, as many facts gradually emerged, was my reaction to Thompson. I came to see him as a man of greater substance, in peace and war, than I had suspected existed. Whilst it isn't essential that a writer should like their subject, it soon became clear that I did; not in a sycophantic way, but as someone with wide experience of life and, hopefully, able to judge complex matters fairly.

This led me to consider the complicated dynamics that existed between Gresley, Thompson and Peppercorn and their respective teams and how their relationships effected events and outcomes.

In assessing these issues for this book, the first stumbling block to progress I found was Thompson's own apparent lack of words on many important issues. It seems that he was loath to commit any thoughts to paper, although in mid-1930 he did write a history of the world when his wife suffered serious illness. I haven't had the privilege of reading it, but it is said that the manuscript is erudite and well written, as befits a graduate of Marlborough and Cambridge. Luckily though, some things have survived to cast new light on his life and work, some he wrote himself, though not with the aim of publication or self-justification. These have come from many sources, some known but not tapped and others that survived in the hands of individuals who may not have understood their significance when seen in isolation.

In the absence of words from Thompson, and most of his contemporaries for that matter, opinion on his career appears to have been formed by later authors who weren't party to these events, the true history, the politics and the reality. They seem to be writers who slipped far too easily into the 'Gresley – good, Thompson – bad' mind set, often basing opinion on conjecture or dubious truths. This was nowhere more apparent than when they described Thompson's dealings with Bert Spencer, Gresley's faithful, dedicated and talented technical assistant. The account that was pedalled as 'true', asserted that Thompson, in a move motivated by spite, made an outcast of Spencer and it was Peppercorn who restored him and his reputation. The reality, as this book reveals, couldn't have been more different, as Spencer, and files held by the NRM and papers in private hands, later confirmed.

Accounts of Thompson's life almost exclusively focus on locomotive design and construction as though this was the be all and end all of a Chief Mechanical Engineer's life. In reality it was only one part of their task, which in wartime was soon swept aside by more pressing demands. Here Thompson's commitment and achievements were largely ignored by earlier historians as though the excessive demands of war weren't important. They still held to the view he was some sort of 'pantomime villain' creeping

One of Thompson's cardinal sins, or so some think, was the conversion of Gresley's 2-8-2 P2s into a Pacific A2/2 during the war years. Here engine No. 60501, *Cock o' the North*, is seen passing through Leeds with the northbound *Queen of Scots* Pullman in 1957. With two new P2s due to enter the preservation movement, the debate over Thompson's actions are likely to find a second wind. My opinion – I like the originals in both states of streamlining but I also find the rebuilds attractive. In many ways Thompson and his draughtsmen turned them into a more traditional Gresley/LNER form. *(PR/RH)*

across the stage deviously planning the demise of Gresley's legacy. It is a wonder that they didn't add a moustache he could twirl, a large black coat and a damsel he could tie to the railway track, such was their apparent bias.

Once I'd read all these accounts, consumed Peter Grafton's astute and erudite book and researched other previously untapped sources, it seemed that John Scott-Morgan's belief that the time was right for a fresh assessment held water and here is the result. Will be it be the last word on the subject? Of course not, because more information may be uncovered that might shed new light on Gresley, Thompson, Peppercorn and the rest. Here I have had odd hints of what else may lie out there. For example, I was allowed to see, but not quote, correspondence between William Stanier and Thompson from the 1930s until the 1950s held by a fellow historian. The tone of these letters, two of which have already

been quoted in other books, is warm and considerate. They also offer an interesting glimpse of their developing relationship, both professional and personal. Each praises the other and, in doing so, reveals how much common ground existed between them.

In writing this book I was given much help by staff at the National Railway Museum and many other people, to whom I give my thanks. In particular I must mention Richard Hardy, who knew some of the key characters described in this book and was very open, balanced and honest in his assessment. Then there is my old friend David Neal. In the fifties and sixties, when so much was being destroyed, David collected many unique items relating to the LNER, including a number of Edward Thompson's albums and papers. He sent me copies of these and gave me permission to use them as I saw fit. To this can be added the efforts of my late uncle, Ronald Hillier. He spent nearly forty years doing the same thing

Thompson's last contribution to the LNER and to railway history. A2/3 No. 500 *Edward Thompson* which appeared days before his retirement in 1946. (*PR/RH*)

as David and continued seeking material up to his death in 1984. He also met or corresponded with many who were part of the LNER's history and could add interesting details to the story. Sadly, this didn't include either Thompson or Peppercorn, but, by luck, did harness Bert Spencer's thoughts on some matters. In due course everything my uncle and I have collected will be donated to Search Engine at York so that others can make use of this archive of material.

In producing photographs for this book some preservation work has been necessary. In some cases their sepia finish, foxing and dilapidated condition could not be entirely overcome. However, because they are often rare pictures or have some historic significance they have been included despite their condition. I hope this doesn't spoil your enjoyment of this book.

PROLOGUE: ACCIDENT OF TIME

Thompson's Class A2/3 Pacifics. Elegant and efficient to some, ugly and ineffective to others. Retrospective views on the man and his work are equally divided. (*PR*)

Whoever first coined the phrase 'timing is everything' may have done so in the sure knowledge of their own success or failure. It can be an excuse or words of modest self-congratulation. Either way, it is a measure of achievement that can only truly be viewed in hindsight when all outcomes are known. But as an axiom, it holds many grains of truth and these are reflected in the life and career of Edward Thompson.

Despite a privileged upbringing and education, plus many inherent skills as a manager and engineer, he seemed destined to be a deputy and never know the satisfaction of being top man in his chosen profession. When chance finally ran in his favour and Gresley, his leader, died in 1941, Thompson stepped up only to find that with war raging, his opportunities were strictly limited and any design ambitions he may have had were unlikely to be fulfilled. Perhaps he didn't mind; after all, he was noted for having a strong sense of duty. Even so, he must have looked around and wondered what might have been if Gresley had retired years earlier, when illness had first begun to show itself and its effects were slowly becoming only too apparent.

It wasn't to be and Thompson, at 60, had to accept that his engineering credentials were unlikely to be improved by being CME at such a time.

Thompson also seems to have been someone history has treated harshly. Anyone who follows a man or woman who has enjoyed greatness and huge success, will always be dogged by fair or unfair comparisons. This is especially true when that person has been feted to the heights and achieved legendary status in the process. Whatever the successor does it will invariably be over shadowed by what has gone before. Who would have wished to replace Winston Churchill and Franklin D. Roosevelt in 1945 or, for that matter, Alex Ferguson at Manchester United in 2013? The engineering world was no different with Brunel, Churchward, Stanier and Gresley standing head and shoulders above the rest, with those who followed inheriting the poisoned chalice of great expectations. In these cases, any slip-up will be marked as a huge failure, made worse if that person seeks to re-model the work of the master who has gone before. Thompson had the temerity to commit this cardinal sin.

410 of Thompson's B1s were built between 1942 and 1952, with the last surviving in service until 1967. (*THG*)

To attempt this, you have to be supremely skilled, self-confident and sure that change is essential. Otherwise, any actions are seen to be merely the whim of a pedant who has to tinker unnecessarily. Here Thompson appears to be guilty as charged, with his reputation suffering as a result. At worst, he was thought to be the man who took Gresley's swans and turned them into ugly ducklings. At best, a mediocre designer seeking to compare himself with one of the greats. As always, the truth lies somewhere else, but to find it means wading through a sea of opinion, some poorly based, and information which is often meagre to say the least. If we are to judge Thompson, we must try to understand the person and the times in which he lived. To do otherwise is unfair and disingenuous,

because these judgements are often based on pre-conceived views or prejudices that should play no part in rational thought or meaningful assessments. Thompson deserves far better than this, even though it might mean questioning some of Gresley's ideas and elements of his legacy.

Time has also added many layers to the Gresley / Thompson debate that focus on their relationship. Whether founded on evidence or myth is now difficult to fathom at times, but a picture of mutual antipathy has been suggested, which if true does neither man any credit. To try and gauge the legitimacy of these assessments, we have to strip away layers of 'evidence' to try and establish where the truth might lie, a process made more difficult because all the

Thompson's Class L1 2-6-4T introduced in 1945. One hundred would be built by 1950. (*BR/RH*)

key players are long gone, and most were very reticent about expressing themselves when alive. Yet to understand why Thompson took the actions he did it is important to evaluate all these factors.

In many ways, it is an analysis made more difficult by contradictory views of the man's nature. Accounts that survive do not always tally up. He is described by some as ruthless, unapproachable, unfriendly, humourless, austere, cutting, unbending and a martinet, none of which are particularly endearing qualities, though quite useful for a senior manager, especially during war. Yet to others he was warm, generous, polite, courteous, reserved to the point of shyness, possessing a wry sense of humour and a self-deprecating manner. Here again we come up against the giant shadow cast by Gresley, who mixed easily and had an immense, outgoing personality and

bred obedience by sheer force of personality, not as an exercise in harsh authority.

In some ways, it seems to me, we can only see Thompson clearly if we take Gresley out of the equation, as much as that is possible, to isolate and describe his successor's life and work. For, despite the many criticisms, Thompson was an able leader and a good engineer. He wasn't Gresley's equal as a designer but that privilege would fall to very few, yet even he wasn't perfect and could, at times, pursue an idea beyond the point of any realistic return on an investment.

So, to understand Thompson and place his achievements in perspective many views have to be put to one side allowing the story to develop in such a way that he is seen as an individual, not as an heir or as a substitute, but as his own man.

Gresley's pioneering A1 Pacific, *Great Northern*, as rebuilt when Thompson was CME, caught in BR days. (*THG*)

CHAPTER 1

BIRTH-RIGHT

WILLS'S CIGARETTES.

VIRTUTE LUDO. STUDIO

SCHOOL ARMS.

MARLBOROUGH COLLEGE.

Wills's Cigarettes.

Arms of

Pembroke College,

Cambridge University.

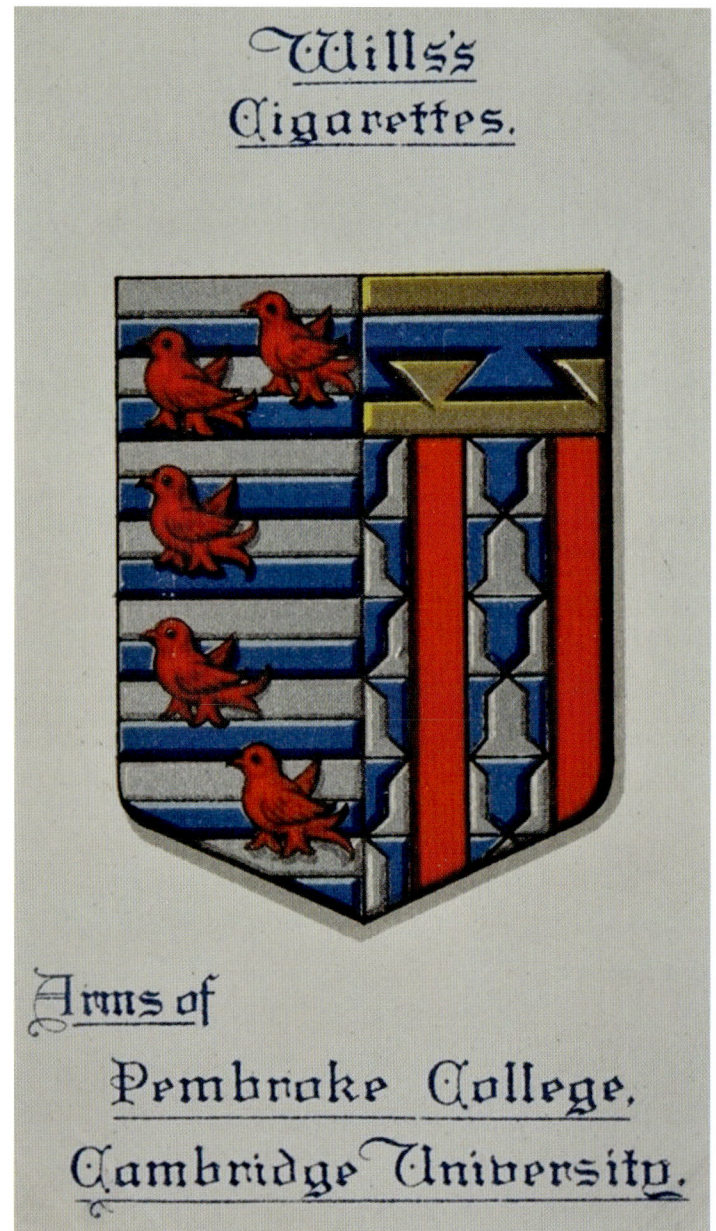

This story begins on a midsummer's night during 1881 with the birth of a boy at his parents' lodgings within Marlborough College, attended by the college Medical Officer, Dr Walter Fergus, and a privately employed nurse.

Edward's father, Francis, was an assistant master having been recruited aged 25 in 1859 by the Reverend George Bradley. By 1869, he had established his position in the hierarchy of the college and married Margaret Powell, late of Bloomsbury in London, and brought her to Wiltshire to live in his rooms there.

In 1870, after much criticism of accommodation at the college, a building programme was set in motion and the architect George Street employed to oversee the design and construction of two new houses. Funding for such a major programme was a key issue and two masters, James Gilmore and Thompson, contributed half the cost of each building and were appointed the House Masters of Littlefield and Cotton House respectively when completed.

Thompson's contribution amounted to £2,500, (a substantial sum at the time) and probably came to him when his father died in 1871, leaving a disposable estate of £12,000. Such a large legacy reflected a family background of some affluence by the standards of the age and also created an income from fees for Francis to collect which supplemented his teaching pay.

It has often been said that Edward was descended from Francis Thompson the noted Victorian architect, who was born in 1808, married three times and spent a great deal of his life in Canada. In a career of some note, he worked closely with George and Robert Stephenson in designing many railway structures. Edward's grandfather was, in fact, a quite different person. This Francis was born during May 1794 in Dartmouth to Thomas and Maria Thompson (Bolsover), who had married three months earlier. Francis married only once, to Louisa Ward. He was an 'Army Clothier' by trade and then developed a tailoring business in the East End of London at Pennyfields. This proved so successful that he opened other shops, one of these being in 11 Conduit Street, just off Saville Row and Regent Street. In time his eldest son, Reginald, managed this establishment, which, at its height, employed nineteen men. With such a prestigious central London address, his business went from strength to strength and this allowed him to have his three children educated privately, his second son, Francis, then going on to Worcester College Oxford, where he read Classics before entering the teaching profession.

Victorian society was one of caste, where the gulf between poor and rich was enormous and little equality existed. For most, the simple act of survival was all they could hope for, with no welfare net to protect those who failed. But it was also an age with a growing, aspirational middle class. Skilled workers and entrepreneurs, by dint

Marlborough College in the late nineteenth century when Edward Thompson was first a resident then a pupil. (*THG*)

Cotton House (left) and Littlefield shortly after construction. Today such properties would each cost more than a £1m to build, so demonstrating the size of Francis Thompson's investment. The young Edward and his sisters would grow up here, attended by servants. (*THG*)

Thompson, the tailor and outfitters, circulated these tokens to advertise their products, to be surrendered to obtain a discount on the next purchase. (*THG*)

of their own efforts, could improve their lives beyond the norm, acquiring status and property along the way. However, one social division would remain between those whose advancement came from 'being in trade' and those of 'old wealth', which seemed to establish a superior birth-right. It was a division best defined by the words 'nouveau riche' and the overtones of snobbery and superiority this suggests. It was this world that the Thompson family inhab-ited and which Francis faced at Oxford, then experienced in the well-heeled world of Marlborough with Margaret and their children. In cases such as this, acceptance often hinged on the suggestion of some important family connec-tion, which in a world suffering endemic social pretentions and posturing is understandable. Today these differences in society still echo, but in the late nineteenth century, and throughout Edward's life, they resonated loudly and undoubtedly affected his life and character, especially as he was a teacher's child. In the circumstances reserve and diffidence were traits to be practiced at all times.

Thought to be Edward Thompson's paternal grandfather Francis who was born in Devon and later moved to London where he set up a successful tailoring business. This photo, which is included in one of Edward's albums, was taken in about 1870, not long before his grandfather's death on 6 November 1871. (*ET/DN*)

Marlborough's Common Room in the late 1870s with Francis Thompson in the back row on the extreme right. (*THG*)

With security of tenure assured, Francis and Margaret prepared to raise their family in the pleasantly cloistered and protected halls of Marlborough. Edward, who was born on 25 June 1881, was the fourth and last of their children. His three siblings were all girls – Margaret, Elizabeth and Katherine – and it is said that he was very close to them all, remaining so for the rest of his life.

Their early years were probably pleasant enough in such wonderful surroundings, though their behaviour would clearly have had to be moderated in respect of

Margaret with two of her children in about 1883. Edward is said to be sitting on her lap. If so, he is dressed in the fashionable style for the age, where small boys wore smocks and their hair was allowed to grow long. This all changed at about the age of four or five when hair was cropped and dress more usually associated with a boy was adopted. In most photographs taken throughout his life Edward appears unsmiling and austere in outlook as portrayed here. Shyness and inbred reserve were often the cause. (*ET/DN*)

their father's position in the school. With his role as House Master, having responsibility for a large number of boys, the family must have been fully involved in the day to day business of education and the pastoral care of those children away from their homes. In such an environment, each day must have been full of interest for enquiring young minds. But the college could not provide education for the Thompson children and it appears that they were privately tutored by a governess, though undoubtedly with the support of their father and other teachers at the college. For Edward, this sheltered existence lasted until the age of eight when he became a boarder for six years at St David's Prep School in Reigate, Surrey.

To tear such a young child away from his family to face the unknown is, by any standards, harsh. This was especially so in the late nineteenth century when attitudes towards children were overridden by a system of ill-enforced discipline and cruelty justified by the crude, inadequate maxim 'spare the rod and spoil the child'. It is sobering to learn that Marlborough's head master until 1876, Frederick Farrar, although noted for implementing contemporary teaching methods and being a sympathetic man, gained the distasteful soubriquet 'Mr Thwackham of Marlborough'. Although he wasn't thought to be a sadistic person or a poor head, his propensity for flogging suggests an accepted standard in schools of that time. Teaching staff would, undoubtedly, have inflicted even more levels of violence, as would prefects and others in authority. To be a pupil away from home at such a young age would have been to face a life of hardship, cruelty and lack of affection. It was hardly surprising that school photos of the time contained few smiling children.

Although 'Thwackham' Farrar was long gone by the time Edward was born, many ideas he set in motion would have a profound effect on teaching methods and the range of subjects taught at the college. His criticism of a system that focussed exclusively on classical antiquity – the history, philosophy, literature and archeology of the Greco-Roman world – was deep and profound. In 1869 he wrote:

'A small boy of eight or nine would be terrified with such incubi and succubi as "quid-quale", "gerundive attractions", "subolique clauses", "spirants".… And I know not what. A public school curriculum was exclusively designed to fit boys for an academic future at university, where some 25 per cent might go. Even these boys had been taught in ways which produced parrot-like repetition and sing-song knowledge, to the abeyance and destruction of intellectual powers.'

Though loath to discard the classics entirely, he wished to expand the curriculum to include more modern subjects, but particularly the sciences. It was during his tenure that Marlborough began to adopt this wider view of education, with his successor, George Charles Bell,

taking these reforms still further before he departed in 1903. How Francis Thompson viewed these changes is unclear, but as a classics scholar and teacher he may have been less than an enthusiastic supporter. To him, it would have seemed as though the Philistines were at the gates and may account for his son feeling throughout his life that he may have been a disappointment to his father by becoming an engineer. Such are the pressures that children of ambitious parents can suffer, even though their lives often prove of greater substance than their forebears. It also suggests the extent of parental pressure he faced and strength of character he had to

Marlborough's two headmasters whose work would profoundly affect the lives and careers of many young men including the young Edward Thompson and Herbert Nigel Gresley. Frederick Farrar (left) and George Bell (whose time at Marlborough ran parallel with Thompson's association with the college, as the child of a master and as a pupil). (*ET/DN*)

display in following his chosen star. Nevertheless, a fear remained with him throughout his life that he had failed his father, which is a burden no child should face.

No records seem to have survived from Thompson's time at school in Surrey, but his education, learnt 'parrot fashion' or not, would have focussed on reading, writing, arithmetic, sport as well as the classics. His interest in the sciences may even have been stimulated by his time there, though the work he undertook would have been of the most basic type. By all accounts, he was an occasional reader with a leaning towards science and engineering, so there was probably a strong element of self-teaching in his studies. Did this draw him towards the railways, which played a significant part in Victorian life and were part of his own world? Reigate and Redhill were served by the South Eastern Railway and his journeys to and from school would have seen him regularly traverse this line to London and then the route from Paddington to Marlborough. On the SER, many of James Stirling's locomotives held sway at the time, particularly his very numerous O Class 0-6-0 tender engines and

Q Class 0-4-4Ts. Then there was the Great Western Railway with its rapidly diminishing broad gauge system still in place. By 1892 work on conversion to the 4ft 8½in. scale was complete and the sidings around the Swindon Works contained many withdrawn locomotives. All this would have been a very familiar sight to Thompson and probably something of interest to him.

By 1895, with his time at Reigate fast drawing to a close, the question of future education came to the fore. It seems that his father strongly advocated a university education and believed that preparation for this would be best accomplished by a period of study at Marlborough itself. With his retirement from teaching imminent that year, though not his business interest in Cotton House, Edward's return to the college as a student was set. For the next four years, as part of Littlefield House under Henry Richardson, he studied a wide range of subjects within the college's broader and now heavily modified curriculum. Though the classics hadn't disappeared, their dominating presence no longer pervaded the lives of these young men, though some elements remained central to their education.

The unavoidable and impressive sight of discarded locomotives at Swindon in the early 1890s and one Thompson witnessed regularly as the GWR converted its system to 4ft 8½in gauge. Before the changeover, Thompson would no doubt have travelled on the wider gauge stock when commuting to school in Surrey. (*RH*)

Littlefield House in 1899. The Housemaster, Henry Richardson, sits centrally in the second row with Edward to the left. More often than not Richardson was accompanied by his pet dog 'Bandy', who appears to be absent on this occasion. (*ET/DN*)

In many ways, Richardson was the perfect person to lead Edward through this crucial stage in his life. He was a graduate of Corpus Christi College, Oxford, and seems to have possessed great wisdom and a very deep understanding of children's needs. But, more importantly, he was a moderniser who believed in the importance of science and used the facilities at Marlborough to encourage his students to develop talents in these fields. When he arrived in 1870, the college had an active Natural History Society in which boys were expected to, 'devote themselves zealously to scientific observations and accumulate and publish scientific knowledge'. However, by 1880 its membership had dwindled to a mere seventeen boys and Richardson became its president in a bid to

instil new life into its fading ambitions. This he did until relinquishing the post in 1886 to be replaced by Thomas Hart-Smith, then Edward Meyrick in 1889, who both continued the good work expanding the range of subjects along the way.

By the time Thompson returned to the college, membership had grown to 240 boys of all ages and embraced a wider range of sciences, both natural and mechanical. In this guise, it encouraged a wide programme of study by experimentation and observation. Having begun to display an interest in science, Edward soon became an enthusiastic member of the society. In this he was encouraged by Richardson, who may also have helped deflect any concerns his father expressed about the direction his son's education was going, though he was now retired and living at 16 Primrose Hill Road in London. As fellow masters, there would have been close contact on many issues and, inevitably, Edward's progress would have featured large in these discussions.

Field trips were a constant feature of College life and this included several visits to the GWR's Swindon Works, which Thompson attended, according to the records that have survived. What he saw is not hard to guess. What is less certain is the impact this had on his interests and choice of career. He remained mute on this point, but later told Bert Spencer, Gresley's technical assistant, that he and Gresley were both impressed by all that happened at Swindon, particularly under George Churchward. From this one might guess that the impact might have been significant.

Although both attended Marlborough, it is unclear whether Thompson and Gresley knew each other at that time. There was a five-year gap in age between them and Gresley spent only three years at the college – 1890 to 1893 – and this when Thompson was away at school in Surrey. So anything more than a passing awareness is unlikely.

Gresley was in B1 House, whilst Thompson, as a child, lived in Cotton House, and by the time he was a student, the older boy had already departed for Crewe and an apprenticeship there. So when they were worked together, many years later, there may have been a loose bond created by a shared school but nothing more substantial than that; if antipathy did develop between them it is unlikely to have found its cause here. However, there is the more prosaic question of birth-right to consider and this can sometimes cause resentment or constraint to form. Gresley had links to nobility, whilst Thompson's origins were 'in trade'. These things mattered so much more then in a country formed on subservience and lack of equality, but did it create a stumbling block between these two ambitious men? One can only say 'possibly' if a sense of rivalry genuinely existed.

Marlborough. Showing the G.W.R. Station on the left, and M. & S.W.J. Station on the right.

On the opening of the G.W.R. from Marlborough to Savernake, all the great people of the neighbourhood were on the train, and the event was probably too much for the engine, as it failed in its first effort to climb the incline, and it is related that a dog running alongside, reached Savernake before its master

Marlborough was served by two lines and two stations during Thompson's time at college there and would have featured in his travels and may have helped focus his growing interest in engineering. (*THG*)

What might have been of greater concern could have been the question of academic achievement. Neither man shone at school and only demonstrated average potential across a range of subjects. But Gresley, with a father whose health was failing fast, chose to begin a long and hard engineering apprenticeship rather than go to university and avoid being a drain on his father's diminishing resources. Thompson, as we shall see, had no such restriction and went to university. However, following this higher academic route may have raised an expectation that emerging sciences might absorb him when qualified. If so, steam's aging technology, though providing sound employment, wasn't likely to fulfil any scientific ambitions he may have had.

His four years at Marlborough seem to have been a fairly positive time, perhaps because his father was no longer a daily presence setting standards that his son would strive towards and, perhaps, not hope to achieve. St David's School must have prepared him for this by helping him develop a sense of self sufficiency and independence. And now he could grow to maturity with parental influence muted by distance, in term time anyway, and seek to become his 'own man'.

He must have made his intentions clear very early in his time at Marlborough, because he was streamed into the Engineering Class, which was overseen by the Reverend Robert Crowther Abbott, a science graduate of Trinity College, Cambridge. As the years passed, the focus of his education became more refined with physics, chemistry and mathematics dominating his work. But in a busy curriculum, time was also found for Divinity, German,

ENGINEERING CLASS (21).
REV. R. C. ABBOTT.

Initials of Housemaster.	Order, by Form work and Examination.	Initials of Housemaster.	Order, by Form-work and Examination.
W.H.M.²	Davison, A. (A D)	F.B M.	Lane, C.M.
J.R.T.	lsMaxwell, G.H. (BCD)	R.C.A.	Walker, H.W.
P.W.T.	Jackson, L.E.S.	F.B.M.	Wilson, H.I.
R.A.	Mitchell, R.F	W.H.M.²	Spence, H.B.
W.H.M.²	Lumby, W.D.R.	P.W.T.	Parker, W.H.
H.S.	Owen, W.E D.	H.R.	Thompson, E.
H.R.	Wright, F.W.	H.R.	Jonas, R.C.
P.W.T.	§Freeman, H.A.	P.W.T.	Greener, H.
P.W.T.	Franklin-Adams, B.I.	F.B.M.	Douglas, C.H.
P.W.T.	Mitchell, A.H.	P.W.T.	Bone, A.F.
R.C.A.	Mann, P.R.		

(A) Form Prize.

(B) Divinity and History Prize.   (C) Mathematical Prize of M Division.

(D) Science Prize.   (E) Dutton Prize for French.

(F) Dutton Prize for German.

§ Foundation Scholar.

Exam results published in 1899. Although finishing in a lowly position, Thompson did at least matriculate and would be far more successful than any of his classmates during his career, although a number of them did have their lives cut short by service in the Great War.

French, Latin, History, English and Geography to ensure a well-rounded education. Edward may have found this a distraction though, because all his final grades were poor. In the key areas he came 19th out of 20 in Physics and 16th out of 19 in Chemistry, and taking all marks into account was rated 17th in the Engineering Class of 21, which was hardly a ringing endorsement of his skills. However, only four of his class went to university and three eventually became engineers of one sort or another, most others joining the Army, the Indian Civil Service or the clergy.

In many ways, the members of this group reflected the way their class was absorbed into careers open to the more privileged in society. Not for them learning a trade, a very lowly military rank or the basest of work with the ever present threat of poverty and the workhouse, but a degree of comfort and affluence no matter what they did or how little they worked.

Another reason for his lack of academic success is suggested by his sporting activities, which seem to have absorbed him since going away to school in 1889. Boys in public schools at the time were known to slip into two distinct groups – 'bloods' or 'scholars'. With his love of cricket, athletics, rugby and more, Thompson fell into the first category. In many ways, part of this creed was to look down upon those who preferred to keep their noses in books. Whilst sport helps to develop many admirable qualities, it can be a distraction from the main purpose of education and may have proved so in Edward's case. In his last term, for example, when crucial exams were pending, he turned out for the college's first eleven in cricket on many occasions and fully involved himself in athletics

He was also known to have become absorbed by photography in his last two years at Marlborough, witnessed by six albums that are known to have survived in public and private hands. This was an interest actively encouraged at Marlborough, especially when linked to the Natural History Society. Could this have been something else that distracted him from his school work? If so,

A photo from one of Thompson's albums. Time and photographer aren't known, though the station is Sutton Coldfield at around the turn of the century. Many of his pictures seem to focus on general views like this, rather than specific things such as locomotives or carriages, and most do contain a strong human element. (*ET/DN*)

many of the pictures he took or collected had a railway theme, suggesting a developing interest in this subject, though perhaps not a passion for its technical intricacies yet.

Although successfully matriculating, Francis Thompson's reaction to his son's tepid results are not recorded, though it is a safe assumption that Edward's future was a hot topic at the time. As a moneyed family, however, university doors could be opened and a place was found for him at Pembroke College, Cambridge. The choice of subject may have proved a difficult one to resolve. With no apparent love of classics and a mediocre performance in other subjects, there was no obvious choice for study at such an advanced level. But with Pembroke's strong reputation for science, and Edward's apparent interest in engineering, the most likely destination for the young man was this faculty. So, in late 1899 he 'went up' to college to study mechanical sciences, which for fifty years had been led by Sir George Stokes, the eminent physicist.

Pembroke has a very long and distinguished history having been established in the mid-fourteenth century and had a heritage that few students could ignore, so places there were much sought after. But like many colleges, it had been forced to embrace the modern world and science in particular, attracting many of its leading exponents in the process. Stokes was one of these and in 1899, though 79 years of age, still directed educational and research programmes with great energy and determination. As a permanent fixture within the college, Thompson would have been only too aware of his dominating presence and come under his spell, as many others did.

When looking at Stokes' long career, it is easy to see him as a scientist well ahead of his time. Much of his research centred on subjects such as fluid dynamics, creeping flow, metallurgy and the theory of light, all of which still resonate today. And with his growing knowledge of the physical and chemical behaviour of metals, his work found a practical application in the design and construction of railways. Such was his importance that he was appointed to investigate the causes of the Dee Bridge and Tay Bridge disasters, in 1847 and 1879 respectively, and recommend changes. In addition, he advised

Pembroke College at the end of the nineteenth century. (*THG*)

George Gabriel Stokes at about the time Thompson arrived at Pembroke College. By all accounts his rather daunting exterior hid a man of some generosity and compassion, though, it seems, he wasn't a person to be treated lightly. He is buried in Mill Road Cemetery in Cambridge. (*THG*)

Two of the photos of the Tay Bridge disaster that Thompson collected or was given by Stokes during tutorials or lectures. With its emphasis on civil and mechanical engineering issues, an accident such as this would be a very useful case study for students to evaluate. Throughout his career, Thompson continued to show an interest in rail crashes, as his albums bear witness. An engineer could learn a great deal from studying cause and effect in some detail, as Stokes clearly demonstrated to him. (*ET/DN*)

a Royal Commission on the wider use of cast iron in railway structures and then the effects of wind pressures and fluid flow on bridges. If the photographs contained in Thompson's albums are anything to go by, Stokes' work clearly played an important part in his education and certainly featured in lectures and seminars during this period. It may also have influenced his decision to focus on railway engineering. Wherever the truth might lie, Thompson's attendance at Stokes' funeral in 1903, a year after leaving college, suggests that the impact he may have had was significant.

Nevertheless, his three years at Pembroke followed a very similar pattern to life at Marlborough, with his sporting activities still taking up a great deal of time, now with golf added. The award of a Class 3 BA in June 1902, although a pass, was barely so. But then, as now, known attendance at Oxbridge, plus a degree, tended to attract greater kudos than those obtained at other universities.

So his status as a graduate was barely dented by his low grades and job opportunities were likely to be plentiful. After some thought, he settled for a short period as a premium pupil with Beyer, Peacock, perhaps revealing much about his interests and ambitions in the process.

Beyer, Peacock and Co of Manchester, lately under the leadership of its Managing Director G.P. Dawson, had become a well-established locomotive manufacturer with a worldwide market for their products. Unlike many builders at this time, they were not affiliated to any particular railway company, but stood alone in a very competitive market producing made to measure engines for a multitude of purposes. From their Works in Gorton, to the south-east of the city, they had supplied specialist engines and machine tools for use on London's first underground railway and then its District Railway, 2-4-0Ts for use on the Isle of Man, a class 4-4-0 for the Tobu Railway in Japan and many more, including railways in South Africa, Sweden, Russia, Norway and Germany. In 1902, they became a limited company and sought expansion with an influx of money that would surely follow. Over the next few decades, their business flourished, particularly in Africa and Australasia where their specialist Beyer-Garratt articulated locomotives found a ready market. In time, they would also build locomotives for the LMS, LNER and GWR, such was their importance to the industry. When Thompson arrived in late 1902, the company were on the cusp of this expansion, though the first visible signs of this might have been hard to detect.

Beyer, Peacock and Co Ltd were a company of some standing for nearly 100 years and their catalogues were translated into many languages, confirming their international status. (*THG*)

Three examples of Beyer, Peacock's work recorded in one of Thompson's albums. Top: Part of an 1870/71 order for the Grand Russian Railway, which Richard Peacock personally accompanied to St Petersburg. Middle: A 2-6-4T 3ft 6in. gauge engine built for the Pretoria-Pietersburg Railway in South Africa. This country provided a fertile market for the company's products and orders were still being placed in the 1950s by them. Bottom: With the rise of Pacific designs Beyer, Peacock were commissioned to build 4 Karoo Class engines for the Cape Government Railway in 1902 for delivery in 1904. These were a modified version of two built by Kitson and Co. The design and construction of these four engines took place when Thompson was in the works and seem to have caught his attention. (*ET/DN*)

The reasons why he selected Beyer, Peacock are now lost to time. The only reference he made to this brief period in his life is contained in his application to join the Institution of Mechanical Engineers in 1929. Here he simply lists against the year 'Premium Pupil'. However, it is safe to assume that he wished to gain some practical experience of a major railway company and so his year would have been one of observing all aspects of their work. It has been suggested that he may have spent time in the Drawing Office at Gorton learning the principles of design and draughtsmanship. As this could form part of 5-year premium apprenticeships in the business, it is probably true, although to what extent this prepared him for such work is debatable. But, as the careers of many of his senior colleagues could bear witness, being an experienced draughtsman or designer wasn't a block to becoming a Chief Mechanical Engineer. In fact, few of them could boast these skills, although they clearly had the engineering qualifications and credentials to create new locomotives, relying on others to fill in the details.

For Thompson, his year at Gorton must have been a challenging one. The world of public schools and university was a far cry from the cut, thrust and grime of heavy industry and demanded strength of character and resourcefulness if you were to survive. They were qualities he seems to have possessed. But with Beyer, Peacock he would have observed more than a series of manufacturing processes.

As a company, they had advanced beyond the norm in the treatment of workers, predicting, by many years, reforms in health, safety and welfare that statute would extend across all industry. It was also a form of altruism that stretched beyond the factory gates to create a new school for workers' children, better accommodation, plus a church and community hall to encourage social lives. As Richard Peacock's obituary made plain, '. . . he took a lively interest in the welfare of his work people. He could be approached by any of them when in difficulty and distress and this was the secret of the whole-hearted loyalty they rendered him'. It was a policy that was embraced by his successors and would have been plain for Thompson to see in his year with the company. It was a lesson not lost on him. In later years, when in a senior position himself, he would also display great concern for his workers and seek to improve their working conditions whenever he could. Whether this was an emotional or practical response is hard to say, but it did display an understanding of industrial and social hardship that wasn't universally held at the time.

Being a premium pupil, for which the company received payment, and relying on an allowance from his father to cover his living costs, there was a constant reminder that paid employment was essential. So, as his year at Gorton drew to a close, he looked for a permanent appointment with potential for advancement. Having sampled the world of manufacturing, it seems as though he wished to expand his knowledge and experience by working for a railway operating company. There were many to choose from and in mid-1904 he applied to and was recruited by the Midland Railway as an 'Improver' at Derby and with this move the major part of his career began.

Mr. Edward Thompson,

With college tie on display Thompson faces the future. (*THG*)

CHAPTER 2

A GROWING INFLUENCE

Thompson simply recorded on this photo 'the Liverpool Express near Harrow'. No date is given but is assumed to be in the early 1900s. (*ET/DN*)

'Sir, – I have read with very great interest the article in the *Railway Gazette* on the subject of Sir Cecil Paget's experimental locomotive. It is of particular interest to me because I was an Improver in the Derby Locomotive Sheds at the time and I remember not only the engine but the secrecy which was observed concerning it. I worked in the shed with a particularly competent fitter who subsequently attained a very high position as a foreman at Derby, and I remember very well on one occasion that he told me he had been out for a run with this engine and that its performance was "absolutely astonishing".

'Unfortunately, in those days I was not allowed to come into any sort of contact with the locomotive, but I am proud to say that in later life the designer became one of my closest friends. I shall always look on him as one of the greatest British railwaymen we ever had.

'Yours faithfully
E. Thompson.'

The first steps in a career are always the most difficult. No matter how highly qualified you are, a lack of experience can quickly expose your weaknesses and leave you open to ridicule or a growing sense of inadequacy. Some will grasp opportunities offered and by sheer force of personality make the transition quickly, while others will be slower and more ponderous in their approach. But in either case, the newcomer will benefit from wise counselling and the guidance of an old hand in the business. To this end, Thompson thought himself very lucky to have met Cecil Paget during 1904. His letter, which is one of the few examples of his writing that seems to have survived, contains a warmth and sense of friendship that belies the rumour that he was a cold and austere man. Here, quite clearly, we see someone in his prime with a strong appreciation of others and a self-deprecating, dry sense of humour.

When recollecting the year he spent at Derby, Thompson recorded very little. But he did recall that the role of Improver meant working with various fitters to ensure locomotives under repair returned to service quickly. In reality, the post seems to have become an extension to his education and given him some experience of running shed work. With the company's drawing office and HQ close by, he also had the opportunity to link up with designers and engineers there and view the latest developments in locomotives and carriages. His collection of photographs grew during this period,

suggesting that he may have travelled widely on Britain's network. Once again, the subject matter is mixed and shows an interest in many aspects of engineering. There were pictures of trains in motion, bridges – across the Tamar, the Tweed, the 'new' Tay Bridge amongst others – and other railway structures. It is as if there was some indecision over the path he wished to follow in his career. Certainly, his degree would have been an ideal lead in to either civil or mechanical engineering.

Clearly, though, seeing Paget's work first hand and sensing the excitement it generated, affected the young man in some way and led to a lasting friendship that the coming world war helped to cement. Although now largely forgotten in railway history, Paget gained a mercurial reputation as a designer and innovator in the years up to 1914. Born in October 1874, the second son of George Paget, the Chairman of the Midland Railway from 1890 to 1911, he, like Thompson, was a product of a public school, in his case Harrow, and also studied at Pembroke College.

Another Thompson photo this time with a date: '*Cornwall* at Gresty Lane 'Crewe' 1904'. This 2-2-2 class locomotive was of particular note having been designed and built by Francis Trevithick in 1847. It was rebuilt by John Ramsbottom in 1858 and ran in main line service between Liverpool and Manchester until 1902. But this wasn't to be the end of its life and the engine was used for inspection purposes for many years and in this role is captured here. When eventually withdrawn from service the engine was listed for preservation and is now part of the national collection. It is little wonder that it proved of interest to Thompson. (*ET/DN*)

Cecil Paget in about 1900. It is possible that he recruited Thompson on the basis that they were both Pembroke College men. (*THG*)

But before this, he became a pupil at Derby Works in 1890 or 1891 under Samuel Waite Johnson and learnt the basics of railway engineering and management in preparation for study at Cambridge. It seems he may have seen service in the Boer War with his older brother George, who died out there leaving Cecil as heir to their father's baronetcy.

Ken Leech, a fellow engineer who served with Paget in the war, left a vivid picture of this singular man:

'A man of such organising ability, as almost to amount to genius, full of energy and fun hidden behind a "poker-face", it is not surprising that tales of his exploits and incidents in which he was involved are numerous. He was popularly supposed to have suffered more "swishings" for pranks at Harrow than any before or since, but the story of his encounter, when an undergraduate, with his old Headmaster, Dr Welldon, is possibly apocryphal. "I'm Paget, sir; perhaps you don't remember me?" "Oh yes I do, Paget; but your face is perhaps not the feature I should recognise best!" After Cambridge he returned to Derby, and by

influence and ability was soon well on the way to a high official position, his youthful exuberance having been – partly at all events – sublimated to the hard work and the driving force so characteristic of him.'

By 1902, he was back with the Midland Railway and quickly rose to become Works Manager at Derby. Despite the obvious patronage of his father he seems to have been a success in this role and used his position to begin developing new ideas that could have far reaching benefits for the company. One of these was prompted by his interest in the Willans high-speed, central valve engine, some of which were in use providing electricity to the MR's offices and Derby Station. From an operational point of view these engines proved to be cheap to run and were very effective with wear 'measured over a number of years as infinitesimal'. Seeing great potential in this concept, he conceived the idea, as part of his studies at Cambridge, of adapting the principle to steam locomotion. But with the company committed to less risky, more traditional designs, there was little support for his idea. So it became a private venture in which he invested his own money. In time, he also took the most unusual step of raising a private order on the company to build the first engine. However, his funds ran out and Richard Deeley, the recently appointed Locomotive Superintendent, took on responsibility for completing the project.

Although planning and initial design work were well advanced when Thompson worked as an Improver, the date when the locomotive first ran is unclear. Some believe it was during 1906, but Thompson, in his letter, suggests that it was much earlier. Wherever the truth might lie, Paget and his experimental engine clearly impressed the younger man in many ways, one being his approach to projects and a determination to be master of events. With No. 2299 Paget failed to do this, as he later described to Leech:

'He explained to me how it had been built at Derby to his private order, and that he spent all his available money on it, only to find that he required another £1000-£2000 to complete it; that the Midland Company finished it for him, but insisted on taking control of all tests and limiting the amount of experimental work that might prove necessary.

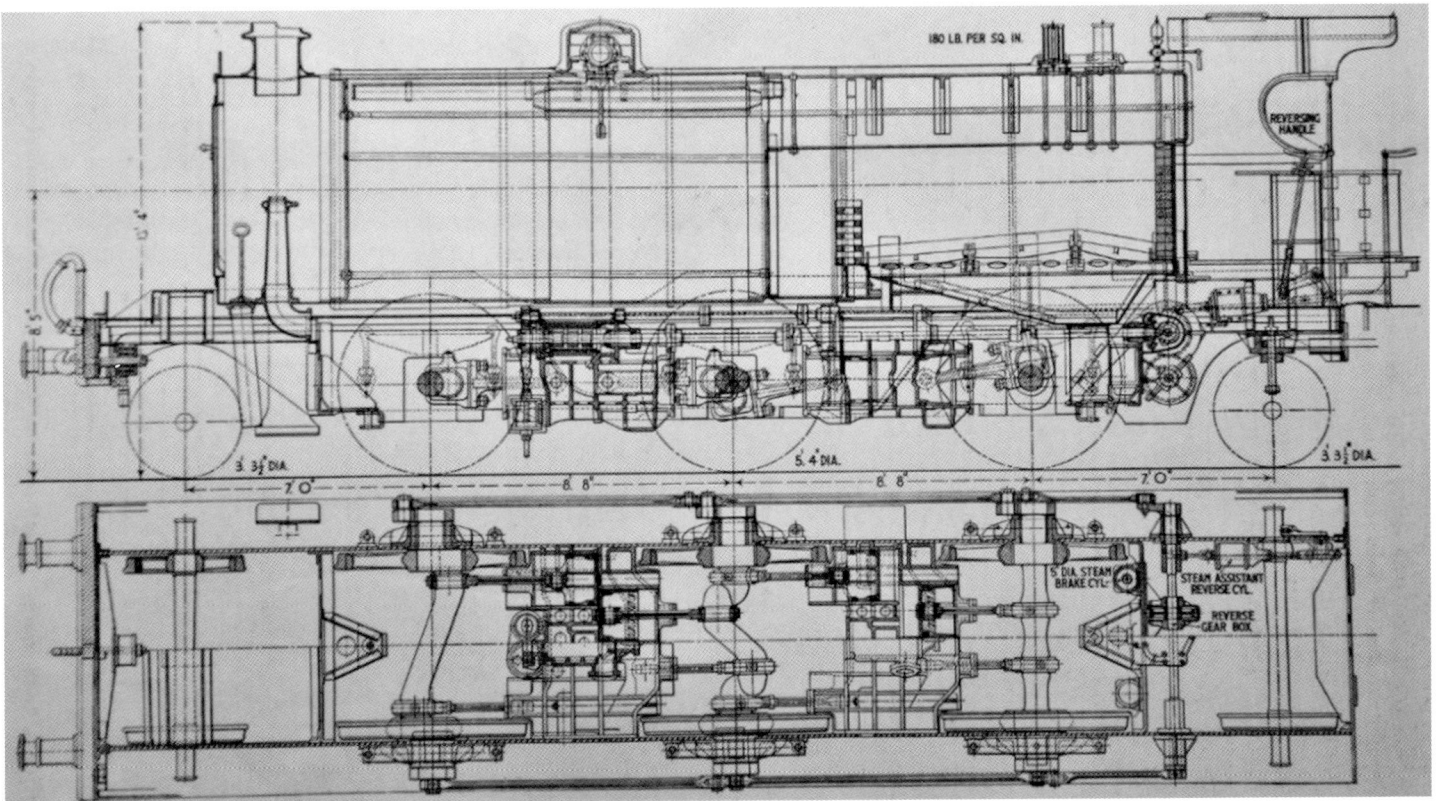

(Above) The end result of Paget's work- the experimental 2-6-2 tender locomotive No. 2299. His intention was to build an engine capable of pulling heavy freight trains at 15 mph to 80 mph express passenger services, with minimum boiler and upkeep costs. Apart from the Willans system the design included eight single acting inside cylinders with rotary steam distribution valves and a most unusual boiler arrangement. This was described as 'simply a brick lined furnace with two fire doors at one end and a steel tube plate at the other; only the steel crown ranked as evaporative surface, for there were no water legs. By this clever stroke, Paget made it possible to dispense with about three quarters of the firebox stays and produced a firebox from which copper was largely absent. In many other ways – location of injectors, water gauges, etc; provision of good look out; and in design of ash dumping devices in ashpan and smokebox – Paget showed himself to be well in advance of his time, and well able to appreciate the needs of those on the footplate'. (Below) One of the very few photographs known to exist of the engine as constructed. It remained a secret project and after Paget left to fight for his country in 1914 the project was quietly dropped and the engine reduced to scrap a year later. (*THG*)

'Although Paget didn't mention it I was aware that right from the drawing board stage, Derby had shown the utmost hostility to the new design, christening it Paget's Folly, and that to hand over the engine to such diehards was to destroy any chance of the locomotive's success.'

Although Thompson may have lacked Paget's ability to innovate, the lesson on managing invention and change effectively wasn't lost on him. But this influence probably went beyond the design of locomotives into the running of a railway. In 1907, Paget became the MR's General Superintendent, taking on the locomotive running department in the process; a role previously undertaken by Deeley. Here he would set about re-organising the traffic management system into a form that some believe became the model for other companies to follow. In this he displayed an ability to think broadly and not be a slave to the past or a predecessor's legacy. It was probably an approach that was reinforced many times over when both men served together, with great distinction, in the Royal Engineers during the Great War. So, it is little wonder that Thompson remembered the man and his achievements with such warmth and enthusiasm.

Just as Paget looked to expand his career and expertise so did his young apprentice. Thompson decided to broaden his horizons and in 1905 left Derby to become a supervisor at the Royal Ordnance Factory at Woolwich.

Production of heavy naval guns underway at Woolwich early in the twentieth century. (*RH*)

Woolwich Arsenal had a long and proud history of providing armaments for the Royal Navy and Army. Its research and development group was, by the time Thompson worked there, reaching for the future, particularly in its production of new heavy naval guns and its work on ballistics. To the casual observer it must have appeared as an attractive option for an ambitious young engineer eager to develop a career where the skills he had developed at Cambridge could find a voice. But it wasn't to the research and development division he went, as the few personnel records that survive bear witness, but to supervise the establishment's sizeable two-gauge railway system and dock machinery. It was a posting that allowed him to live at his parents' home from where he could commute to work.

The railway at Woolwich Arsenal as it would have appeared to Thompson whilst working there in 1906. Right – the 18 in gauge running shed showing the variety of types of locomotive operating within the establishment. The one on the far right appears to be one of the newer oil-fired engines for use in areas containing explosives. Bottom – Moving staff around the site was an essential part of the railway's day to day work. This train is apparently divided into two classes, one for industrial and the other for non-industrial workers. (*ET/DN*)

Heavy industry was often served by extensive railway systems in the days before road vehicles became commonplace. Narrow gauge was used for most internal workings, supported by standard gauge, which also provided a link to the national network, through transfer sheds. Things would change with the advent of the internal combustion engine but in the nineteenth century, steam was the primary form of motive power in many factories and workshops. Woolwich was no different and from the early 1870s built up a sizeable 18in. gauge system, estimated to contain more than 50 miles of track, and a less extensive standard-gauge network.

By 1905 there were upwards of 50 narrow gauge engines operating, supplied by companies such as Manning Wardle, the Vulcan Foundry, Hudswell Clarke, Bagnall, Kerr Stuart and Hornsby. Alongside this fleet there was an extensive range of rolling stock, all supported by running sheds and workshops where the full range of maintenance tasks could be undertaken. There were obvious dangers in using steam locomotives in an explosive environment. To overcome this, the Arsenal successfully developed spark arresting gear and, less successfully, experimented with a compressed air-based system before acquiring a number of oil based internal combustion engines in the 1890s.

Although no detailed description of his duties has survived, it is safe to assume the post would have focussed on all aspects of running shed life. It must have been a useful experience so early in his career, but the chances of promotion at Woolwich were limited. In reality, there was a well-established hierarchy which was dominated by the two services it supported, so opportunities for newcomers or 'outsiders' were limited, a fact that Thompson must soon have realised. During the year he sought fresh employment and found a post with the North Eastern Railway at Hull. Here Wilson Worsdell, the Chief Mechanical Engineer, held sway, with Vincent Raven his deputy.

Why he chose this post is unclear but having briefly seen an alternative world and its restrictions, the NER must have seemed to offer good prospects for an aspiring man. Was he influenced in any way by old friends or people who may be considered mentors from his brief time at Derby? Judging by his admiration and respect for Paget this may well be so. But witnessing the apparent discord within the Midland Railway, a return there may not have seemed an attractive option. Alternatively,

there may simply have been no opportunity there for him to exploit, so pastures new beckoned. The NER, with its Eton and Cambridge educated chairman John Wharton, seemed to offer him the best opportunity to progress into senior management.

The NER came into being during 1854 with the amalgamation of the York, Newcastle and Berwick Railway, the York and North Midland Railway, Leeds and Northern Railway and the Malton and Driffield Railway. Its growth continued as the NER gradually acquired numerous other companies in the years that followed. Although providing key passenger services, including part of the East Coast main line, it relied heavily on the lucrative mineral traffic around its region.

If success is measured by profits then the NER regularly produced healthy dividends for its shareholders, with income exceeding outlay by an average of 30 or so per cent per year until 1913 when there was a £4.5m deficit. This healthy state of affairs fed the ambitions of the directors and their senior managers and allowed a certain amount of innovation and expansion to take place, including electrification.

Wilson Worsdell had succeeded his older brother Thomas as Locomotive Superintendent in 1890, with the post later being re-titled CME. From the beginning, he launched an ambitious development programme. In this he may have been encouraged by his great friend George Churchward, whose work for the GWR was reaching new heights of invention. In addition, he had spent four years as a pupil at the Altoona Railroad Works in Pennsylvania, under the wing of his brother who was a Master Mechanic there. At the time, innovation and experimentation across the US system had become almost commonplace and Worsdell would, undoubtedly, have been influenced by all he saw there. One of his obituaries neatly summed up his contribution during twenty years in charge:

'He was connected with the NER during one of the most important periods of British locomotive history. He produced more than 20 different types of engine and rebuilt some of those designed by his brother to improve their performance. He designed and built an outside cylinder engine of the 4-4-2 type, which ranked amongst the largest in Great Britain, which performed excellent work. He was the first to introduce the 4-6-0 type of engine in this country for

(Left) Wilson Worsdell (1850 to 1920), CME until 1910. (Right) Vincent Raven (1859 to 1934), Worsdell's Deputy then CME when the older man retired. He remained in this post until 1922. They were both men of great standing in their profession. Raven, in particular, would have a profound effect on Thompson's life and career. (*THG*)

passenger work. He took an active part in connexion with carriage and wagon work, and was an advocate of the larger capacity types. His dynamometer-car has been of the greatest service, and marked the beginning of a new era in the creation of accurate data regarding tractive effort. He was chiefly responsible for the North Tyneside third rail suburban electrification programme, one of the first in this country.'

These were days when the CME's role held great autonomy. They could run their organisations autocratically if they felt so inclined and influence was exercised, often in a miniscule way, on all aspects of day to day work. In many ways they became personal fiefdoms, where the leader's merest whim could easily become law and woe betide any transgressors. But it was also a world of birth-right

and patronage, where the favoured few could forge careers based on personal connections and not necessarily outstanding abilities. In this it mirrored the Victorian world of privilege, monocracy and subservience. Great if you were part of the 'club'; an endless struggle if not. In such an environment, the wise would cultivate contacts and feed into this inherent conceit whilst seeking position and influence. No wonder that the phrase 'climbing the slippery pole' is often applied to worlds such as this. And it was in these circles that Thompson found himself operating, with his Marlborough and Cambridge background giving his professional credentials added weight. In assisting him onto the first rank of management, Worsdell and Raven clearly played a part.

There has been some speculation that Vincent Raven may have been chiefly responsible for Thompson's rapidly advancing career. In the years ahead, the young man would also be welcomed into the Raven household, becoming a regular visitor in the process, suggesting a proprietary interest. He would in time foster a close friendship with their eldest son, Norman Raven, who was five years his junior and fellow golfer, and then marry their second daughter in 1913. So, there is every reason to believe that the Ravens and their patronage played an important part in his life. However, Worsdell would also have been involved in his recruitment and carefully monitored his progress hoping to see the potential suggested by his qualifications. Until 1910, he was chiefly responsible for postings and promotions, no matter what Raven may have thought or suggested. After that, of course, it would be a different matter, but the years from 1906 to 1910 were crucial to Thompson's development and helped establish him in the railway profession.

Did he see it this way himself? He had, after all, moved away from this industry looking for alternative and perhaps more challenging areas in which to work, suggesting ambition and an open view of the future. It is impossible to say, but it seems likely that Thompson was astute enough to judge these issues and see where the best chance of promotion and success existed. Woolwich hadn't fulfilled this objective and the NER, with its sound finances and its desire to move forward, may have seemed a far better option for someone imbued with ambition. The warmth of his contact with the Raven family may simply have strengthened this bond. Wherever the truth might lie, the NER seemed to meet Thompson's needs.

His first appointment was as assistant to the Superintendent in charge of the Dairycoates Sheds in Hull. It was a post that would have given him first-hand experience of all aspects of locomotive work from an operational viewpoint. Having been established in the early 1860s, it had, by 1906, expanded to become the major shed on the NER, though now is largely forgotten. With two large round houses and maintenance facilities, it played an important role in the day to day life of the company and became the centre of his working life for three years. Although little is recorded of his time at Hull, there is some evidence that he frequently took the opportunity to take footplate rides to experience, first hand, what this entailed. It was a practice he followed throughout his career. His responsibilities also seem to have included attendance at railway accidents, both major and minor, and not those simply involving Hull engines; perhaps as a nod to his time at Cambridge under George Stokes.

The worst of these crashes both came in 1907. On 26 March, buckled track caused the derailment of a passenger train at Felling in County Durham, killing two and seriously injuring six others. Five months later, on 27 August, a goods train failed to stop at signals near Goswick and came off the track killing two more people. His role in the investigations that followed is unclear, though is not difficult to gauge, bearing in mind his job, qualifications and background.

Hull Dairycoates as it appeared a few years after Thompson worked there. This well-known photograph was taken during a visit by George V, with many of the engines specially prepared for the occasion. This picture demonstrates the size of the sheds and its complement of locomotives. (*RH*)

The rail crash at Felling on 26 March 1907 which Thompson attended (the photo above appears in one of his albums). Unusually for March the weather was deemed hot enough to buckle the track and cause this passenger train to derail. The inquiry that followed exonerated the train's crew but found that the fishplates may have been too tight so making it difficult for any expansion to be absorbed. (*ET/DN*)

Five months later, on 27 August, Thompson recorded the crash at Goswick in a series of photos with emphasis on the loco-motive's condition. (*ET/DN*)

For a budding engineer hoping to improve his credentials as a designer, there was little direct involvement in this type of work at Hull. No matter how much he learnt about locomotive performance and engineering, this was no substitute for the very specific skills acquired and practised in drawing offices. Some increased their knowledge of this work by study at local colleges, but Thompson doesn't appear to have done so. Of course, his degree would have given him some insight into the engineering issues involved, as would his friendship with Paget, but there is nothing more. In fact, he seems to have been deliberately routed down an operational path, suggesting that is where his skills were deemed to be.

Nevertheless, there was much for him to observe, even from the confines of Hull as Worsdell's time in charge drew to a close and Raven took over. Perhaps the most interesting of these developments was the NER's electrification programme, which by any standards was pushing back boundaries in a steam dominated world. The project came about as a result of the rapid expansion of the tram network and the threat this posed to the level of commuter traffic around towns and cities. Although there had been some pioneering work in this field across Britain, most notably with Volks Electric Railway in Brighton, the slowly developing London Underground system and the Liverpool Overhead Railway, many other proposals for main line

A postcard published in 1904 to commemorate the opening of the 'Tyneside Electric' scheme. One hundred of these three car trains, plus some parcel vans, were constructed in the NER's York workshops and were equipped by British Thomson-Houston, of Rugby. (*THG*)

schemes didn't get beyond the drawing board until the new century dawned.

It fell to the NER and Lancashire and Yorkshire Railway to take the initiative and by 1904, their separate projects had come to fruition. The L and Y, whether by chance or design, opened their 625 V DC fourth rail system, between Liverpool and Southport, a week before the first stage of the NER's 'Tyneside Electric' 600V DC third rail network on 22 March. Although there was no direct competition between these two electrified lines, the desire to be the first in service was a pressing one as it would attract great attention and much kudos.

The complete electrified line, from Newcastle to Tynemouth, opened on 25 July and this was followed, in June 1905, by a freight only branch to Newcastle Quayside, operated by two specially constructed 0-4+4-0 ES1 class shunting locomotives. With this, the electrification programme came to a temporary halt which allowed the commuter service to establish itself and begin to recoup the substantial outlay on construction. It would be another nine years before the experiment reached its second stage. This time, under Raven's guiding hands, a line between Newport and Shildon was electrified with the installation of a 1,500V DC overhead system. It was served by 10 EF1 Class 0-4+4-0 locomotives designed by the drawing office team led by R.J. Robson and were built at Darlington with the capability of pulling 1,400 ton mineral loads at 25 mph on the level.

Construction work began in 1914, with the first stage being completed in 1915 and the final section in January 1916. With these programmes proving successful, Vincent Raven felt empowered to extend electrification, only to be thwarted by the coming of war, a shortage of funds, then amalgamation in 1922. Even so plans were laid down by Raven and his board to begin work on the East Coast main line, but in a rapidly changing world there would be little forward movement on these proposals until the 1970s.

Thompson's thoughts on this subject aren't recorded but having grown so close to Raven, professionally and socially, he would probably have been a strong

Thompson's photograph of one of the two ES1 0-4+4-0 electric shunting engines built for the Newport to Shildon line. (*ET/DN*)

Five EF1s ready for duty in the roundhouse at Shildon. These engines remained in service until the early 1950s, but none made it into preservation, although one ES1 did and is displayed by the National Railway Museum. (*PR/RH*)

advocate of electrification and supported his greatly respected father-in-law. In many quarters, Gresley, who became the LNER's first CME in 1923, stands accused of ending Raven's modernist dream of the future, preferring to build more steam locomotives instead. The reality is that the 1920s were a period of great austerity as the country recovered from war. And things grew worse with the financial crash triggered by events in 1929 and the Depression that settled on the world in the decade that followed. The LNER, like any company at the time, had to draw in its belt to survive, making the huge costs involved in electrification unsustainable without government sponsorship. This would not be forthcoming until the next world war approached.

Gresley, despite an interest in this new technology and a desire to experiment and expand, would find it impossible to take it forward until the late thirties, despite being a member of an influential parliamentary commission advocating these projects from the late 1920s onwards. Finally, he received approval to begin work on the Liverpool Street to Shenfield and the Sheffield to Manchester Lines only to find these projects shelved due to another world war.

There was much else for Thompson to absorb in his years with both Worsdell and Raven. Yet it is interesting to note that neither man attempted to get him involved in design of engines or rolling stock, perhaps sensing that his true talents didn't lie here. If so, a transfer to Gateshead as assistant to Charles Baister, the Running Shed Superintendent, in 1909 tends to support this view. Here, it seems, is a man considered strong on organisation and management, but, perhaps, not possessing a true designer's skills or gifts. However, at Hull then Gateshead he would have been in charge of some maintenance facilities and he seems to have displayed some understanding of these processes. His albums also focus on the construction of engines and carriages at Darlington and York, suggesting a growing interest in production line techniques. As his career developed, this would be an area in which he would become something of an expert.

With the war over, Raven tried to revive interest in electrification. In 1920, the company felt able to begin planning conversion of the York to Newcastle main line and Raven was authorised, as part of this project, to design and build a prototype locomotive. A 2-Co-2 (4-6-4) wheel arrangement was chosen and the unit, numbered 13, was completed in May 1922 at Darlington, with electrical equipment supplied by Metropolitan-Vickers. But seven months later, after a series of trials, the NER was absorbed into the new LNER and the project was suspended. No. 13 would spend almost three decades in reserve and would eventually be scrapped during December 1950. (*ET/DN*)

By 1910, Thompson had also become a very experienced accident investigator. In November of that year, he was called upon to use these hard earned skills when examining and reporting on a major incident that took place at Bank Top, Darlington, in the early hours of the 15th.

He was one of the first on the scene and superintended rescue work, including the removal of the dead driver and fireman from one engine. As soon as day had dawned, he began the difficult task of assessing cause and effect. At the same time, the company reported the accident to the Board of Trade and they immediately assigned Lt Colonel P.G. von Donop RE to the inquiry that followed. Over the coming weeks, he and Thompson worked closely together and appear to have developed a very close rapport.

They established that on this clear moonlit night, a goods train from Parkgate to Hull, which arrived at Darlington at 12.38 am, had been pulled up with its engine opposite the water column. After standing there for about eight minutes, the engine and the leading fifteen wagons were uncoupled and moved forward into the sidings. This left the rear portion of the train, consisting of twenty-eight wagons and a brake van, standing on the up main line. At this moment, it was run into by the 10.45 pm goods train from Newcastle to Leeds. In the collision that followed, Driver Connolly and Fireman Lough, on the Leeds train, were both killed. In addition, their 2-6-0 tender engine was flung sideways and badly damaged, along with twenty or so of the trucks it pulled and another twelve attached to the other locomotive. However, they absorbed much of the impact which probably saved the other engine and its crew.

Above, opposite and overleaf: Thompson kept extensive records of this accident, including a number of photographs, some of which are reproduced here. (*all accident photos - ET/DN*)

At the board of inquiry that followed Thompson reported that:

'I am Assistant Locomotive Superintendent and I am stationed at Gateshead. About 10.30 am on the morning of the 15th I carried out an inspection of the engine of the Leeds train. The engine was then lying on its right side in the position which it had been after the accident. It had only been moved since the accident sufficient to release the driver [who had been badly crushed and burnt]. The regulator handle was in the shut position. I could work the regulator handle quite freely. It bore no signs of having been placed in the shut position by a blow. I had the dome cover broken so as to examine the valve. I found it in perfect working order. It worked correctly in unison with the regulator handle and at the time I opened it the valve closed. As far as I could see the regulator and valve

were both in thoroughly good working order after the accident.

'I then looked at the position of the brake handle before the driver's brake valve was touched and it was in the emergency position. This means that the brake was fully applied. I had the driver's brake valve taken off and taken to pieces and found it in excellent order. As far as I could see all the braking arrangement on the engine were all in perfect working order. The brake gear underneath the engine was broken and the brake blocks were hanging loose. From their position, therefore, no conclusion can be drawn as to whether they were applied to the wheels. The engine was in back gear. There were bright marks on the wheels indicating that the wheels had been skidding. These marks were on the six coupled wheels of the engine and on the tender wheels. I should not, however, say from these marks that the engine had been skidding for a long distance.

COLLISION AT BANK TOP.
DARLINGTON. NOV 15th 1910.

COLLISION AT BANK TOP.
DARLINGTON. NOV 15th 1910.

DARLINGTON BANK TOP NOV 15 1910

DARLINGTON BANK TOP NOV 15 1910

'I found that the steam valve which admits steam to the Westinghouse donkey engine was open showing that the pump was being worked at the time of the accident. This is the normal position in which it should have been as it works automatically during the whole journey.'

When he spoke at the inquiry, Thompson had already reached the conclusion, having spoken to signalmen, shed foremen, station masters and others, that driver error was most probably the cause of the accident. Once this conclusion had been reached, he and Donop considered any mitigating factors. They discovered that Driver Connolly was reputed to have had a drinking problem and this may have contributed to another accident, in May the previous year, near Berwick-on-Tweed. Although there was no medical evidence post mortem to support this conclusion, witnesses reported that the train had been moving faster than usual on this run. In addition, the driver did not seem to notice the signals 'lowered for the train' and braked late and suddenly when the danger of collision became only too apparent as detonators on the track went off.

It may have been the words and actions of the dead fireman that sealed Connolly's fate. Thompson discovered that two weeks before the Bank Top accident Lough, being seriously concerned about his driver's drinking habits, had asked to be transferred to other duties. Connolly was later questioned by Collinson, the Locomotive Foreman, and admitted that he had partaken of brandy for 'medicinal purposes'. Collinson accepted this and took no further action, for which he was later severely criticised by Thompson and the inquiry.

This and many other accident investigations were handled expertly by Thompson during the early years of his career. In the process, he revealed great awareness, common sense, professionalism and a depth of engineering knowledge which allowed him to understand and assess many complex issues. These are all skills essential for anyone hoping to reach senior rank in any field, particularly one as broad and as demanding as a CME. There was still much more for him to learn, particularly on questions of design, but the basics were there for all to see. And there was much else for Thompson to observe if he wished to know more about the construction of steam locomotives and rolling stock.

Worsdell, in particular, was prepared to experiment and improve what was available, encouraged by the company's continued financial buoyancy. In this he was ably assisted by his Chief Draughtsman, Walter Smith. During his time in charge, twenty different types of engine were produced, whilst some that his brother introduced were rebuilt. In this he doesn't seem to have been deterred by any considerations of filial loyalty, but did restrain himself for a time when, for four years, his brother acted as a consultant to the company.

Although Worsdell wasn't noted as an inventor, having only one patent to his name (GB190716980 – Improvements connected with the blast pipes of locomotives – published on 23 July 1908), he was prepared to innovate and test ideas current at the time. One of his first steps was to move away from the concept of compounding, which as a rule held little appeal for him. In addition, he believed that engines with 'single' driving wheels had reached the limit of their development in pulling heavy express trains. His major project, the M1 4-4-0, of which twenty were built between 1892 and '93, reflected his thoughts, but also, in time, his ability to seek improvements to his own designs when necessary. As events would prove, he wasn't someone hidebound or narrow in his outlook. Here he demonstrated a characteristic not always found in his fellow engineers, who seemed happy to stay fixed and unmoving in time.

It seems that Worsdell chose to fit the M1 with steamchests outside the frame plates, rather than inside, in a bid to make the valves more accessible and easier to service. This solution meant that motion was applied by a Stephenson valve-gear via rocking shafts. But by 1903, this solution went out of favour and the CME re-introduced inside cylinders, which seemed to improve performance as well as confirm his ability to be flexible and magnanimous in approach. This was followed in 1894 by a rebuilding programme in which two-cylinder compound engines began to be converted into two-cylinder 'simples', as they were called. This work meant that the Joy valve gear used on these engines was replaced by the Stephenson system. Worsdell was no fan of David Joy's concept, which had been introduced in 1879, unlike his brother, who showed a marked preference for it.

With an ever-growing demand for bigger, more powerful engines to reduce the amount of double-heading necessary, Worsdell began to experiment with 4-6-0 designs. The first engine of this type he produced was built at Gateshead and appeared in 1899. S Class No. 2001, which would be one of 40 produced, had 6ft 1in. driving wheels, which were generally thought to be too small for express work. In addition, a boiler was fitted with an unremarkable 23.7sqft grate area, which was shallower than some existing types running on the railway. There were two outside cylinders and the first seven had slide valves, with the remainder being fitted with piston valves. They were long engines and, in a bid to make them fit turntables, the cabs were made too small and were cramped and uncomfortable, even by the standards of the age.

During tests, the engines were found to be mediocre performers, offering little or no advantage over his sixty R Class 4-4-0s that were being built concurrently. Inevitably improvements were made to ease some of the shortcomings. 8¾in diameter piston valves and Schmidt superheaters were fitted and, with an assurance that turntable restrictions would be eased, the length of the locos was increased by 2ft to allow the cabs to be extended.

Despite this, the class were seen as failing and Worsdell sought to develop the class in an effort to prove the 4-6-0 concept. In doing this, he was mirroring the work being undertaken by George Churchward at Swindon, which would result in the Saint Class of 1902 and his classic Star Class four years later, just as Thompson arrived at Hull. Undaunted, Worsdell followed suit and continued experimenting with the concept, bringing out his S1 in 1900.

The new class sought to eradicate some of the shortcomings highlighted by experience with the earlier version. The wheels were 7in. greater in diameter and the piston valves were 8¾in, to reflect the modification made to later S engines. This, by all accounts, made them more fleet of foot, though not substantially better than the R Class. It needed a bigger grate, ash pan and higher combustion rate to help achieve this. Where it did improve on the 4-4-0s was in producing a higher rate of adhesion which allowed them to get bigger trains away on steep gradients without assistance.

SIX COUPLED EXPRESS LOCOMOTIVE, NORTH EASTERN RAILWAY

Worsdell's elegant S1 Class 4-6-0 makes its appearance. (THG)

However, this wasn't a noteworthy requirement on most of the NER's system. Armed with this information, Worsdell only built five of the S1s, though allowed production of the modified S Class to continue until 1909. With his R, then R1 Classes proving successful the need for more 4-6-0s proved unnecessary and, possibly, unsustainable with electrification costs to be met.

In some ways, the S and R Classes were of lesser importance to the NER than freight engines and tank locomotives Worsdell designed and constructed, in terms of revenue at least. The north-east, being a heavy industrial area with coal mining at its core, needed to move large quantities of goods to support these businesses. The most successful of these engines were the 0-8-0 Class T and T1 tender engines, of which 90 were built, and the E1 0-6-0Ts, the U Class 0-6-2Ts, and the W (4-6-0T), X (4-8-0T) and Y (4-6-2T) Classes. All these engines appeared between 1898 and 1910 in what may be seen as Worsdell's most creative period. So successful were some of these designs that they were still being built by the LNER many years later and some saw long and active service – Ts, Ys and the E1s, lasted into the 1960s and 1950s respectively.

For Thompson, working hard at Dairycoates and then Gateshead, all these new designs would have been of the greatest interest, especially when innovative, such as the number of cylinders used, electrification and the rejection of compounding. In his role at both sheds he would have dealt with all the nuances of these developments and much more, including the reaction of the drivers and firemen who manned them. Amongst good engineers it became a common refrain that you only learnt about an engine by riding on the footplate and listening to the crew. If so, Thompson seems to have been one of them, though whether he fully understood the gradations of design in the way that Worsdell did is debatable. Still, he had a good master to learn from and Raven was able to continue his valuable education when becoming CME on 1 June 1910.

Vincent Raven was an NER man through and through, having become an employee of the company in 1875 when taking up a premium engineering apprenticeship at Gateshead under Edward Fletcher, the Locomotive Superintendent. He was the third child of a clergyman and was educated privately at Aldenham School, near St Albans, so had much in common with Thompson in terms of class and status. Once qualified, in 1880, he was able to find permanent employment as a fireman, then became a foreman in the workshops at Gateshead. So great was his progress that in 1893 he was appointed Assistant Mechanical Engineer to Worsdell and sat on the cusp of even greater success.

Although eventually thwarted in his ambitions for electrification, steam still offered him an outlet for his talents, ably supported by Arthur Stamer, his deputy, and Chief Draughtsman, George Heppell, who had replaced Walter Smith in 1906. But the coming of war gave him only a short period in which to make his mark before the conflict consumed all effort. With such a strong industrial background, this saw him, in September 1915, appointed by David Lloyd George, then Minister of Munitions, to be Chief Superintendent at Woolwich. Before this happened, though, he pursued a number of locomotive projects.

The R Class, built between 1899 and 1907, to supersede his M1s. (*PR/RH*)

The NER's Y Class Pacific tank engine, twenty of which were built between 1910 and '11 at Darlington. The 4-6-2 configuration was still a new concept in Great Britain at this time and only the GWR had committed themselves to building one – their 1908 prototype engine No. 111 *The Great Bear*. Worsdell's Y Class was one of four tank designs being considered by companies in Britain during 1910. With their three cylinders,5ft 6in boilers, 7½ piston valves, 23sqft grate area and 4ft 7½in coupled driving wheels, they proved more than adequate for the task and provided a fitting swan song to Worsdell's long career. (*PR/RH*)

Aware of Worsdell's work with 4-6-0s, in which he had actively participated, Raven sought to keep this programme going, taking advantage of the larger diameter boilers then being produced by the NER. The first ten S2s began appearing from Darlington Works in 1911 to be followed two years later by the final ten. Although his ambition was to fit the 4-6-0s with three cylinders, as well as bigger boilers, this requirement wasn't included in the specification. Post 1918, he would achieve this with the S3, so the S2 can be seen as a transitory design. But the idea wasn't ignored completely in the pre-war years. There was, of course, Worsdell's tank engines with three cylinders and their success allowed Raven to develop the idea further with a new generation of Atlantic class locomotives. As an experiment, he took the Class 4CC 4-4-2 design and fitted it with three cylinders. Two of these engines had in fact been built in 1906, under the direction of Walter Smith. Despite Worsdell's

apparent rejection of compounding, he allowed Smith, a truer believer, great latitude in pursuing the concept and two four-cylinder engines were constructed as a result. Despite their success, no more were built, but the design was capable of adaption to carry three cylinders, which Raven duly did. In 1911, the first of his Z Class appeared, with another forty-nine being added by 1917. Raven proved to be a very strong advocate of three cylinder designs, believing that they produced a more balanced torque and smoother running, both desirable qualities for fast running express engines. But his Z Class engines contained much more. The NER were assessing the advantages to be gained by superheating at this time, so when twenty were constructed, ten were built with saturated boilers and the rest with Schmidt superheaters. This entailed different sized cylinders (15½in and 16½in) and boilers producing different pressures (175psi and 160psi respectively). In tests that followed, the superheated engines proved themselves superior and others in the class were converted to this form during the war. Such was their success that they were recognised in one professional journal as being the 'North Eastern's best big passenger engine'. So it would remain until Raven experimented with a large Pacific design in the early 1920s.

Although Thompson was sitting on the periphery of all these developments he couldn't have failed to take note of them and may have discussed them with his CME, especially as they were soon to be related by marriage. In late 1911, he was also invited to join a party led

by Raven going to the USA to study electrification projects, a sign, perhaps, of his growing status. It seems to have been an important tour for Thompson, not so much in terms of railways per se, but in revealing the way senior managers operate. Whether by chance or design, he was also invited to view other industrial concerns, most notably the new Ford Car Plant at Detroit. The impact of its production line technology and systems seem to have been significant and his albums contain many photographs and articles about these works. However, he also followed Raven's lead in studying the East Coast railway systems, particularly that operated by the

As part of his experiments with 4-6-0s, Raven introduced Stumpf Uniflow cylinders to locomotive design and had them built into the last S2 constructed in 1913 (No. 825 – portrayed above). The system first came to notice in Britain during 1827, but a patent did not appear until 1885, submitted by Leonard Todd. The system found its primary application in large, static engines and it was Professor Johann Stumpf, when teaching in Berlin, who adapted it for use in mobile steam engines. This work then appeared in four patents submitted between 1908 to 1910. When designing his engine, Raven anticipated that the system would reduce or eradicate condensation in the cylinders and make the engines more fuel efficient. This was achieved, or so it was hoped, by having separate intake and exhaust ports, with steam flowing in one direction only. Comparative trials showed sufficient improvement to justify extending the system, post-war, to the last Z Class engine built. But the work went no further and in 1924 No. 825 was rebuilt with conventional cylinders. (*PR/RH*)

(Above) One of Walter Smith's experimental four-cylinder Class 4CC locomotive as captured in Thompson's photograph albums. If these pictures were a true representation of his thoughts, they reveal someone with a deep interest in locomotive engineering and the possibilities inherent in the exploration of new or alternative ideas. He showed the same interest in carriage design. (Below) A Z Class engine in action. (*ET/DN*)

One of many photographs and articles concerning Ford's production line techniques which Thompson collected. His interest in this method of working wasn't confined to the car industry but covered many other areas too. His advocacy of these processes would have a profound impact on the workshops for which he was responsible and even office layouts. In some ways he was predicting the time and motion business that would become a basic part of industry. (*ET/DN*)

Pennsylvania Railroad Company, which also features significantly in the items he collected during the tour.

Whilst Raven's patronage may have helped Thompson's career prospects, advancement may still not have been as swift as he wished. So, in 1912 he applied to become Carriage and Wagon Superintendent with the Great Northern Railway and was recruited by Gresley, then the GNR's Locomotive Superintendent. There has been speculation that this move may have been arranged so that accusations of nepotism within the NER might be avoided. However, there is no evidence to confirm this,

so it may simply have been a case of an ambitious man seeking promotion where none appeared to exist within the NER. He did, after all, move from Derby to Woolwich and then Hull seeking advancement, so it was probably no different when choosing to join the GNR.

Whilst at Hull, then Gateshead, he had learnt much and observed even more but this wasn't simply a result of Worsdell and Raven's leadership. Two other key figures in his development were Charles Baister and Arthur Stamer, both of whom became personal friends as well as colleagues. Baister in particular did more than

Above, left and opposite: Judging by the photos and postcards Thompson collected during his visit to the USA in 1911, he was impressed by what he saw on the Pennsylvania Railroad. By 1910, this company, though dominated by steam locomotion on its 10,000-plus miles system, had begun experimenting with internal combustion and electrification. The top photograph is simply inscribed with the words 'the PRR's senior managers and supervisors 1911', with no names added. The left picture shows a McKeen Motor Car which the PRR purchased from its builders in Nebraska in 1909 and which ran until 1920. The postcard that follows portrays a day to day scene on the New York Terminal Area third rail electrified system which opened in 1910 and was a major draw for Vincent Raven during the tour. The second phase of this PRR project adopted overhead wires and was opened in 1915. (*ET/DN*)

The Pennsylvania Tunnels, New York.

anyone else to ease Thompson into a senior management position and then guide him through an important phase in his career. It was a period in which the skills of a leader had to be learnt and honed, with an emphasis on operational efficiency, target setting and achievement, the economics of day to day life in a major industrial concern, an awareness of politics and personnel management. But underlying it all was an astute understanding of engineering issues and the need to balance many factors if success were to be achieved.

Stamer's impact on Thompson's career was less obvious than Baister's but longer lasting. He was described as urbane, astute, sporting and a natural leader with excellent engineering credentials. He developed a close relationship with Thompson from 1906 onwards, an association that would last until Stamer retired in 1933. Unlike Raven, who gained an unenviable reputation as a tough, uncompromising manager of staff particularly industrial employees, with whom he could be crushing and inflexible, Stamer preferred negotiation and a more reasoned approach. In a rapidly changing world, where

equality and democracy were becoming prominent features of working life, Stamer's approach was more likely to succeed.

This was a lesson Thompson came to appreciate, although early in his career he had a tendency to copy Raven's demigod approach, occasionally causing unnecessary offence in the process. But he wasn't alone in this. The long-established principle of worker subservience and deference were deeply rooted in Victorian society and many found it hard to let this go. It was, after all, very easy for leaders to work in this way – cheap labour glad of any work, no serious consideration of health and safety issues and few if any employment rights to worry about. Many like Raven found it difficult to change and would struggle as industrial democracy spread. So, perhaps, he was lucky to retire in 1922 before this became a significant problem. Thompson, voluntarily or not, did at least embrace change and seek to replicate Stamer's more balanced approach to these issues. The civilising influence of his marriage in 1913 may have helped this process still further.

Charles Baister (left) and Arthur Stamer (right). Both men were long term friends and associates of Vincent Raven and each had been working with the NER for many years by the time Thompson arrived; since 1881 and 1891 respectively. Baister had in fact begun his apprenticeship at the Stockton and Darlington North Road Works in 1869 and remained there until 1876 before searching for pastures new. For five years, he moved around the industry spending time working at the docks in West Hartlepool, then with the South Eastern and Chatham Railway and, finally, working on a tramp steamer. He returned to Darlington and the NER where he soon found favour and by 1893 had risen to become Raven's assistant and Superintendent at Gateshead. Stamer was the son of the Rt Reverend Sir Lovelace Stamer and attended Rugby School before becoming an engineering pupil with Beyer, Peacock. Joining the NER at the age of 22, he rose quickly from Assistant Shed Foreman to become Raven's Assistant Mechanical Engineer in 1910. During this period, he became a strong advocate of the electrification programme as well as being closely involved in the locomotive development programme. During the war years, he became acting CME when Raven was seconded to Woolwich. (*THG*)

Raven's second daughter was in her mid-twenties when she met her husband to be. She was born in 1884 and christened Edith Gwendoline according to her birth certificate, though she seems to have varied the spelling of her second name. So Gwen, Guen or Gwendolen were used at different times in her life. In childhood it was discovered that she suffered from a congenital heart defect, which appears to have been exacerbated by an attack of scarlet fever. As a consequence, a nurse was employed by her parents to tend to her needs and she carried ill-health into adulthood, where she was noted as suffering from chronic mitral stenosis, a debilitating, long term condition for which there was no cure. There were also periodic bouts of rheumatic fever, which in the days before antibiotics carried very severe risks.

How much her husband knew of this when they married we shall never know, but her condition would have required careful handling, making the thought of children inadvisable if not impossible. In his biography

Gwen or Guen Thompson (pictured here in the 1930s) was by all accounts a friendly person who was very close to her parents. Health problems beset her from childhood and would have affected her marriage. Although Thompson appears to have been a devoted husband, vague rumours of infidelity did surface at the time. This photo of him appeared in the 1930s but seems to have been taken much earlier suggesting a slight vanity. As always, he is well-groomed with a quality of suit that suggests that his family's tailoring links were still close. (*ET/DN/RH*)

of Thompson, Peter Grafton contemplated the nature of their relationship and considered the rumours that their marriage was possibly not as happy as it might have been. Even stories of infidelity began to surface. This must remain speculation, of course, but if true it followed a pattern that was quite common in the upper echelons of society at the time, where men were known to 'take a mistress'. But unless either husband or wife chose to make reference to this free behaviour it was given no public face, so stifling rumour. In truth, Thompson was nearly thirty when they met and as a healthy young man, is unlikely to have lived a celibate life. So, being married to someone with such a serious, long term illness would have been difficult on many levels.

Their wedding on 25 June 1913, at the Holy Trinity Church in Darlington, was a major social event attended by family and friends as well as many colleagues from the NER and GNR, including Gresley. In addition, his nine-year-old daughter Violet was one of four brides-maids, suggesting a warmth and closeness between the two families. Equally, it might simply have been the display of an ambitious man seeking to get close to his leader. Either way, Gresley's presence is interesting in the light of the many rumours that surround their relationship.

By this time, Thompson was already living in a GNR house in Thorne Road, quite close to Gresley and his family. It was here he took his young bride after their honeymoon in Switzerland. And so life might have gone on, except that in the background old European enmities were beginning to unravel and create problems that diplomacy was failing to resolve. In ignorance of this cataclysm, Edward and Gwen settled into a domestic life and, like the majority of the population, lived entirely unaware of what lay ahead and the disruption and sorrow awaiting a country soon to be at war.

Their house had many benefits apart from being large, spacious and supported by servants. It was close to Doncaster Works and a golf course where Thompson played regularly, occasionally with Gresley, who had just recovered from blood poisoning and phlebitis which nearly cost him his leg and brought him close to death. Sport continued to play a major part in Thompson's life, with cricket in particular providing a pleasant distraction from an increasingly busy work schedule. On occasions, he turned out for the Works' team and seems eager, despite any reserve he might have felt, to contribute fully to all aspects of life at Doncaster. In this he was probably influenced by Gresley and Stamer who were willing participants in all such things, as many surviving pictures bear witness.

As Carriage and Wagon Superintendent, Thompson was following in Gresley's footsteps. The older man held this post from 1905 to 1910 before succeeding Henry Ivatt as Locomotive Engineer, or CME as it became known. At the comparatively young age of 32, Thompson must have expected that this posting might take his career in a similar direction, which but for the war it may have done. When he arrived at Doncaster, all seemed set fair and in his first few months he took time to observe all that was going on around him and establish the limits of his authority. Gresley would, undoubtedly, have monitored his new recruit and set him challenging targets. As ex-head of C&W, he might have been forgiven for retaining a paternal interest in the work they were doing,

The peaceful and pleasant scene in Thorne Road, Doncaster, at the time the Thompsons lived there. They were noted for keeping an open house and welcoming many guests, all carefully recorded in their visitors' book. Her father would undoubtedly have been pleased to note that they re-named the property 'Litchfield', in so doing adopting his second name. (*THG*)

having invested so much time and effort in developing new rolling stock, and may have been tempted to micromanage his deputy because of it. But there is no evidence of any disputes, though it is likely that two such forceful men may have gently locked horns at some stage as they tried to establish their respective positions.

At this time there were few public meetings between the railway companies, although many of their leading engineers were members of professional institutions where ideas and information might be exchanged. One of the few exceptions to this was the periodic meetings of the Locomotive Engineers and Carriage and Wagon Superintendents held at the Railway Clearing House, Seymour Street, in London. The RCH had been established in 1842 to manage the allocation of revenue when one company's trains used another company's lines.

However, over the decades that followed it gradually took on a broader function. By the early twentieth century, it had become a place where companies could discuss issues of concern, debate common practices and resolve any disagreements that had arisen. These covered a wide range of technical subjects, but would have been supplemented by many informal and unrecorded discussions that could, potentially, have had long term benefits in locomotive and rolling stock design.

So, the RCH went beyond providing a central accounting function to becoming a body with some professional status in railway engineering. As such their meetings were attended by many of the leading lights of the day including George Churchward, Gresley, William Stanier, Alfred Hill, Oliver Bulleid, Richard Maunsell, Charles Collett, Frederick Hawksworth and many more.

A day to day scene of life in the carriage works at Doncaster that would become only too familiar to Thompson and which he recorded in his albums. (*ET/DN*)

The work that Thompson managed had many different facets, including maintenance of all the company's horse drawn vehicles as this picture reveals. It is interesting to note the number of female employees captured in this pre-war scene. During the conflict, the number would rise significantly, as war devoured young men at an alarming and unsustainable rate. Without so many women workers coming forward, heavy industry would have ground to a halt with alarming consequences for the war effort. It is also interesting to note that both Gresley and Thompson were early advocates of a mixed work force and actively recruited women well before the war drove such a need. It was a policy that Thompson pursued throughout his working life, suggesting quite modern views on equality. (*ET/DN*)

The offices of the Railway Clearing House in Seymour Street in London as they appeared when Gresley and Thompson attended the Locomotive Engineer and Carriage and Wagon Superintendents meetings there. (*THG*)

Shortly after arriving at Doncaster, Gresley had developed sufficient trust in Thompson to send him to these meetings in his place, though occasionally accompanied him. This carried on well into the late 1930s and suggests a high level of trust between the two men, which is interesting especially in the light of an often described cooling in their personal relationship which took place when they both served with the LNER. There is also the interesting issue of contacts Thompson may have established across the industry during these sessions and the part they could have played in his development as an engineer. Judging by later correspondence, he certainly befriended Stanier and shared many common ideas on production and design.

One of the first tasks Thompson managed on arriving at Doncaster was to supervise an active carriage building programme that Gresley had initiated. The GNR doesn't seem to have enjoyed the NER's economic success, so at times had been forced into a more active programme of make do and mend. Nevertheless, Gresley's dynamism drove change and he overcame some restrictions by using articulation to turn old six wheeled carriages into something more modern, with greater capacity. At the same time, he was able to get Board approval to modernise the fleet and, amongst other things, build a range of new dining cars. He, with others, sensed that customer needs were changing and these new carriages would tap into a new, more profitable market. It fell to Thompson to take on this work which he duly recorded in a series of photos. He in turn began to look more closely at carriage design, prompted in part by the many accident investigations in which he had participated over the years. Because of this, he became a firm believer in the need for stronger, more robust designs, seeing traditional wooden carriages as intrinsically unsafe. The few papers of his that remain make this point very clearly, but it was an issue that would take many decades to resolve satisfactorily. Nevertheless, he was an early advocate of change and pursued the issue tenaciously.

During 1913, correspondence records that he was in regular touch with William Lysaght, of John Lysaght Ltd, who by then were producing 175,000 tons of rolled steel a year in their 42 mills around Newport in South Wales. The two men shared a common interest in safety issues surrounding the use of wood in vehicles that might sustain impact damage. It was a subject brought into sharp focus by an article in the *Illustrated London News* that year. Having followed a number of accident investigations around the world, journalists questioned the wisdom of continuing to build wooden carriages when the damage they sustained was so much greater than steel-based types. There were, of course, good commercial reasons for Lysaghts to advocate this change and produce steel panels for the railway industry. But their concern for safety seems to have been genuine enough and in Thompson they found someone of like mind, who, it seems, was prepared to argue this case with great determination.

All this was to prove of little avail though, with wooden frames and teak external panelling continuing to dominate construction of carriages on the GNR and then the LNER under Gresley for many years, despite its known shortcomings. Safety was one issue, but in a memo of November 1913, to the Locomotive Engineer, Thompson raised the additional problem of rotting wood in window frames due to an ingress of water. Gresley's preferred style seems to have been square cornered, rectangular windows carried up to the cantrail just below the roof. Such a design was known to leak and considerable effort was expended in damage repair. Thompson pointed this out and suggested using steel as well as applying modifications to eradicate the problem of water damage. Despite this, the design remained unaltered and it wasn't until the mid-1930s that the policy began to change. To produce a sleekness of line, the special rake of coaches for the streamlined Silver Jubilee service were built with steel panelling over the wooden frames. However, they retained the square cornered windows as preferred by Gresley.

This seems to have been one issue on which the two men didn't agree and as the years passed the list seems to have increased in length. Before any dispute might deepen between them, a rather more serious campaign consumed all their effort and attention. The war some politicians and military leaders had predicted for many years finally found its trigger on a hot summer's morning in Sarajevo. Within weeks, events escalated, in an atmosphere of mutual distrust and provocation, into a conflict so easily avoided if men of goodwill had prevailed. But it wasn't to be and a remorseless timetable was set in motion, with leaders either unwilling or unable to stop the descent into horror in which millions of lives would be lost.

Above and below: Two photos commissioned or taken by Thompson in late 1912 showing the external and internal layouts of one of the new eight-wheeled dining cars (No. 3250) built at Doncaster that year. (*ET/DN*)

Right and overleaf: Thompson's heavily creased copy of the *Illustrated London News*'s illuminating article on carriage safety published in 1913. (*ET/DN*)

SHOULD RAILWAY-CARRIAGES BE CONSTRUCTED OF STEEL?

Thompson must have watched these events unfold with as much consternation as anyone else. But he, like millions of others, would soon be swept up in the Herculean effort to wrest victory from an enemy who seemed likely to sweep all before them. Whether he welcomed this isn't recorded, but many did and in the first few months of war volunteered in huge numbers for a duty few of them could understand and many might come to regret. Thompson would have felt the fear and reservations common to all those about to fight and yet he did his duty and would serve with great courage and distinction at the Front. And like men of true bravery, he remained silent on the subject and took his memories of these dreadful days to his grave. Was he marked by these experiences? It would be impossible not to be.

CHAPTER 3

THE BLEAKEST WAR

To say that Britain was ill-prepared for a land war in Europe in 1914 would be an understatement. With a relatively small standing army, whose primary aim was to police the Empire, supported by reservists and a few territorial regiments, its chances against an advancing German Army numbered in millions were slim. Luckily, the French were better prepared, in numbers if not tactics, and in the mobile battle that followed, both sides fought themselves to a standstill then went to ground. Lines of trenches soon spread from the Belgian coast down to the Swiss border and the industrial slaughter now seared into our national conscientiousness began. Whilst this happened, Britain's only true military might lay at sea, where the Royal Navy sought to strangle the enemy by blockade and counter the threat of German U Boats before they starved Britain of essential supplies. These were invaluable tools, but inevitably they were long term strategies unlikely to effect the course of war on land quickly.

It wasn't simply a case that the British Army had insufficient numbers to fight this war. It was also ill-prepared when it came to weaponry. In 1914, an established regiment would be lucky to have a single machine gun and artillery fortunate to have sufficient shells for more than token resistance. If anything, the territorials were in a worst state, with many going to France and Belgium without ever having fired their guns and clips of bullets that wouldn't feed into rifles, a problem first realised when the enemy were bearing down on them. The least said about their strategies the better. Fighting a well-organised, well-equipped force made up of seven individual armies with tactics little advanced from the Battle of Waterloo, was naïve to say the least. Things needed to change and change quickly if the Germans were to be held or defeated. Sadly, whilst weapons and numbers improved, the sheer industrial muscle of both sides and their ability to feed troops and equipment into the front line on a conveyor belt, ensured stagnation. The impasse this created remained unbroken until mid-1918, when a war of some movement returned. But in the meantime, each attempt to break the deadlock led to a massacre and the defilement of millions of young lives.

THE ROYAL ENGINEERS

Regtl. Button. 1772   Present Day Button

The static, heavily industrialised war that ensued soon demanded a vast team of engineers and other specialists to sustain it. By 1918, the Royal Engineers alone had nearly a third of a million men in their ranks, broken down into Field Companies, tunnellers, signallers, men to build and run a huge railway network and much, much more. To all this was added the sheer physical effort of the infantry who, when not fighting and dying, dug, wired and resupplied their own lines. But it was the Royal Engineers that absorbed Edward Thompson and many other highly skilled men.

Railways became the cornerstone of all that happened on the Western Front, on both sides. A battlefield of such size, with millions of men tied down in a war of attrition and little movement, required constant re-supply. The French railway system soon proved inadequate for the task and a rapid expansion was essential if the war was to be fought to a successful conclusion. Soon the countryside was covered by a latticework of track, employing tens of thousands of men, including specialists such as Edward Thompson. Later analysis has suggested that it was the efficiency of the railways that contributed to the stalemate. Each side was able to feed men and equipment into the front line when the enemy threatened a breakthrough more quickly than the other side could in support of their attack. True or not, it took a mighty effort to keep the system going and the use of 600mm track, as shown above, proved essential. This system had been developed in France by the Decauville Company during the 1870s and used readymade track fastened to steel sleepers, in portable easily laid sections. It linked the front line to the broader gauge system through a series of transfer areas and it proved tough and flexible enough to stand the rigours of war. (*ET/DN*)

When trying to trace his war career we face one stumbling block – his army personnel records don't seem to have survived and he chose not to write or speak about his experiences to any great extent, although several letters have survived. In the National Archives, only a single card exists which states that he went to France in December 1916 as a Major with the Royal Engineers and became a Lieutenant Colonel, after a period acting in this role. For this he was entitled to wear the British War Medal and the Victory Medal. However, the absence of records is not unusual. During the Luftwaffe's Blitz on London in 1940-41, the archives containing all personal files, held at Hayes in West London, were bombed. In the fire that followed, it was estimated by the MOD in the early 1980s that a considerable part of 1,900 tons of First World War personnel records were destroyed, Thompson's files most probably amongst them.

In their absence, biographers have had to settle on some very basic details indeed. He served initially at Woolwich then joined the Movements Branch of the Directorate of Transportation in France. He was mentioned in despatches twice, 'demobbed' in 1919 and was awarded the OBE in recognition of his services. Thompson added a little to this when asked to provide a brief resume of his career for both Marlborough and Pembroke Colleges. For his old school he simply stated, 'RE France 1914-1918, Lt Col OBE 1919' and for Cambridge, 'Lt Col RE, OBE (Military – March 1918), mentioned in despatches'. Like so many veterans of this terrible war, he was very modest about his achievements, which were, in fact, quite considerable. But whilst rank and an OBE are one thing, two 'mentions' is quite another. They were awarded for 'gallant and meritorious action in the face of the enemy' and entitled the bearer to attach a spray of oak leaves, cast in bronze, to their Victory Medal. These didn't go to people far away from the lines and didn't 'come up with the rations' as many soldiers described some decorations. Thompson would have earned these citations under fire and at great personal risk. Such things can come at a terrible personal cost and rarely, if ever, leave someone unscarred or unaffected by their experiences. It is this crucial issue that earlier accounts of Thompson's life have failed to describe when assessing his personality, behaviour and attitudes. For it seems to me that the pre-war Thompson was significantly different to the person who emerged from the conflict. And this in an age when millions of seriously disturbed men returned home without treatment or help, to a world that neither knew or seemed to care about their suffering.

The photographs that Thompson collected of the battlefield were more often than not general views that surveyed a scene; assessing and evaluating. These three battered pictures, covered by heavy foxing, from one of his albums, capture the battlefield in front of Ypres at the end of 1917. They note the geography of the area, the battle damage and the difficulties faced in laying the essential narrow gauge railways and roads needed to keep the front line supplied. It is probably safe to say that he himself served on this particular battlefield and lived in these appalling conditions. There are other photographs of the trenches at Arras, Cambrai and Messines, plus pictures of battle damage behind the front line. Another group covers the in depth preparation of defences on the Somme early in 1918, days before the German Army launched its last big series of offences lasting until July and their aftermath. (*ET/DN*)

Thompson, whether with the Army, the GNR, NER and LNER, was always eager to collect pictures of those with whom he served, though not of himself. Being in charge, and financially sound, it is most probable that he took the photographs himself or arranged for the work to be done by professionals. This says much about his interest in people and events, particularly on the railways where he was eager to record their contributions and honour them in this way. On the back of this picture he has simply written,' One of my parties of engineers who fought at Messines Ridge – June 1917'. Although there to construct gun emplacements, railways, strengthened defences and much more, they often took part in the fighting, particularly when the enemy counterattacked. Engineer casualties, although not as heavy as the infantry, were severe and resulted in about 15-20 per cent of deaths, with three times that number mentally or physically wounded. 'Shell shock' was barely recognised at this time let alone the long term effects of what we now know as Post-Traumatic Stress Disorder. (*ET/DN*)

The reality of war in 1914-1918 is now barely understood, because all the veterans are long gone. In many ways, our interpretation of these events has become clichéd and stereotyped by familiarity. This has helped create a blindness which inhibits our ability to fully comprehend the true impact of such destruction and its lasting effects on lives. And as veterans would later utter in the many books that appeared in the years that followed, 'if you weren't there you couldn't possibly understand'. So, we have become distant and desensitised to the true

horrors of this war and the impact it had on even the toughest, most resolute of individuals. It has become too easy to recall that such and such a person served on the Western Front, then look winsomely into the distance as though true understanding exists, when it doesn't. So to truly comprehend Edward Thompson's life after the war we have to appreciate what he went through and try and assess how the horrors he witnessed affected his personality. From the evidence available, it seems to have been profound indeed, adding new layers to an already complex, highly intelligent character. It is probably true to say that these changes didn't always sit easily in his relationships with friends and colleagues in the peacetime world.

In 1920, Philip Gibbs, a war correspondent, perhaps best summed this up when writing of returning soldiers:

'Something was wrong. They put on civilian clothes and looked very much like the young men who had gone to business in the days before the war. But they had not come back the same men. They were subject to queer moods and tempers. Fits of profound depression alternated with a restless desire for pleasure. Many of them were easily moved to passion when they lost control of themselves. Many were bitter of speech… Something seemed to have snapped in them.'

It was a theme that Stuart Cloete, another veteran, picked up when writing of the isolation that he imposed on himself in the years that followed the war:

'I realised that this is what I needed. Silence. Now that I could let go, I broke down, avoided strangers, cried easily and had terrible nightmares . . . Something in the works was broken, never to be repaired.'

Today, it is almost impossible to understand the scale of this tragedy. The statistics are mind numbing in their enormity. Shattered minds and bodies afflicted millions in this country alone. For those with the most severe medical conditions, 113 special hospitals existed, supported by 319 separate surgical clinics, eye clinics, heart centres and 48 huge special mental institutions. To these many tens of thousands were committed and restrained for life without hope of recovery or release. One of the last of them, David Ireland, a despatch rider in 1916, spent 77 years in Stratheden Psychiatric Hospital, dying there in the early 1990s.

With such a sea of suffering to manage, the authorities could do little more than skim the surface of this overwhelming problem. As a result, the silent majority were left to their own devices and had to cope as best they could with their mental and physical scars. Some appear to have achieved a sort of balance relatively quickly, depending on their experiences and the support of family, but for others it didn't happen for decades, if ever.

It was also a process made more difficult by a largely war-weary population at home, to whom surviving soldiers saw themselves as being an embarrassing legacy. And for many veterans, those who hadn't served were seen as 'shirkers', especially if they had profited in some way from the war in wealth or position, so were shunned as a result. The gulf between those who were there and those who weren't was infinite.

So how did these war experiences affect those who were there and what may Thompson have seen and suffered in two continuous years at the Front? To understand this, we need to appreciate the nature of the war in France and Belgium and the way the body and mind were flagellated by its worst excesses.

The first thing to realise is that there were few safe billets where people could hide from enemy fire, with heavy artillery capable of hitting targets twenty or so miles behind the lines and aircraft also striking deep into friendly territory. And the guns rarely ceased their pounding, the front line being particularly vulnerable to all manner of explosive devices, killing and maiming indiscriminately. The noise, impact and shock waves of these bombardments were described as capable of 'destroying the body and the mind'. But their torment began well before the explosion. The experienced soldier could pick out each gun or mortar, note its sound, calibre and trajectory and where they might explode. But this knowledge didn't add a layer of protection because rarely was there anywhere to run or hide. In some ways, the newcomer was protected from all this by their innocence though they too quickly succumbed to the shock, as days turned into months.

Beyond the incessant shell fire, there was the constant threat of small arms fire, trench raids, snipers and much more, all ensuring that soldiers could only live a troglodyte existence if they were to stand any chance of survival. Yet in such a war, remaining in trenches or underground and simply holding ground could not be allowed. Maintaining the offensive was practised no matter what the cost and by the time Thompson arrived, the main slaughter was well established, with the haemorrhage of men becoming a daily occurrence to be endured.

For many soldiers when looking back, this became of lesser importance to the living conditions they endured. Memoirs are full of descriptions of mud, rats, rain, extreme cold and all the illnesses such things imposed.

Another of Thompson's photographs of a group of Royal Engineers in camp 'enjoying' a break from the front line. On the reverse of this picture is written 'Sutton has hold of the dog'. At rest pets such as this attached themselves to the troops and sometimes remained with them going back to the Front, providing a rare source of affection and domesticity in unbearable circumstances. (*ET/DN*)

This is a relatively well-known photograph of an unidentified working party, possibly Royal Engineers, trudging to or from the front line. By some means Thompson acquired an original copy of this picture, suggesting that it moved him in some way. (*ET/DN*)

Worst still, there was the need to live side by side with the unburied dead, as Norman Gladden recalled in his book *The Somme*:

'The dead were everywhere amidst earth and broken timber. Never before had I seen a man who had just been killed. A glance was enough. His face and body were terribly gashed as though some terrific force had pressed him down, and blood flowed from a dozen fearful wounds. The smell of blood mixed with the fumes of the shell filled me with nausea. Only a great effort saved my limbs from giving way beneath me. I could see from the sick grey faces of the file that these feelings were generally shared. A voice seemed to whisper with unchallengeable logic, "Why shouldn't you be next?"...'

The dead could lie undisturbed, except by shellfire, for long periods, whole or in bits, in various stages of decay, filling the living world with a stench that became worse in summer, attracting millions of flies and rats grown fat on flesh.

The cumulative effect of all these things couldn't be avoided by anyone who lived daily near the Front for any length of period. Some endured longer than others, with the responsibility of command helping many officers and NCOs cope more effectively with the strains, but even this had its limits. What often tipped the balance between survival or disintegration, apart from luck that is, was the bond of comradeship and shared experience. Yet even this could be a doubled-edged sword, because if friendships were torn apart by sudden death, the sense of loss could be overpowering and

The day to day reality of war on the Western Front was about survival, but it was also about living, perpetually, with the dead. Very few photographs such as this, showing the horrors, were allowed to be published at the time. The likely effect on the morale of a war-weary population was deemed too serious to be risked. For the soldiers, there was no such escape except illness, wounds or death. (*THG*)

A suggestion of a lost friendship? A photo which Thompson kept of a Captain Jack Richardson who was 'killed in action'. The writing on the back appears to be Thompson's, but there are no other details. His cap badge suggests that he served with the York and Lancaster Regiment and one wonders whether he was one of many officers on detachment to the Royal Engineers. (*ET/DN*)

isolate the victim even more. My maternal grandfather, a 1913 intake territorial, who served with the Post Office Rifles in France from March 1915 to May 1918, recalled that he was the only one of his original draft who survived in service until the end of the war. And as he remarked 'this was without all the others who came and went between times. It was a very lonely business being a survivor'. In his case it was a 'business' from which he never fully recovered, even with the benefit of a stable career and a happy family life.

Did Thompson lose many friends and colleagues? Being an Engineer didn't come with an added level of protection and casualties were high, so, inevitably, he must have seen many familiar faces disappear. Did he live in the appalling conditions that were the common lot of troops along the front line and behind it? Undoubtedly: the Engineers, by the very nature of their work, had to be in the thick of things and experience the shellfire, poison gas, mud, rats, lice and carnage. Was he good at what he did? Decorations and promotion suggest he was. As a Major, then Lt Colonel, would he have fallen victim to the war weariness and severe stress that affected so many others? His strength of character would have helped considerably as would his experience as a leader, and he seems to have avoided physical wounds. But two Mentioned in Despatches suggests he didn't spare himself, as other senior officers might have done, and regularly faced the enemy taking his chances with his men. Leading by example is a commendable thing, but the consequences can be severe and damaging even for the most resolute.

Here was a brave man serving his country and leading by example, but inevitably it was a 'game of blood', which would tax even the strongest and leave them depleted and disturbed. In Thompson's case, the evidence suggests he went from being a man who in pre-war days seems to have been a gregarious, though occasionally aloof person, to one more inward-looking, impatient and less accepting of other people at times. But, as it did for many, it also seems to have created a sense of restlessness and frustration which drove him hard. Could this have been a reaction to the disturbing effects of his war service? I think it most likely.

For him, though, the war had a slow start. Many railway employees were given reserved status, their work being deemed essential to the war effort, though many chose to ignore this and volunteer. In some ways, Thompson had been prepared for some elements of army life at Marlborough, where there was an active military training programme and a cadet force. Many classes were, in fact, set up specifically to prepare boys for the Army and by the time they left, they were imbued with the culture and a basic understanding of the military world, though, ultimately, nothing they learnt here or at Sandhurst could prepare them for what they would face in France.

As the war settled into a static but violent pattern, Britain quickly expanded its forces until in 1916 it had millions under arms and a force equal to its French allies. They were spread over a Front stretching from the coast down to the Somme, where, in July that year, they began their greatest battle to date. Whilst this happened, Thompson remained at Doncaster, with Gresley, involved in essential war work and the production of armaments. But as the conflict deepened, and losses increased, a life at home, no matter how important it might be, became too much to bear for many and they too joined up. Feeling a heavy obligation to serve at the Front, Thompson was undoubtedly pulled in conflicting directions, none more so than in the need to care for his ailing wife. Gresley may also have felt this way, but at 40, with a large family to support as well as being CME of an essential service with commitments to the war, he clearly felt it important to remain.

Did the two of them debate service at the Front and did Thompson express his wish to go? We shall never know, but it was a conversation that is likely to have taken place especially between a leader and one of his senior managers, both with heavy obligations at home. In reserved industries, it did become custom and practice for those wishing to volunteer for active service to seek the approval of those in charge and in this case Gresley would undoubtedly have expressed his opinion. But whether he acquiesced or resisted became immaterial when Vincent Raven took the matter out of his hands.

During 1915, Raven had been seconded to the Ministry of Munitions as Chief Superintendent at Woolwich, with Arthur Stamer temporarily taking his place as CME, and some months later he drew his son-in-law into the organisation. This might smack of nepotism, but Raven's actions can also be seen as seeking to resolve a problem for Thompson. If Gresley didn't agree to release him and his assistant was determined to go, there would have been an impasse between two stubborn, strong men. Raven, with the power of Lloyd George, his Minister, behind him, could claim exigencies of war and bring in whoever he so wished. So he laid claim to Thompson and to Woolwich he went for a short period before transferring

Engine No. 1290 'jacked up' and undergoing maintenance whilst serving with an unidentified unit on the Western Front in 1917 or '18. This 2-6-2T locomotive was one of a 100 built by Alco at their Cooke Locomotive Works in New York in 1917. They are thought to be the largest and most powerful engines run by the British Army on their narrow gauge system. (*ET/DN*)

to the Engineers in late 1916 and departing for the Front in December. In so doing, he released the care of his wife into the hands of his mother-in-law, with whom she apparently lived until her husband returned, judging by the few letters that have survived from this time.

One can only wonder at Gresley's reaction to this. With so many pressing demands on his time and energy it was probably an inconvenience but no more than that. Yet some years later, when recalling her father's relationship with Thompson, his daughter Violet remembered Gresley using the word 'disloyal' in relation to his assistant, but provided no other details or clarification. A harsh word

indeed and one wonders whether events in 1916 may have given rise to these thoughts, especially when considering that their relationship before the war seems to have been relaxed and friendly. One thing is certain though, once the war was over, Thompson would only return to the GNR for a brief period before transferring back to the NER.

Although records for this period are sparse, it is generally agreed that Thompson joined the Director General of Military Railway's staff in France. In late 1916, Eric Campbell Geddes, a Conservative MP and businessman, had been appointed to the post, which he combined with that of Inspector-General of Transportation.

Eric Geddes (left) as DG of Military Railways in France, with the rank of Major General. He remained in this post until becoming First Lord of the Admiralty in July 1917. This dynamic man had built a career working on railways in India. On returning to Britain, he joined the NER and became its Deputy General Manager in 1911 before moving on to greater glory as Deputy DG at the Ministry of Munitions in 1915, then DG of Military Railways. He, of course, had worked alongside Raven with the NER and would have been aware of Thompson's burgeoning career, which may account for his posting to France in 1916. However, Geddes may have been aided in this by his former assistant on the NER, Ralph Wedgwood (right), a Trinity College Cambridge man, who had been Chief Goods Manager before the war. In 1915 he joined Geddes, as a Lt Colonel then Brigadier, at 'Munitions'. With Geddes, Raven and Wedgwood working together it was hardly surprising that someone with Thompson's background and organisational skills was chosen and granted senior Army rank during 1916. In 1923 Wedgwood would rise to become the LNER's Chief Officer, where his influence on Thompson's career would continue. (*THG*)

He'd made his name earlier in the war when recruited by Lloyd George to find ways of boosting production of weapons and ammunition. With a small team of experts, he reorganised and streamlined industry to ensure they began to meet the Army's ever increasing demands. Having achieved this success, he was then set the challenging target of improving the railway system on the Western Front. Haig, Commander in Chief of the British Expeditionary Force, had come to realise that his ambitious plans for the offensive depended upon being able to feed men and material from ports to trenches and gun lines as rapidly as possible. His experience to date had been far from impressive, little helped by the inability of so many of his senior officers to predict and plan need effectively. And as had been shown during the early battles, the ability to move reserves quickly to support any

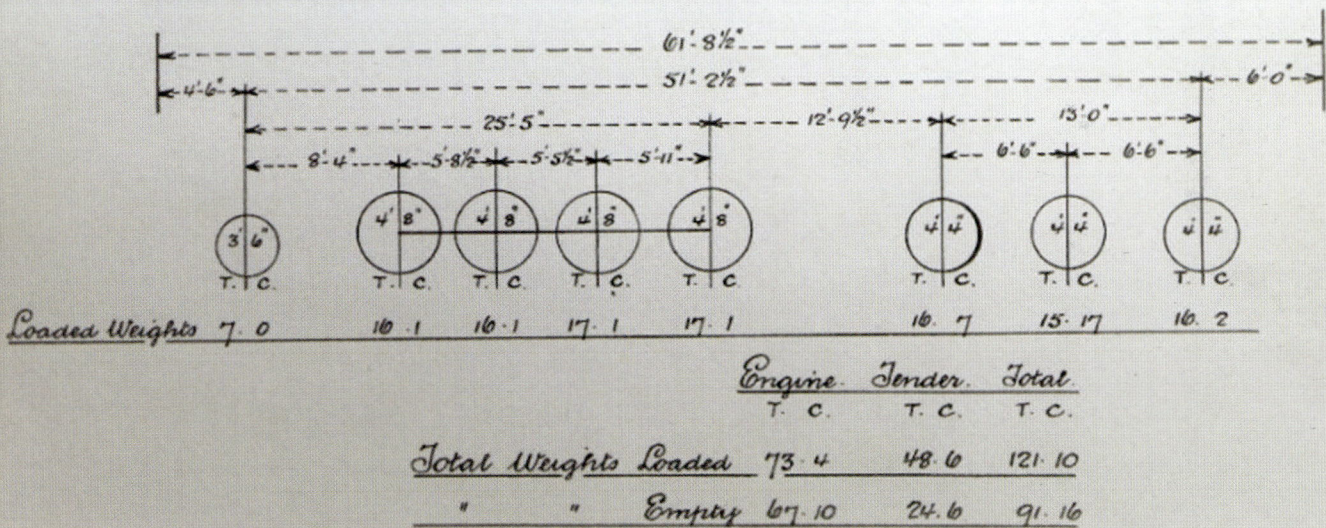

Above and overleaf: As the war on the Western Front grew in scale the BEF found that it couldn't rely upon the French and Belgium railway services to meet its broad-gauge needs. To fill the gap, the War Department requisitioned some 600 locomotives from many of Britain's railway companies. But it gradually became apparent that some degree of standardisation was necessary and the Great Central Railway's Class 8K 2-8-0, which first appeared in 1912 under the guiding hand of John Robinson, the company's CME, was chosen. By the end of the war, 521 had been procured and would clearly have been noted and possibly admired by Thompson. Post-war, many were loaned to a number of companies, with 400 plus eventually being inherited or purchased by the newly formed LNER (and re-designated as Class 04s). In due course, and in another war these sturdy locomotives would again feature in Thompson's life, by which time he was CME.

The 8Ks were probably the most successful of the standard-gauge locomotives employed by the BEF and their history is captured in these four pictures. The two pictures, above and on the facing page, were collected by Robert Thom, who at the time was with the GCR, and kept in his album of locos built by the company. The record card on page 77 gives the history of just one of the GCR locos from those that went to France, with a marked lack of information for the period 1916/1918. The final picture, on page 77, shows engine No. 1718 on duty at the Front. (*RT/THG*)

Class 8K Type 2.8.0. Total Engines ... 129.								
Maker	Year Built	No of Engines	Maker	Year Built	No of Engines	Maker	Year Built	No of Engines
G.C.R.	1911	9	North British	1912	48	G.C.R.	1914	15
"	1912	21	" "	1913	2	"	1919	3
Kitson	1912	20	G.C.R.	1913	11			

CYLINDERS.
Diameter .... 21"
Stroke .... 26"
Centres .... 6'-8"

BOILER.
Class .... No 6 Standard
Working Pressure .... 180 Lbs. per □"
Barrel Dia. Outs. Max. .... 5'-0"
Barrel Length .... 15'-0"
Barrel Thickness of Plates .... 5/8"

TUBES.
Large No. 22 Dia. Outs. 5¼"
Small No. 110 Dia. Outs. 2"
Length between Tubeplates .... 15'-4⅜"

SUPERHEATER.
Kind of Header .... Front Cover
Elements { Dia. Outs. 1⅜"
Dia. Ins. 1¹/₁₆"
Number 22

IF FITTED WITH
Draft Retarder ....
Circulating Valve .... Yes
Header Discharge Valve .... Yes
Pressure Release Valve ....
Combined Pressure Release and Piston Valves } .... Yes

FIREBOX SHELL.
Length Outs. at Bottom .... 8'-6"
Width ,, ,, ,, ... 4'-0½"
,, ,, ,, Top .... 5'-2¾"
Thickness of Plates—
Back 21/32 Casing 5/8 Throat 3/4"

COPPER FIREBOX.
Length of Grate .... 7'-9¹⁵/₃₂"
Width ,, ,, ... 3'-4⅞"
Depth to Top of Ring, Front .... 6'-5½"
,, ,, ,, Back .... 5'-3"

Width of Ring.
Back and Front 3" Sides 3"
Thickness of Plates—
Back 9/16 Casing 9/16 Tube { 7/8"
9/16"

HEATING SURFACE.
Firebox Outside .... 154 Sq. ft.
Large Tubes .... 404 ,,
Small Tubes .... 895 ,,
Superheater Inside .... 242 ,,
Total 1745 ,,

GRATE AREA. .... 26 Sq. ft.

WHEELS. Diameter. See Diagram.
Tyres Thickness .... 3½"

JOURNALS. Dia. Length.
Leading Bogie or Truck .... 6" 9"
Leading Coupled .... 8" 9"
Driving .... 8½" 9"
Intermediate .... 8" 9"
Trailing Coupled .... 8" 12"
Trailing Bogie or Truck ....

Tractive Power at { Lbs. 30,913
85% Boiler Pressure { Tons .... 13·75
Adhesion Coefficient. Lbs. per Ton 465
Height. Rail to Top of Chimney .... 13'-3½"
,, ,, Centre of Boiler .... 8'-6½"

VALVES. Kind .... Piston Inside Admission

CYLINDER LUBRICATOR. Kind Mechanical
If Fitted with Steam Sanding Apparatus .... No
,, ,, Train Warming ,, ... Yes

BRAKE. .... Steam & Auto Ejector

TENDER. Capacity. Water, Gallons 4000
,, Coal, Tons 6

WHEELS. Diameter .... 4'-0"

JOURNALS. Dia. 6" Length 11"

breakthrough was often a wish that died still born. This wouldn't improve significantly during the war for various reasons, but there was much else that the railways could achieve in keeping the Front supplied.

In fact, it was Thompson's old friend, Cecil Paget, who had played a leading role in developing the railway system, both standard and narrow gauges, before Geddes arrived in France. It fell to Lightly Simpson, in a meeting of the Institution of Locomotive Engineers, to provide a brief glimpse of these early days when ad hoc arrangements were the norm. As a mechanical engineer, he had been gazetted then appointed as a captain to the Engineers during June 1915, two months after the Railway Operating Division (ROD) was formed for service in France. This followed the deployment of the Engineer's 8th Company to the Front in August 1914, under the command of Lt Colonel Twiss, to begin the task of building an effective railway service to support the BEF's activities; in essence a standard gauge system from ports to a transfer point then a narrow gauge system to take men, armaments and stores to the Front. Simpson recalled that:

'Very soon after our arrival (in France) the OC/ROD, Lt Colonel Paget, came over from the HQ train, then at Calais, to our quarters in a sugar beet factory at Pont d'Ardres. He explained that the authorities wished us to relieve the French engineers who were then working the Hazebrouck-Ypres line, the doubling of which was just being completed. 35 engines would be found waiting for us. These were in a terrible state owing to their not being touched since they were rescued from Belgium and were the first consignment of a large number. To help us with our work we had five or six machines, which the OC had begged, borrowed or stolen from his own railway at home.

(Under) 1970 No. 1236 6236 63583 3.11.46	MAKER North British Co, 63583 3340 &

DEPOT.	CLASS.	TYPE.	BUILT.	REBUILT.	BRAKE.	H.A.	PICK-UP.	VALVES.	REMARKS.
Staveley	8K	2-8-0	Nov		Vac & Steam		Jas. Robinson		
Meaboro 30 9 19		04	1912						
Staveley 13 11 19									
Sheffield 24 1 34		2/19 Circulating & Header Discharge Valves.							
To G.W.R. 23 11 40	BLAST PIPE								
SHEFFIELD 30 4 41									

Robinson Superheater

HEAVY REPAIRS.

	SENT TO GORTON	DATE IN	AT.	BOOKED OUT	BACK IN TRAFFIC.	REMARKS.
14/8/16 5¼"		22 4 16	Gorton Shops	24 6 16	14 8 16	
28/3/19 5¼"		16 11 18	" "	1 2 19	28 3 19	3/19 Collapsible valves.
		12 3 21	" "	28 4 21	13 6 21	6/21 Top feed.
		22 9 23	"	10 11 23	13 11 23	
		6 1 26		16 3 26		
		3 9 28		17 12 28		
		1 12 30	"	5 2 31		
		24 5 33	"	13 7 33 (46,492)		
		30 9 35	"	9 11 35 (52,307)		
		4 2 38	"	19 2 38 (63006)		Fountain Lubr to Archbox w 2/38
		31 7 40	"	17 8 40 (67292)		
		2 3 43	"	10 4 43 (68567)		
		W.R.A	"	12 10 47	C.	
		8 8 50		30 9 50	G 6236	

The threat posed by enemy fire and bombardment from the ground or air was a constant threat resulting in many casualties even well behind the lines, as this ROD locomotive bears witness. (*ET/DN*)

'More men came and more engines, and during the next few months, until August, I was partly occupied at Pont d'Ardres, but most of the time working with Paget at Calais on plans for the future. A move was made to Caffiers Station at the end of August where the detachment continued to grow and were joined by HQ ROD a month later.

'In the early days of the war Lt Colonel Paget had been consulted as to the improvements to be made in the yards and sidings at Boulogne Harbour to support an Army that, in time, would grow from 6 to 60 Divisions. It was stated that a division would need 200 tons of deadweight stores (a day) to keep it supplied. We were told that ammunition, which then did not exceed 600 tons a day, would not be likely to exceed 1,500 tons, though by January 1916 the total daily amount touched 2,300 tons and continued rising. It is interesting to mention that the Germans fired 1,350,000 tons of shells at Verdun, which required 135,000 wagons to carry them, such was the need for an efficient railway system.'

By 1917 it was estimated that there were a 1,000 miles of light railway track, with weekly traffic often reaching 200,000 tons and much higher when an offensive was due:

'After careful study of the probable requirements, Lt Colonel Paget produced a scheme of working that held good for the war. He, with his precise knowledge of the French language and unrivalled skill in railway operating and organisation, had no difficulty in working with the French or in carrying out the orders of higher authority. This involved the complicated movement of men and materials, and it is entirely due to him that the ROD took such a large and important part in contributing to the success of our arms.'

Paget led by example and remained with the ROD until the end of the war, seeing it constantly expand. It is said that he turned down promotion to Brigadier as he didn't wish to be based at the C in C's GHQ, but lived on his own sixteen-carriage train and 'moved from north to south, from one siding to another, as the demands of the railway service changed'. For all his efforts, he was awarded the DSO, the French Legion d'Honneur, was mentioned in despatches and became a Companion of the Order of St Michael and St George.

Despite his best efforts, Paget couldn't manage this huge expansion by himself. Geddes' arrival may be seen as adding much needed weight to the organisation at a crucial time. To do this, he began recruiting more railway specialists to ensure the best minds could be applied to such a crucial task. Thompson would be amongst their number and was soon engulfed in a huge programme of work essential to the success of a series of planned offensives in 1917. With the French on the point of collapse, the pressure on their Front had to be relieved and the new year would see British and Empire forces committed to this thankless task.

If Thompson was recruited to plan and direct some of this work, he seems to have gone beyond this brief and become more involved in actions more akin to infantry work. The line between service in the trenches and the

During daylight hours, smoke from steam locomotives became a giveaway sign for enemy observers to spot and then direct artillery fire. To allow some movement in daylight hours, without giving away these tell-tale signs, combustion engine vehicles such as this were introduced. Though appearing to be 'Heath Robinson' in concept they proved to be remarkably effective, but did lack a steam locomotive's pulling power. In this case the locomotive appears to be a cut down Model T Ford hurriedly pressed into service. Other more effective designs were produced, most notably, by the Motor Rail Company with their Simplex engines. (*ET/DN*)

back areas was one that was easily blurred by the need to construct a railway system that went as far forward as possible. So, in many ways, coming under fire was a necessary part of his work and, judging by his gallantry awards, it was something he did little to avoid.

By 1917, some 40,000 railway workers were attached to the Engineers and another 140,000 or more serving with other units in France. Despite the large numbers involved and the dangerous nature of much of their work a resume included in the Official History makes light of their contribution:

'It was not till the end of 1916 that any great development of the light railways in France took place. The adoption of an extended system was then decided on. Thence forward the personnel employed on light railways increased very largely, and, by the end of the War, there were thirty Light Railway Companies of various descriptions in France.'

It seems that Thompson was first attached to the C in C's General Headquarters staff. Here he would have acted as an advisor, visiting different parts of the line to counsel and instruct operating and construction companies on many specialist issues. But as a Lt Colonel, which he became in late 1917, he would have filled one of a number of Commanding Royal Engineer posts, attached to the Headquarters of a particular Army. They would each be responsible for a number of construction companies, Railway Survey and Reconnaissance teams, workshops, train crew, traffic sections, oversight of the massive new military railway workshop being built at St Etiennee Du Bouvray south-west of Amiens for the BEF and much more. All in all, a microcosm of his life within the NER and GNR, so it is little wonder that he proved successful in this role.

Before he departed for the Front, there was one death to mourn, before the sight and sounds of decease became a daily ritual. His father reached the end of his long and

A perfect picture to illustrate the problems Thompson and his comrades faced in constructing and then maintaining a railway system across a churned up wasteland, constantly traversed by gunfire. They were always under observation from tethered balloons and enemy aircraft throughout daylight hours so making it necessary to carry out a great deal of work under the cover of darkness. (*THG*)

active life on 18 February, aged 82, maintaining his link to Marlborough College to the end as a member of its governing council. His widow seems to have inherited his entire estate, with Edward, and two of her sons-in-law, Henry Beauchamp-Walters, who had married Margaret, and William Johnstone, a Military Outfitter, and Katherine's husband, managing the estate of some £12,000 on her behalf.

With these events still fresh in his mind, and with responsibility for his much loved mother to be considered, Thompson crossed the Channel and entered the battle. As the months passed, he immersed himself in the task at hand, rarely, it seems, ever taking leave. But with action rapidly intensifying as one major battle followed another in quick succession, as Haig tried to achieve an increasingly elusive breakthrough, this isn't surprising. Yet worse was to come at the third Battle of Ypres between July and November 1917, where

Thompson it seems, from the surviving records and photographs, was deeply involved. Passchendaele, as it became known, has become a byword in the English language for all that is awful about war.

In the minds of those who survived its mud-encrusted ravages and appalling casualties, nothing would ever compare to its barbarity. Courage and the ability to endure were all that mattered and the eternal wish for it to end was a constant prayer. It was a battlefront that Thompson came to know only too well. The few letters of his that survive, muted in their content to spare his family at home, still speak of the horrors he faced daily. Words such as so and so has 'gone west', 'a locomotive and crew disappeared into the mud', 'the casualty trains can barely cope' and 'I will be greatly relieved to be away from all this, but must do my duty' punctuate his writing, barely suppressing the depth of his feelings.

Another picture from Thompson's collection. It is dated 1917 and shows a rail mounted portable generator used by the ROD. On the back three names are listed – Thompson (left?), Simpson and Joseph, but this isn't to say that this information relates to the three officers in the picture. (*ET/DN*)

If conditions on the Western Front were appalling in the summer months, in winter they were infinitely worse. Rain created a quagmire, snow and ice compounded the misery as portrayed here in late 1917, early 1918. The warmth of the fire in the cab of this Royal Engineers Railway Operating Department (ROD) locomotive must have made it an inviting place to be. (*ET/DN*)

The allied armies were exhausted by their fruitless attacks in 1917 and needed time to regroup. But the Germans, strengthened in numbers by the Russian surrender, which released huge numbers of men and equipment, were determined to force a decision in 1918 before the Americans arrived and tipped the balance in the Allied favour. Their main blow, across the old Somme battlefield, fell in March and was followed by ever more desperate attacks along the whole British Front until July. During these battles, the Engineers carried on their essential work, but were also pressed into service as infantrymen at times, as the enemy pushed forward and threatened to overwhelm the defences. It seems that Thompson found himself in this role, judging by later citations and official regimental histories.

The final year of the war was one of desperate defence and then a sudden return to a war of movement. From August onwards, the enemy retreated so quickly, destroying anything that might been of use to the Allies, that the BEF's railway system couldn't keep pace. It didn't help that they were advancing over the wasteland of past battles, where effective civil engineering was near impossible and by November when surrender came, the area to be traversed was still huge.

One can only imagine the sense of relief Thompson and his comrades must have felt as the guns were finally silenced. Inevitably it would have been tinged with sadness at the losses they had all endured on a long path to victory. But for some, there was also a sense of anti-climax. With Germany brought low but not yet beaten,

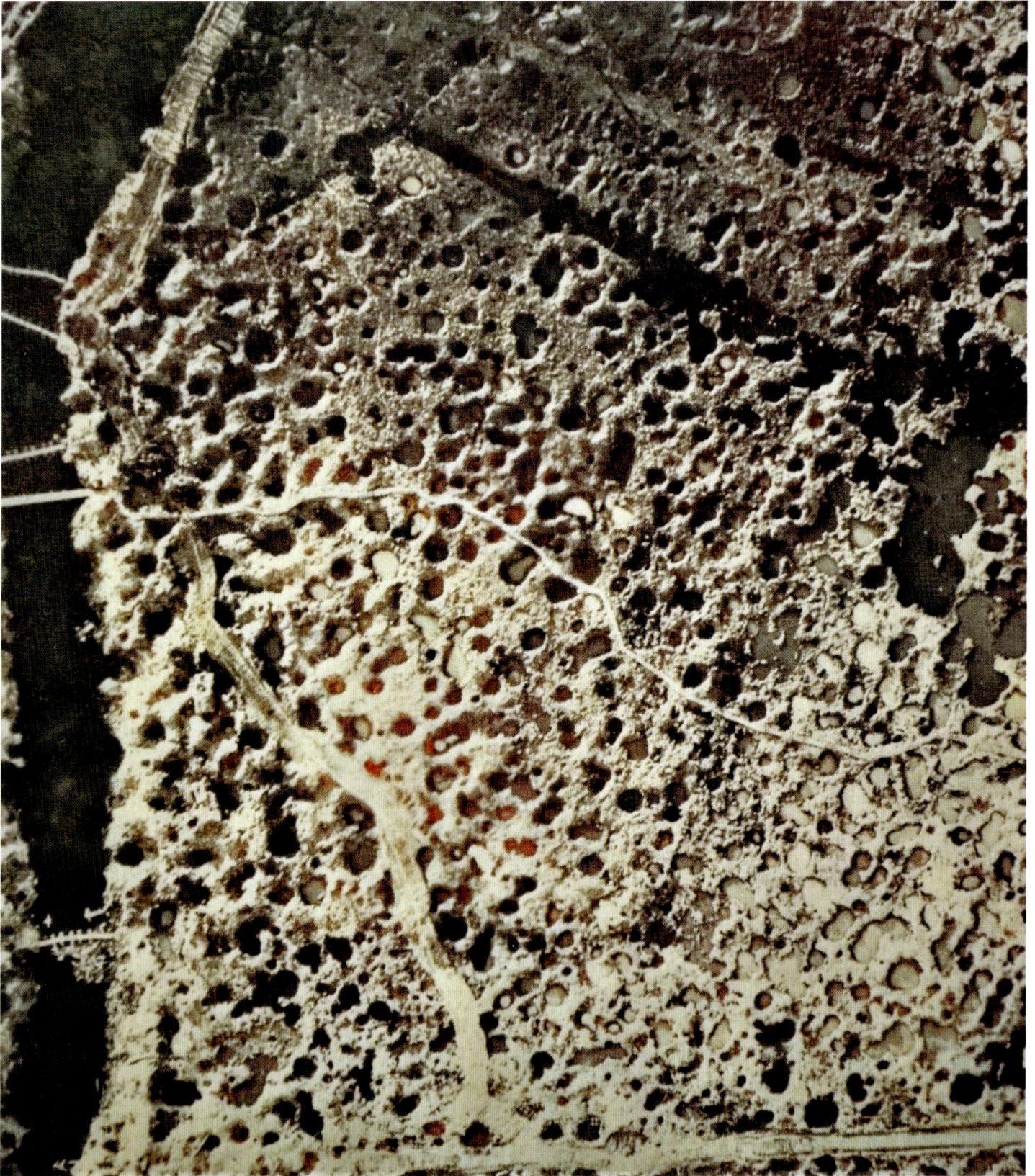

An aerial photograph that Thompson kept of the battlefield in front of Ypres during the autumn of 1917. Pictures such as this were crucial in planning where railways or roads might be laid so that the Front line could continue to be supplied and any advance be supported and sustained. At Passchendaele, this would prove impossible despite the best efforts of the Royal Engineers. (*ET/DN*)

there was a strong feeling that their army should be pursued and destroyed, behind their own border if necessary, to make sure they didn't rise again quickly. It was a view Thompson seems to have shared.

In November 1918 he wrote 'we are here, fully equipped and ready to go, and should finish the job'. Bearing in mind later events, who is to say whether he was right or wrong. But for his family at home, the view would have been quite different, especially for the Ravens. In 1917, they had to endure the death of their youngest child, Frederick, a captain with the Royal Engineers, and had the constant worry of their other son, Norman, still serving at the Front. Frederick was near the Front line when a shell exploded close-by. Severely wounded, he was taken from a Casualty Clearing Station to the military hospital at Le Havre, usually the last port of call before shipment to Britain. Although appearing to make a recovery, sepsis

set in and he died. Thompson, hearing the news, was able to visit him briefly and later attended his funeral at the St Marie Cemetery nearby. Sir Vincent journeyed to France a little later to view the grave and mourn.

It would take some months after the fighting had ended for the terms of the Armistice to be agreed. But following the surrender on 11 November, the Germans began evacuating the battlefield, followed closely by the Allies, swiftly consolidating their gains. Yet, despite this, it was a troubled peace with concern in many quarters that the enemy might re-group on their border and begin fighting again. To guard against this possibility, the BEF and its Allies were kept up to full strength, much to the frustration of many servicemen and women who longed for home and civilian life again. For Thompson, still a GNR employee and on full pay for the duration, the need was less pressing.

On the ground at Passchendaele things looked even worse. British casualties during the battle were estimated to be 275,000 missing or wounded, with very little ground gained. The practical problems in running a railway over such heavily flooded, churned up ground are only too apparent. The casualties amongst the Engineers were as great as for any other unit engaged in the struggle. The only cover to be had whilst working in this nightmarish land was to be one of darkness. (*ET/DN*)

Tanks arrived in France in greater numbers during 1917, but these lumbering beasts needed the railway system to get them close enough to the Front to be truly effective. Here a fascine-laying Mark IV tank is loaded ready to be moved forward. It would have been a key part of Thompson's work to ensure that these war winning weapons could be deployed to the Front quickly and in great numbers. (*ET/DN*)

The massive locomotive workshops constructed by the BEF at St Etienne du Rouvray captured here in early 1918 in another photograph from Thompson's collection. It seems that he was a frequent visitor during its construction and his knowledge of production techniques would have been put to good use. This works would provide maintenance facilities for both standard and narrow gauge locomotives, with many engines from Britain, the USA, Canada, France and Belgium (and occasionally captured German engines, it is said). (*ET/DN*)

Thompson's last photograph from the Western Front. He has written on the back 'September 1918 the Lens Canal. Light railway laid along canal bed to protect it from enemy fire – unsuccessfully'. (*ET/DN*)

After a period of leave, he returned to France to help superintend work on the railway system, which was now being turned towards the clearance of the battlefield and the restoration of life there. The scars would take many decades to heal, but the railway system that fed the battlefield now helped in its repair.

This period of watching and waiting gradually drew to a close with the Armistice and an Army of Occupation taking control in western Germany, making a renewal of fighting unlikely. Demobilisation could begin and by the end of 1919, Thompson was a civilian again, ready to return to the GNR and Gresley. It is unclear whether he and his wife returned to live together at their house in Thorne Road or if she remained with her family in Darlington. After the death of her brother and such a prolonged period of stress and disturbance, there may not have been an immediate return to peacetime life. It was a situation not helped by the influenza epidemic that scarred many lives anew after the war and would have been of particular concern to Gwen, whose health was never good.

All we know for certain is that Thompson took up the reins of his old job at Doncaster that year, deeply affected by a war that had scarred so many people. On returning to civilian life, he would soon have been faced by the dichotomy of those who had served, being with those who hadn't and the irreconcilable differences this could create.

Adjustment after a period of intensive, gut wrenching action is always difficult. The danger is that veterans become detached from a peacetime reality and then judge it too harshly. The civilian world with its reliance on seemingly tedious routines, laboured decision making and measured actions will quickly pall, making the returning soldiers long for the cut and thrust of action again. Then there is the re-adjustment to the domesticity of family life, which many found to be an unbearable strait jacket of conformity. Some never re-acclimatised and spent the rest of their lives in a slowly unravelling turmoil. Yet those who could make the transition and

A key part of the Engineers' work was not only constructing and running railways all along the front line but also ensuring they were adequately hidden from prying eyes. This was nowhere more apparent than when dealing with trains on which senior officers lived and worked as they directed the war, as captured in this photograph. Thompson has written by this picture 'HQ train Fourth Army October 1918 – south-east of Honnechy' (near Le Cateau where the British Army had last fought in 1914). It is likely that the train contained a detachment of Engineers from the DG or Transportation along with Army Commanders, hence Thompson's interest. It is noticeable that the standard-gauge line has a number of narrow gauge lines emanating from it. By this stage of the war, the Germans were withdrawing so quickly that the railways could barely keep up, but it was often the case that the land now being fought over was in far better condition than the old stagnant battlefields, so possibly easier to lay track. (*ET/DN*)

allowed the day to day routine to absorb them without too much questioning, quite often found their sanity restored. But it wasn't something that could happen overnight and could take many years of calm existence to become reality.

To judge the effect of this return to a peacetime world on Thompson it is interesting to note the response of his great friend Cecil Paget, with whom he had served for two years. Ken Leech recorded that:

'After the war, Paget was too big a man to be acceptable to those who had remained on the Midland Railway during the war, so he quit railway work for good. His stocky figure, with iron mouth and jaw, the

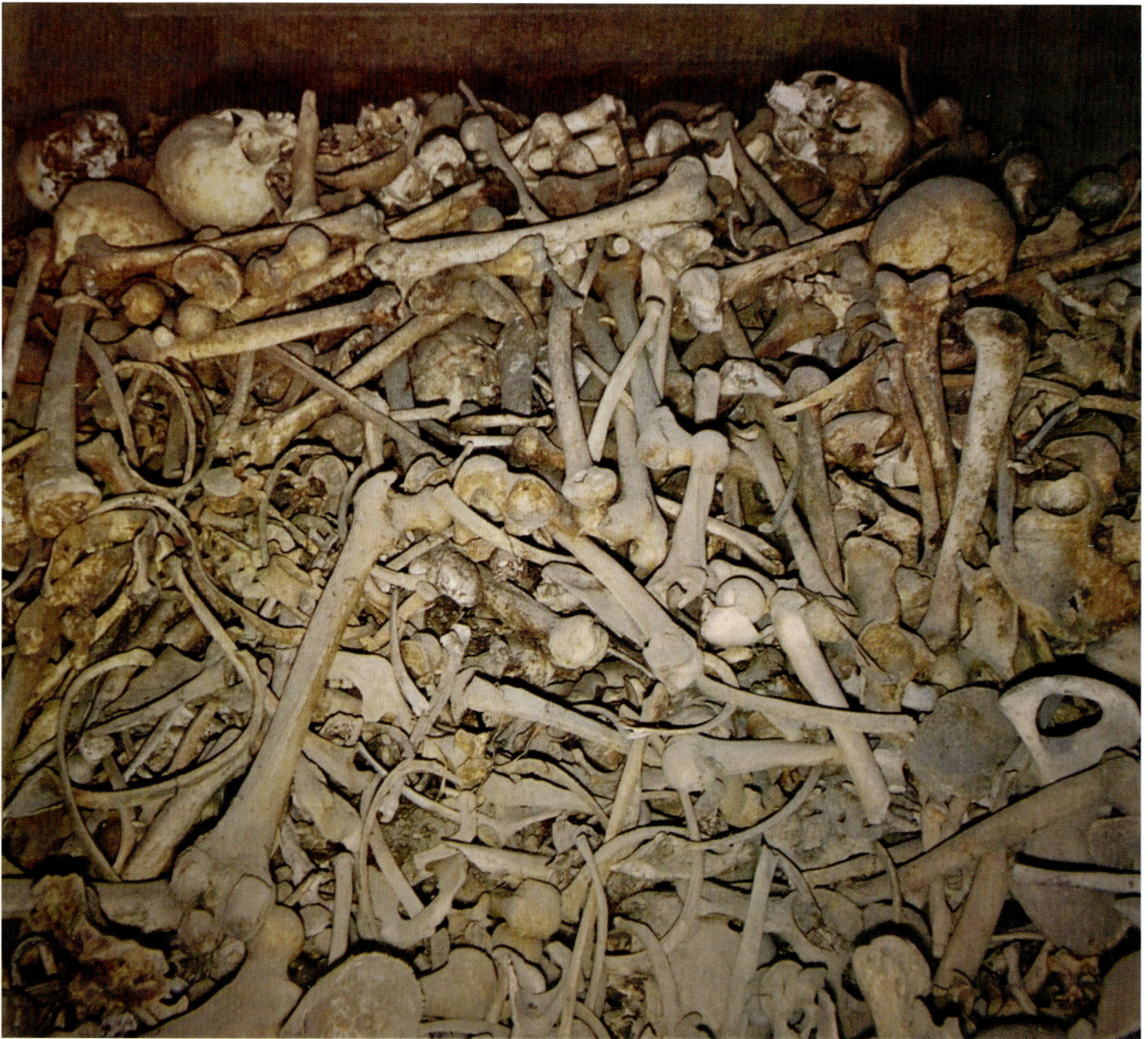

The physical reality and legacy of the Great War I captured on a visit to the Ossuary at Douaumont. For most of the survivors, the mental wounds had to be borne in silence and stoicism. Love of family and a return to work in a peacetime world provided succour, but the personalities and behaviour of many were irrevocably changed by these experiences – for better or worse. (*THG*)

sandy moustache and hair, and those frosty blue eyes, which could twinkle so merrily in one of his inimitable after dinner speeches, will long be remembered by any who were brought into contact with him. As will be his habit of conducting all work by means of long detailed telephone conversations, often lasting well over an hour and involving the making of innumerable drawings and diagrams to his meticulous instructions.'

In war, men such as this are essential. Their ability to think on their feet, to be imaginative in finding solutions to critical problems, often in the face of the enemy, and to be resolute and flexible is crucial to success. But they are not necessarily qualities that fit in well with a staid, sedater peacetime world. And for many it was even worse. Some young men who went to war as inexperienced fledglings, ended the conflict as officers with responsibility for the lives of hundreds if not thousands of men. Yet in 1919, they were expected to return to the bottom rung and bow to the will of an old order with little understanding of their experiences or skills. Thompson was saved this

indignity by the GNR but he would probably have sympathised with Paget's situation. The only real difference between them was that Paget was immensely rich, would soon inherit a baronetcy and had the ability to choose what he did, so lived a life that reflected his changed personality. Without such freedom, only time would tell how deeply the war's effects would continue to colour Thompson's life and affect his relationships at home and work.

According to Paget's diaries, he and Thompson met regularly at the Oxford and Cambridge University Club in Pall Mall and remained close friends. This carried on until Paget's death in 1936 and one wonders whether their shared experiences were a topic of conversation. The veterans' world was a very private one that only those who 'had been there' could truly understand. For many, this was their only means of true self-expression, if biographies are to be believed. Yet, it only seems to have given temporary relief. Only the ability to endure counted and the grit to carry on and forge a new life, despite the trauma and sense of loss. They were, by any standards, a remarkable generation, and Thompson was a very worthy representative of them all.

CHAPTER 4

A DIFFICULT PEACE

When Thompson returned to Doncaster in 1919, he set about recording the lives of the people who had served the company during the war in the Carriage and Wagon Works. The pictures commissioned focussed on the tasks they undertook and groups of people from each office or workshop. The hundred or so photos taken also became a record of his life in the months before transferring back to the North Eastern Railway in 1920.

Throughout his career, he seems to have taken an interest in people and celebrated their work and achievements. In a world based on unquestioning subordination and few privileges, this was unusual. From the correspondence that remains, it appears that he was a strong believer in the need to improve working conditions and was an advocate of women's rights and employment. How strongly Gwen Thompson influenced him in this way isn't known. But the war changed many landscapes and brought social issues and the need for greater equality sharply into focus. It seems he was sympathetic to these issues and remained so for the rest of his life.

Looking at these pictures now, one is left with a sense of a time now long distant and alien to us. Things we take for granted, such as equality, the welfare state, health

The uniform of the working man in industry during 1919. Flat caps for the workers, bowler hats or trilbies for managers and foremen, plus collars, ties, waistcoats, watches and chains. There is little evidence of safety clothing, which helped to contribute to a shameful level of industrial injuries and illnesses. (*ET/DN*)

and safety and a good education for all, were at best just emerging, if they existed at all. Poverty was the lot of most and poor living conditions ensured that illnesses rarely seen today were endemic, particularly tuberculosis and rickets, though smallpox still struck regularly. Child mortality which now runs at about 0.5 per cent, and seems shocking in an advanced, supported society, was then nearly 14 per cent, with few families in poorer areas being spared this tragedy. In addition, the average life expectancy was well below 70 in many communities, at which point the means tested state pension system, introduced in 1909, clicked in. If you were lucky enough to survive to such an age it ensured a married couple 7s 6d a week, when an agricultural labourer typically earned fifteen shillings, which did little to lift the threat of ending your days in the work house, which still existed then.

Then there was the extreme sacrifice of the Great War that most endured in one way or another, which did little to improve the lives of those who survived. However, it did lead to the vote being extended by the Representation of the People Act in 1918 to women over 30 and 7 million more men, including many who had fought in the recent war. The effects of this huge change would take decades to be felt, during which recession, austerity and another world war would afflict society.

For those lucky enough to have enjoyed the safety net and affluence of being managers or owners in the early twentieth century, the battle between capital and labour was just beginning. Such a driving need would require a quite different approach if businesses were to succeed. Those returning from the trenches, such as Thompson, seemed better able to cope with these challenges than

A mixture of staff gathered in front of a J13 0-6-0T (possibly No. 1236) during 1919. This class were derived by Henry Ivatt from the J14s that first appeared in 1892 when Patrick Stirling was the GNR's Locomotive Superintendent. They would become a familiar sight to Thompson throughout his career, especially this one which appears to have undertaken shunting duties around Doncaster. The last of these engines would survive in service until 1961. (*ET/DN*)

those who hadn't served. But there would still be many clashes as the old order sought to fight a rear-guard action, with the General Strike of 1926 marking a low point in this struggle.

Over the coming decades, it would fall to Gresley, Thompson and many more in the rail industry to manage these growing expectations and seek a balance between profitability and equality. Some would fail badly, but others wouldn't, although the path to enlightenment was often paved with examples of harsh behaviour, even brutality. This can be witnessed by William Stanier, a seemingly moderate man then serving with the GWR, turning hoses on workers during the General Strike of 1926, though by comparison to Vincent Raven,

who reportedly showed an intransigent hand in all matters concerning labour relations, this act seems almost restrained in nature. In rapidly changing times, this was a short-sighted and heavy-handed approach when sensible negotiation and arbitration would have proved more fruitful. Thompson was remembered as being equally tough but seems to have coloured his approach with greater pragmatism, especially in the case of women workers and the adoption of evolving employment principles and practices.

We shall never know how Thompson was received when returning to Doncaster by Gresley, though his leader's reaction was unlikely to have been anything but courteous and accommodating, especially to someone

The ever-growing presence of women in industry. In offices and on the shop floor, the number grew during the Great War and their general employment continued when hostilities ended. The number did decline post-war, as men returned from the war demanding work and armaments production diminished, but the die had been cast and a mixed work force remained a daily reality, though not equal pay. This group of office workers, according to his notes, included Thompson's secretary (smiling confidently for the camera front row fifth from the left). It is rumoured, though not confirmed, that this is Ivy Shingler who remained his secretary when he moved to York and for many years after. (ET/DN)

who had served so gallantly. His departure in 1916 may have caused ripples at a time when every experienced hand was needed to keep the railway going, but service to one's country in its hour of need was still an ingrained ideal with the power to over-ride all other considerations. Gresley's approach would probably have been sanguine and measured. However, by nature, he seems to have been a man who preferred to exercise close control of all aspects of work for which he bore ultimate responsibility. Delegation, as Bert Spencer later recalled, was 'hard earnt under Gresley and came with many checks and balances that some found onerous'. Thompson, having achieved senior rank in the GNR and then in the Army, with power over life and death, was probably not best placed to handle too close a marking. The wish for autonomy and more responsibility would have been a pressing one indeed. And he may have harboured ambitions to become CME himself, but with Gresley only five years older this was an ambition likely to remain unfulfilled at Doncaster.

It is most unlikely that Thompson didn't see all this clearly when returning to the GNR and had to consider whether he wished to remain a deputy or find somewhere where his ambitions might find an outlet. There is little doubt that the matter became a pressing issue, possibly encouraged by Raven, but also by actions being taken within the influential precincts of central government.

In anticipation of a major war in Europe, a Railway Executive Committee had been set up in 1912 to act as intermediary between the War Office and railway companies to manage the network effectively in the event of a war. Following mobilisation in August 1914, the REC grew rapidly in power and influence under the leadership of Alexander Butterworth, General Manager of the NER, who held both positions concurrently. To all intents and purposes, this was nationalisation in all but name, with the railways remaining under government control until 1921. During this period, serious consideration was given to the way they should be operated in future; an issue that Eric Geddes had begun to consider when becoming Minister of Transport in 1919. Many favoured permanent nationalisation, but he resisted this in favour of retaining commercial management, with worker participation, and companies gathered together into a small number of regional operating groups. It was this model that was passed into law by the 1921 Railways Act.

During 1920, this process still had some way to run. But rumour and conjecture, fed by the inevitable leak of information which accompanies these things, would have furnished men of ambition with the information they needed to plot an advantageous course. With promotion to CME at Doncaster blocked by the presence of Gresley and knowing that Raven, now approaching his mid-60s, was likely to retire in the near future, Thompson may have thought that a return to the NER held more benefits. Yet there was probably more than this to consider. The NER may have seemed a more progressive company under Raven than the GNR under Gresley. With the war over, the NER quickly resurrected their electrification plans, as well as producing an active steam locomotive programme, so were looking to the future. And, if pre-war levels of business returned, this company looked more likely to be profitable and grow more rapidly as a result, so becoming senior partner in any grouping that might be created by the Ministry of Transport. All of this would have been self-evident to Thompson, with a further attraction being a senior post within the NER's Carriage and Wagon Works in York then becoming vacant.

Whilst considering his next move, Thompson's primary task at Doncaster was to oversee the restoration of rolling stock badly affected by overuse and reduced maintenance during the war. He would also action Gresley's development plans for carriages. Though the CME is best remembered for his work in producing locomotives, much of his early career had been spent on the wagon and carriage side of business, where innovation and experimentation became the cornerstones of all he did. As a result, he had developed a very close and lasting interest in its design and construction, including the principle of articulation. During 1919 and 1920, this focussed on the development of a five coach 'jointed' set for use on the King's Cross to Leeds line, which Thompson oversaw. It was during this period, just before departing for York, that he came into closer contact with Oliver Bulleid.

Like Gresley, Bulleid began his career as an engineering apprentice, but like Thompson, he also followed a university path attending classes at both Sheffield and Leeds where he studied the purely theoretical side of his business to an advanced level. This bright and gifted young man soon rose through the ranks to become Gresley's personal assistant in 1912. Like Thompson,

During Thompson's brief post-war period at Doncaster, a key part of Gresley's development plans reached fruition. In February 1920, his pioneering three cylinder H4 Mogul No.1000 appeared with its conjugated valve gear, which would become a defining feature of the CME's designs and an issue of great controversy between Gresley and Thompson much later. The design must have interested the younger man because this picture, and several others, appear in one of his albums from this period. (*LNER/RH*)

Another photograph Thompson collected in 1920. This time it features the Henry Ivatt designed Class C1 4-4-2 of which 94 were built between 1902 and 1910. These elegant engines were deemed to be a success but their role was largely taken over by Gresley's Pacifics during the 1920s and '30s. Thompson seems to have taken an interest in the development of this class, but his reasons for doing so are now lost to time. (*LNER/RH*)

he could not resist the call to arms, saw wide service on the Western Front and played an active part in the Directorate of Transportation's work. In so doing, he rose to the rank of major. Post-war he returned to Doncaster and took up the reins as Gresley's assistant again.

Bulleid's memories of both men are important. He was able to observe their relationship and also assess them as individuals. Of Gresley and Thompson he wrote:

'Gresley was the best chief I worked under . . . He gave me orders when he should. He asked my opinion if he wanted it. He expected to receive suggestions and be given particulars of any developments in any field which might not come to him direct . . . His manner at times could be gruff and was obstinate especially when his designs were criticised, but he was a great engineer . . . He had a wonderful memory, was extremely observant, and amongst other things could read a drawing in a way given to few. Disloyalty was the one thing he did not tolerate.

'Thompson was a clear thinker and a good organiser. When I arrived at Doncaster to replace Thompson he took great pleasure in giving me the best possible introduction to the carriage side, probably sensing my intention to liven things up. He showed me round and explained the organisation generally and could not have been more helpful. I thought him a good engineer, but do not think him the equal of Mr Gresley, although that privilege would fall to very few.'

Even though only remaining at Doncaster for such a short time, Thompson continued his habit of collecting photographs showing many tasks for which he was responsible, including this view of carriages under construction or simply being maintained. (*ET/DN*)

Bulleid, through his son Henry, also left a brief picture of Thompson and the friendship and informality that punctuated their relationship, with golf at its centre:

'After the war golfing enthusiasm swept into the Plant affecting, in order of competence, Groom, Thompson, Peppercorn and my father. They were all friendly players as well as friends, but utterly different. Groom was icy calm and reckoned to do every hole in what was then called bogey. Thompson was an efficient 10-ish handicap and always immaculately attired. Peppercorn played with immense vigour and my father kept seeking refinements of technique. I believe they all got on well together because they had served on the Western Front and this created a bond especially in those early years after the war. Certainly my father always spoke warmly of Thompson and held him in high regard. When he was promoted to become CME of the Southern Railway Thompson was one of the first to write offering his congratulations. During the Second World War they often met and offered support to each other at a difficult time.'

Thompson's move to York in 1920 has been likened to a level transfer, although in this case it did offer greater autonomy and authority, the NER's CME being based at Darlington and not alongside him as was the case with Gresley at Doncaster. There was also a greater challenge in developing production ideas he'd studied when visiting Ford's car plants in the States before the war. With this in mind, he set about modernising construction and maintenance processes, with the full support of Raven and his deputy Arthur Stamer.

In many ways, this work played to his strengths. He had proved on many occasions that he was a very effective planner and administrator, with the ability to see valid solutions when faced with a mass of facts and figures. This is a rare ability indeed, particularly in an industry not noted for great efficiency in this field. But having grown used to cheap and plentiful labour for so long, railway companies lacked the impetus to move forward. Post-war this was changing, so woe betide those who didn't embrace modern production methods and seek to check spiralling costs.

The only aspect of work at York that Thompson might have found unsatisfactory or frustrating was the absence of design tasks. Any engineer worth their salt, and hoping to reach a very senior position, needs to be exposed to this type of work. But throughout his career, the opportunity hadn't arisen. He would have been aware of developments in locomotive and rolling stock design, though hadn't been drawn into this field in any meaningful way, although, as a peripheral issue, he had studied accident damage and analysed how design might be improved to reduce damage and casualties. But this fell far short of taking a specification and developing a new locomotive, carriage or wagon.

In some ways, this was to be expected. The mechanical engineering world is made up of many specialities, but those hoping to reach senior level in the railway industry tended to go down one of two routes – design or production. The skills needed for either role were complementary, but there were clear differences, which the careers and achievements of Thompson and Gresley best illustrate.

Gresley was first and foremost a designer. He had an enquiring mind that sought to understand engineering issues and develop new or alternative solutions. His life was spent in studying scientific papers, books and attending learned conferences and advancing his own ideas. He may not have been the most gifted at doing this and perhaps placed too heavy a reliance on other peoples' work at times, but his instincts were for innovation and analysis. However, this could come at too high a price. Sometimes, he was criticised for seeming to be too dogmatic and unbending about his creations, then failing to modify them when a better solution presented itself. His advocacy of engines with three cylinders, equipped with his conjugated valve gear, was just such an example. But if this is a failing, it is entirely understandable, though frustrating at times for those supporting him. Yet he had a sound understanding of the economics of his business and rarely, if ever, pursued something to the point at which a huge or unnecessary debt was incurred. And for the most part, his ideas worked. So whilst he was a designer at heart, he saw a bigger picture, understood the restrictions that existed and could map his ideas successfully to the needs of the business.

Thompson seems to have been more comfortable as a production engineer. His favoured way of working was more about method and systems than the specifics of design. Although he may have wished to be an innovator and inventor in his chosen field, talents that evolved

Thompson seems to have taken a keen interest in all matters relating to the railways and captured many daily scenes in his album, including this undated photograph of North Eastern engines 'on shed'. (*ET/DN*)

at school, university and during his career do not speak of someone with a pressing urge to create a machine of any type. Until, that is, he became the LNER's CME in 1941. But did this late flurry of activity reflect long harboured ambitions or was it simply a case of finding practical solutions to operational problems?

He, like Gresley, did have an enquiring, innovative mind, but in his case it seemed better able to focus on manufacturing and operational issues rather than the fine detail of creation itself. And, to be frank, he seems to have made little effort to cross over, if the papers that remain are anything to go by. Of course, it may simply have been that he lacked the opportunity to do so and was placed in positions that others believed best suited his talents. But this doesn't quite ring true, because in many cases this strong and resolute man chose the path

his career took. Quite simply, he sought no opportunity to improve his design credentials by a posting to a drawing office where these skills might have been honed and his imagination be allowed to flourish.

Lack of design input doesn't necessarily mean lack of interest. He didn't join any learned engineering institutions, until encouraged to do so by Gresley, who also acted as sponsor, in 1929. But he does seem to have collected papers they produced where locomotive and rolling stock design was involved. In addition, he read magazines such as *The Engineer*, the *Railway Gazette* and others which contained many items of interest about design and were formally circulated amongst officers of his rank by their CMEs. Some samples of this still exist with his signature and occasional comments attached. One interesting example is a paper produced by George Hughes for the Institution of Mechanical Engineers in 1909, when CME of the Lancashire and Yorkshire Railway. Under the title 'Locomotives designed and built at Horwich with some results', he reviewed the company's development programme. Thompson appears to have underlined many sections of this paper. The most interesting of these is:

'When the works at Horwich were opened, the company had 1,000 engines, namely, 353 passenger and 647 goods. There were 29 different types of passenger engines and 26 types of goods engines. Realizing the great importance of having as few classes as possible, Mr Aspinall, then CME, resolved to reduce the number, and to introduce standardisation, and, wherever possible, interchangeability. This policy, no doubt, from a commercial point of view is correct, but requires to be judiciously handled, at the right moment, otherwise it may have a tendency to impede progress'

Thompson also highlighted Hughes' comments on the size and number of cylinders, linked motion, the need for greater power to cope with heavier, faster trains, types of boilers, the use of the Belpaire fire boxes, maintenance issues and much more. However, despite this interest, he doesn't appear to have drawn any conclusions from this or any other paper he collected or sought to develop a debate on the subject. Nevertheless, it does denote an underlying interest in the subject of design and performance, suggesting a thought process beyond the production work in which he specialised.

One thing is certain, though, design and production engineers have to work in harmony if a business is to succeed. And it is in the less glamorous world of production that Thompson's understanding of organisation, manufacturing flow and operational issues seemed to find true vocation. In these fields, he demonstrated a rare talent that probably found its metier when serving with the army in a world of intense operational extremes. In fact, Bert Spencer probably summed this up best when writing that:

'he [Thompson] was a planner, organiser and strategist. By nature, he was a reformer who would take on an organisation and make it run very effectively. I often felt that he might be better suited to be a General Manager of a railway than a CME. His talents certainly seemed to lie in that direction'.

There is another factor to consider in this – the teams each man employed to make their ideas come to life. In my book about Gresley, I quoted the aviation expert Paul S. Baker who, in the 1940s, when asked about assigning credit for the design of a particular aircraft replied,

'The day of one-man engineering projects are long gone. You might as well print the organisation table of the engineering department.'

It is this issue that underlines Gresley and Thompson's work and achievements. Whether by accident or design, each man inherited or put together teams that seem to have reflected their own personalities and working methods. In this the outgoing, sociable and astute Gresley proved

Three examples of carriage work that would fall to Thompson to manage between 1920 and 1923. Major design developments would follow with Gresley in charge of the new LNER, but the NER under Raven did much good work too. (Opposite) A non-corridor third class coach designed for commuter traffic. In the past, most companies used clerestory style roofs; Raven introduced elliptical types with this model. (Above) The extremely plush first class dining saloon that was used on Newcastle to Liverpool and Leeds to Glasgow trains. (Below) An exterior view of this coaching stock. (*ET/DN*)

When taking over the reins at York, Thompson mounted these two photographs in one of his albums. On the first of these he has simply written 'the oldest working locomotive in the world' and added 'Darlington'. There are no other details and one is left to ponder the engine's history and the 'Heath Robinson' side cab arrangement. The second picture captures *Aerolite,* which was built as a 2-2-2T in 1869 as replacement for an engine constructed for the 1851 Great Exhibition at the Crystal Palace in Hyde Park, but destroyed in a collision during 1868. It was converted from 2-2-2 configuration to 4-2-2 in 1892 then to 2-2-4T ten years later. In this form it was often used to haul the Mechanical Engineer's saloon, as portrayed in this photograph. This unique locomotive was withdrawn in 1933 and was marked for preservation and is now part of the national collection. Thompson's interest was clearly aroused by both engines, perhaps revealing a deep interest in the evolution of locomotion. (*ET/DN*)

particularly adept and undoubtedly lucky. Without the likes of Robert Thom, Arthur Stamer, Oliver Bulleid, Bert Spencer, Arthur Peppercorn, Tom Street, Harry Broughton, Edward Windle and Thompson himself, his achievements might have been far less. But without doubt, he was able to lead them effectively. Once they had gained his trust, he allowed them to manage with a certain amount of autonomy and exercise their creative talents in a cohesive way that paid dividends. The same might not be said of Thompson.

Before the war, he seems to have been eager to learn as well as lead and involve his staff in work for which they all bore responsibility. But army service seems to have changed and hardened his attitude. He returned a much more austere, even troubled person who was often unnecessarily impatient and cutting when faced with the foibles of those around him. But it wasn't always so, as Bert Spencer again relates:

'He ran a tight ship and woe betide anyone who stepped out of line or tried to assume uninvited familiarity, at which point he could be strong in his criticisms. But if allowed to take the lead and given due respect his approach did change. At these times he showed interest in other people's ideas when presented in a measured way, wished to know more and would modify his own views if the case was strong and well argued. Nevertheless, there was a tendency to put people too firmly in their place when it wasn't strictly necessary, which was a weakness. But for those who gained his respect he could be generous in his praise and appreciative of their efforts, especially Peppercorn, Thom, Edge and staff, both senior or junior, on the shop floor or in the offices. I gained the impression that if he drove people hard, he drove himself even harder.'

Thompson, it seems, was a man of contradictions, whose balance seems to have been slightly askew at times. Such people are often unpredictable and testing to those around them and the word martinet is often applied in these cases. One doesn't expect a leader to be all charm, sweetness and light, but be able to exercise authority in a firm, measured and flexible way, leaving outrage and cynicism to one side. It was here that his ability to manage people could be out of sync with day to day needs and served him ill at times. By contrast, Gresley's

personality and sense of authority were better suited to creating and leading a diverse and talented team before setting them challenging targets.

Thompson's personality may have presented problems but he was also unlucky. When eventually becoming CME, he not only had to manage when the Second World War was at its height, but also when time and promotion had stripped him of some men who had served Gresley so well. Thom, in particular, was sorely missed when he retired in 1938. Here was a man of exceptional skill and energy who drove through the CME's ambitious locomotive programme whilst Mechanical Engineer at Doncaster for eleven crucial years. To make matters worse, he had been preceded into retirement by the hugely talented and phlegmatic Arthur Stamer, who departed in 1933. To lose one such man can create problems, but two can be damaging in the extreme. Gresley struggled to replace them and probably suffered because of it. Thompson had similar difficulties when his time came to lead. But the problem went deeper than this.

Gresley was always careful to include people of great ability in his immediate entourage at King's Cross and was prepared, at times, to listen to those who had gained his trust. Although other very senior managers in a company can offer their leader advice and help alleviate the need for closer control from the centre, it is often the case that the man in overall charge needs a few carefully selected specialists close at hand to provide more immediate support and guidance. In this, Gresley had the expert assistance of the dynamic, headstrong and occasionally erratic Bulleid and the more measured and astute Spencer. It was he, having been personally selected by the CME in the early 1920s, from whom Gresley received the most valuable and balanced support for 18 years.

Spencer acted as a filter and advisor on locomotive matters and was trusted by Gresley. In a sensitive and understanding way, Spencer was able to take often sketchy ideas, fill them out, even modify them, and guide his greatly respected leader to alternative solutions. With his ability to translate basic, delineated ideas he also acted as an important link between the CME and the drawing offices who did the final designs.

Strong leaders can often only bear 'yes men' around them. Dissent, no matter how well meant, is not encouraged, especially if the person in charge has a flawed master plan which they are determined to pursue no matter how limiting this might be. Gresley was prepared

The sprawling mass of the Railway and Carriage Works at York, which at its height was one of the largest employers in the area. (*RH*)

to listen and consider alternatives, the post-Great War Thompson seemed less so. But this was a long way in the future when Thompson left Doncaster for York in 1920, although the signs of his developing intransigence were there for the astute to see.

In many ways, the Carriage and Wagon Works was an ideal place for him to exercise his talents. A move into a design post, though likely to have broadened his knowledge and experience, could have exposed his shortcomings or deficiencies in this field of work. We shall never know, but his father-in-law, who had sanctioned his recruitment and promotion, may have seen something lacking and astutely kept him where his talents would be best employed.

Nevertheless, there was still a major challenge at York, of lower profile admittedly but important nonetheless. In many ways, workshops such as this have slipped from our view. We remember the places where the locomotives

A day to day scene that became a familiar part of Thompson's life for three years. The shops at York with their rapid turn round, high density workload, were an ideal place to introduce car plant production line practices. These proved to be very successful and, by all accounts, increased output considerably. (*ET/DN*)

were built and see their work portrayed in hundreds if not thousands of pictures. Due to the nature of these tasks, they tend to have greater appeal to those interested in railway history and their designers are more famous for that reason. Yet the complexity of rolling stock design, the level of innovation and standard of craftsmanship the task demanded were of a comparable standard. And in the post-war period, they shared a common problem – manufacturing and maintenance programmes were often managed in slipshod, time consuming ways. However, mass production to meet war needs and the spreading influence of production line technology and processes had begun to change this.

Thompson had seen this happening and his brief at York included a commission to complete the reorganisation of the shops to improve productivity and flow rates. It was a programme begun by his predecessor Robert Pick, who retired in 1920. Their combined contribution would change the layout and see modern machinery procured and installed, but they also considered the wider effect of higher output on working conditions and pay. It was a subject few had broached in peacetime, because a workforce was both cheap and easy to employ and just as easily let go. But the demands of war had begun to tip the capital/labour relationship slightly in favour of the shop floor. Unquestioning obedience was still expected in many quarters and lack of adequate employment contracts continued, but the world was changing rapidly. Thompson was aware of this, judging by several papers that have survived, and seems to have been in favour of reform.

In July 1920, a party of ILocoE members toured York, before Thompson's arrival, and in a short article painted a picture of life there as they observed it:

'Some parts of the Works were built as far back as 1867. Considerable extensions were made in 1873-6, and the greater part of the goods and merchandise wagons are built here. About 40 per cent of the total stock of wagons are also repaired here. The number of men and boys employed is 1,180.

'In the wagon building shop we were shown various classes of open goods, coal and ironstone wagons under construction. There were special features to be seen in the saw mill, machine shop, boiler house and engine room . . .

'The party next inspected the carriage works, which were opened in 1884. Since that date, year by year, considerable extensions have been made, and at the present time the works are replete with modern machinery and up to date equipment for building and maintaining the carriage stock of the principal Northern railroad.

'These works occupy an area of slightly more than 13 acres of roofed buildings. Here the whole stock of the NER is built, and the greater part of the repairs necessary to keep the vehicles in running order is carried out. A considerable portion of the East Coast Joint Stock and Great Northern and North Eastern Joint Stock is built and maintained at the works.

'The number of men, women and boys employed is about 1,500, and the works are capable of turning out one bogie carriage per day. To the ordinary observer this may not seem a great turn-out for a works of this size, but when the notice of the visitor to the works is drawn to the various processes to which the ironwork is subjected between its raw state and when it emerges into finished ironwork, and also of the timber from the log to the finished woodwork, the completion of one finished bogie carriage in one working day will be fully appreciated.'

By any standards, these workshops were a huge concern requiring men of substance and skill to keep them going, but the ILocoE touched on one serious issue in a diplomatic way. For its size, the output seemed small and it was this problem that would tax Thompson, as it did his predecessor. With costs rising, company finances struggling to recover after the war and a backlog of maintenance work to clear, the NER needed to change its working practices very quickly if it were to grow or even survive. Spend to save, though an admirable concept, wasn't really an option in this instance when there were so many other calls on company finances. So proposals had to be low cost, if involving any cost at all. In such circumstances, someone with Thompson's eye for detail and process and, as proved by his service on the Western Front, an ability to manage ingeniously in extreme circumstances with limited resources would be key to success.

Apart from the day to day running of these labour intensive workshops, he had to change methods of operation and improve output, with minimal disturbance to the task at hand. He does seem to have delegated much of this work, but, nevertheless, his involvement was more than just being a leader. In the weeks that followed

As Thompson settled into his new post at York, Raven continued with an active locomotive building programme. By comparison with Gresley's work at this time, his designs had a dated quality, as though a throwback to a bygone age. When the time came to consider who best to be CME in the newly formed LNER it is, perhaps, not surprising that they believed that Gresley better represented the look and ambitions of a modern company. All this, of course, ignored Raven's ambition for a much more modern solution in electrification. A cornerstone of his steam programme would be the NER's Pacifics, but this ambitious programme was supplemented by the two classes pictured here – the three cylinder T3 and S3. (Top) The first of the T3 0-8-0s was built at Darlington in 1919 and was followed by another fourteen (four in 1919, the remaining ten in 1924). In the same timescale, the company built 70 S3s. Both classes remained in service until the early 1960s and became Q7s and B16s under LNER ownership. Both these photographs come from Thompson's albums. The S3, No. 927, is pictured under the coaling chute at York.

his arrival in late 1920, he began a close and very detailed examination of layout and task to identify pinch points where improvement was essential. He was even noted working on possible layouts using drawings overlaid with simple scaled cut outs to represent machinery and matchsticks forming flow lines for a 'conveyer belt' system. Gradually, by trial and error, a solution was found, aided by his workshop managers and J.W. Dow in particular, who had assisted Pick before him. From here, his persuasive manner and ability to argue his case ensured that the proposals were accepted and funded by the NER's Board.

Implementation was not immediate and took two years to complete but the results proved worthwhile. In time, these revamped workshops were seen to be at the cutting edge of manufacturing processes and were greatly admired for this reason and often visited. And it was in this state that they passed into the hands of their new owners in January 1923, when Britain's railways faced the amalgamation presaged by the 1921 Railway Act.

Although ensconced at York, which was important to the NER but peripheral as far as the dynamics and politics of the company were concerned, Thompson would have followed these changes very carefully. Undoubtedly, rumour would have fuelled speculation and contact with his father-in-law would have focussed on many issues arising from these changes. These debates would have grown in strength when the future structure became known and the shape of grouping was made clear. As predicted in many quarters, the NER, GNR, Great Central Railway, Great Eastern, Great North of Scotland and the Hull and Barnsley Railways came together under the banner of the new LNER.

Confirmation of this inevitably set off a race amongst senior officers in these companies for positions of power in the new organisation. With so many CMEs and Locomotive Engineers in post, the competition would be fierce. For some, age was against them. John Robinson, of the GCR, was in his 67th year, Raven nearing 65 and Alfred Hill, who had served the GER for 46 years, was 61. Each of them could have provided the new Chairman, William Whitelaw, and the new Chief General Manager, Ralph Wedgwood, with a short term solution. But with the talented and dynamic 47 year old Gresley waiting in the wings, a longer term solution presented itself.

In quite short order, Hill and Robinson retired, removing themselves from the field of battle, but Raven remained, apparently eager to become the LNER's first CME. The level of competition between him and Gresley can be witnessed by the efforts of both men to design and build high profile prototype Pacific locomotives in the months before amalgamation. As a result, during 1922, these engines duly emerged – the GNR model to great acclaim and publicity in April and Raven's, seven months later, attracting far less attention. Second place is rarely newsworthy and it proved so again in this case. As a result, Gresley may have appeared the more astute of the two, with his work on the Pacific project and his other development work on steam locomotives and rolling stock impressing the powers that be with its energy, foresight and, perhaps, its prudence. Although of equal merit, Raven's work, particularly his strong advocacy of electrification at a time of great austerity, may have appeared unrealistic, even unsound to men of commerce.

With neither man likely to back down, Whitelaw and Wedgwood were forced to consider a competition for the post, or, at least, a compromise arrangement. There were, of course, other potential candidates from outside these companies, but the new managers seemed loath to consider them or they simply didn't have the right credentials. There has been much speculation over the conduct of the selection process. But all that can be said with any certainty is recorded in the minutes of the Locomotive Committee meeting of 22 February 1922, which tracked the Board's decision making process:

'Item 20 – Resolved that it be recommended that Mr H.N. Gresley be appointed Chief Mechanical Engineer of the company at a salary of £4,500 pa.'

It is said that Raven enjoyed a cordial relationship with Gresley, although tempered, as it must always be in a relationship between two hugely ambitious people, with caution. But despite this, Raven felt unable to serve under the younger man and decided to take retirement on the last day of 1922 instead. Perhaps in respect of his exceptional past services to company and state, a short term consultancy was arranged, for which he was given the title Chief Technical Advisor and paid a substantial sum. In this role he was asked, amongst other things, to consider how operations could be rationalised and reorganised.

Although the desire to pursue his dreams of electrification once the war had ended ran strong in his veins, Raven also engaged in an active steam locomotive programme of which Thompson was only too aware. Interest in the 4-6-2 Pacific concept was slowly growing in strength and, following Churchward's work on such an engine with the GWR, other designers in Britain began to take note. There was a strong desire for larger and more powerful locomotives and the 4-6-2 configuration was considered one way of achieving this. Gresley and Raven were both intrigued by the possibilities and pursued their own designs in the year or so before amalgamation. With the merger becoming a reality this may have appeared short-sighted but undoubtedly reflected a measure of rivalry between the two men. Of course, they may simply have wished to be first in the field, but bearing in mind the level of competition to become the LNER's first CME, construction of such prestigious engines held a deeper meaning. Gresley's classic Pacific, *Great Northern*, No. 1470, entered traffic in April 1922 and Raven's *City of Newcastle*, No. 2400, appeared in December (above – Raven's Pacific when unveiled at Darlington, with the men who had constructed the engine, and (below) *Great Northern* at New Southgate on the way from King's Cross to Doncaster in 1922). In the years that followed, Gresley's design dominated whilst the five Raven Pacifics that were built ended up on lesser duties. The CME chose to rebuild No.2404 *City of Ripon* in 1929, and then condemned and scrapped all five between 1936 and '38 at Doncaster, the last when Thompson had succeeded Thom there. Bearing in mind his great admiration for Raven, who died in 1934, this must have been a sad sight to witness and, perhaps, a bitter pill to swallow. (*ET/DN/RH*)

With the coming together of so many different companies, it was essential that they operate as one and not continue past practices. His far reaching report, which recommended that the running department should be separated from the CME's organisation, was adopted in July 1923. And more was to follow from Raven in the last months of his consultancy. He reviewed the company's workshop capacity and led a committee in looking at the electrification of the GNR suburban line to Hitchin. But this arrangement couldn't last forever and he gradually took on tasks away from the LNER, including a directorship with Metropolitan-Vickers.

Throughout this period, Thompson must have wondered what his future held. With Raven at the helm he would probably have looked forward to promotion, even succeeding him in time. But with Gresley taking the top post, and unlikely to relinquish it before retirement at some indeterminate point in the future, his own elevation grew increasingly unlikely. Beyond the LNER things looked little better. Amalgamation had reduced the number of CME posts considerably and the industrial world outside was entering recession, as wartime contracts dried up. Without an influx of new work and with austerity beckoning, companies couldn't expand so any opportunities for advancement for those such as Thompson were few and far between. But the Works at York had a future of sorts and whilst it lasted he was secure in a senior post and could ride out the storm. The only unanswered question seemed to be whether Gresley might be a help or hindrance to him in this new world. If their relationship had indeed soured with Thompson's departure to the Western Front and then later to York, the future might bode ill.

If Thompson had gambled that returning to York gave him a long term advantage when amalgamation came, it proved to be a short lived hope. With Raven in charge this might have been so, but without him, the chances were far fewer with more candidates likely to enter the fray. Nevertheless, he still had some advantages. There were two ex-NER colleagues in senior positions who might be considered influential allies – Wedgwood and Arthur Stamer, who became Gresley's deputy as well as Mechanical Engineer at Darlington in 1923.

During these years, Gwen's health remained a constant worry and with the possibility of children receding the future may have seemed a little barren. But at least they had the security of status and good income. It is hard to paint a picture of their domestic life at this time, as they slipped into middle age. They seemed to have enjoyed entertaining visitors, with his widowed mother, until her death in 1925, and parents-in-law being frequent guests. Yet, in general they appear to have led a quiet but sociable life. However, Thompson does seem to have maintained a degree of privacy and rectitude, features probably compounded by his experiences in the trenches. Nevertheless, he seems to have found some relaxation, even comfort in pursuing a number of activities. His continued interest in photography is noteworthy, as was the growing appeal of carpentry. Playing golf, if not an obsession, was a pleasant pursuit very often enjoyed with Gwen's brother Norman, with his love of cricket continuing, more as a spectator than a player now. But to this he added angling, in which he was encouraged by a developing friendship with Robert Thom.

On amalgamation, Thom, who had had a long association with the Great Central Railway, became Area Mechanical Engineer at Cowlairs before moving to Doncaster, as Mechanical Engineer and Works Manager, in 1927. As two very senior managers in the LNER, they would have met through work and this gradually grew into a closer relationship through this shared interest. Thom, like Gresley, was a highly intelligent and outgoing man, who had an easy way with people of all backgrounds and with Thompson he found friendship. And they must have made an interesting pair – the short, rotund, humorous Scot and the tall austere, rather prim Englishman.

If Thompson feared that he might find his career stalling with Gresley in charge, then he may have been mildly surprised when the new CME appointed him to become the company's North Eastern Area Carriage and Wagon Works Manager at Darlington in mid-1923. If there was any ill-feeling between the two men, this promotion suggests that it wasn't allowed to get in the way of good business practice. By any standards, Thompson was a very effective leader whose skills couldn't be ignored by even the most biased person. It was this attitude that seemed to underpin the approach both men adopted in the years to come. If there was mutual distrust or antipathy, they don't seem to have allowed it to boil over into petty bickering or point scoring, though some resentment may have simmered underneath.

The LNER's Angling Association which Thom led for many years and which proved extremely popular amongst returning soldiers, including Thompson who became a very keen member from the 1920s onwards. Thom sits to the right of the annually awarded angling trophy with Thompson behind in a light coloured suit. (*LJ*)

Thompson would remain in this post until 1927, extending more modern working practices across his bigger empire. But, if anything, this period in the LNER's history was more about locomotive policy than rolling stock. Whilst there were new developments in this field, the main focus centred on new engines and modifications to existing types. Gresley had always displayed a keen interest in carriage design and so it wasn't forgotten now, but took second place to his constantly developing locomotive programme.

The Pacific programme went from strength to strength with 52 entering service by 1924. N2 0-6-2 tank engines rolled off the production line from 1920 to 1929, until 107 were built, and 25 more heavy goods 2-8-0 Class 02s were constructed at Doncaster during 1923/24. He also began his experiments with 2-8-2 tender engines, beginning with two P1 heavy mineral locos in 1925, and developed the new J38 0-6-0 goods engine and the D49

4-4-0 passenger class as well. And to this he added existing engines already in the GNR programmes. The H4 2-6-0 begun in 1920 continued until 1925 with 193 locomotives being built and re-designated K3s. In addition to this, there were locos inherited from all the constituent companies to consider. By any standards it was a substantial bank of work.

The business practice usually applied in such situations is to rationalise and standardise to save money and improve efficiency. But Gresley doesn't seem to have been constrained by this mantra. Thompson, on the other hand, appears to have been a strong advocate of this approach and applied it wherever he could. In this he had much in common with William Stanier, then with the GWR as Principal Assistant to the CME, and soon to rise to become the LMS's CME. He too had focussed on production issues or running shed matters, not locomotive construction and, like Thompson, had never served in a drawing office.

Nevertheless, he appreciated the need for greater standardisation and commonality of parts across a fleet of locomotives and rolling stock. In this the GWR, under Churchward, had become experts and advanced accordingly. When taking command of the LMS, Stanier took a similar, very effective line, not so the LNER which seemed unable to grip this issue under Gresley. As a result, the problem seemed to grow worse and the company ended up with an array of different types of locomotives, many inherited from companies with diverse operational needs, to which the CME added more types.

It is here that closer co-operation between Gresley and Thompson might have paid dividends and made the most of their combined talents, one as the creative leader and the other as his immediate deputy, offering sound guidance and operational advice. Whilst each may have recognised the strengths of the other, their increasingly strained relationship made such a positive relationship difficult if not impossible to sustain. So Thompson sat on the periphery of the organisation until time and opportunity brought him closer to the true centre of the CME's world.

In the circumstances, and bearing in mind their like-minded approach, it isn't surprising that Stanier and Thompson went on to develop a strong professional relationship, which, judging by the correspondence that has survived, lasted for a long time.

In the meantime, Thompson threw himself into the Area Works Manager role overseeing amalgamation and rationalization of the rolling stock in an effective way. During his three years in charge, the shops under his control grew more efficient. In addition, new construction tasks were beginning to increase as the company's financial position improved and customer need grew. Gresley was attuned to this and realised that passengers demanded much more in the way of comfort and facilities. This helped stimulate ideas he'd begun developing with the GNR and it fell to Thompson, now vastly experienced in carriage work, to take on and manage this task.

Was Gresley impressed by this and did Thompson's success improve his reputation in the eyes of the CME?

The N2 tank programme derived from Henry Ivatt's N1s which appeared in 1907. These engines were primarily designed to pull suburban commuter trains. To service this need, 107 N2s were built between 1920 and '29. This engine, an N2/4, was constructed by Hawthorn, Leslie and Co, and appeared in January 1929 (*PR/RH*)

Gresley's design ambitions ran in many directions, the results of which Thompson logged in his archive. The Pacific programme was of note, but so were his efforts to produce two 2-8-2 P1 heavy goods engines, represented here by No. 2394. Experience gained in building these 2-8-2s eventually led to the P2 programme in which Thompson would 'dabble' post-1941 to the detriment of his reputation. Perhaps of greater value to the LNER was Gresley's work on smaller engines, in this case the J38s, with the first of the class, No. 1400, rolled out of the workshops at Darlington in 1926. Thirty-seven more followed that year. (*PR/RH*)

We shall never know with any certainty, but it is unlikely to have passed unrecognised or ignored. In fact, Gresley chose this development programme as the subject of a lecture he gave to the Federation of Railway Lectures and Debating Society in York during 1928. It contained a detailed account of the work undertaken in the carriage side of business when Thompson was in charge. Although not mentioned personally, he could take credit for much that the CME marked as being a success. Some of his words even harked back to Thompson's efforts to get steel used in construction as a safety measure, although Gresley chose to take a contrary view in his assessment. In his lecture, he touched on three key issues – construction, equipment and general design – and the direction research was taking the company. Some of the points he made were:

'Various experiments in the use of steel had been made before the war, but it was only after the war that the development of all steel carriages seriously commenced. The influences which brought this about were the high cost of timber and the desire to help the British steel industry [bearing in mind their pre-war correspondence this may have produced a wry smile from Thompson]. The adoption of steel carriages in this country was a more difficult matter than in America and on the Continent, where carriages with doors at each end only are in general use. Carriages of this design are much simpler to construct out of steel than carriages having side doors to every compartment.

'An effort had been made to construct a vehicle offering the greatest resistance to shock, the whole being in the form of a tubular girder. The bodies are built entirely of steel plates riveted together and welded at joints. When travelling in coaches of this type on express trains I found a remarkable absence of vibration and noise.

'Steel carriages were heavier than wood, notwithstanding the efforts made to lighten them by means of aluminium allows, etc. Experiments made on the LNER some two years ago [under Thompson's direction at Darlington] showed that open thirds, 60ft long, built of steel, weighed 34tons 5cwt, as compared with 32½ tons of similar coaches built of teak. A steel coach also costs rather more than the teak-built coach, although teak is one of the most expensive woods used in carriage construction . . . [For this reason] LNER carriages were made almost entirely of this wood.

'In considering the construction of wooden carriages one of the most notable developments of recent years has been the introduction of sectional building. In this method of construction several sections forming a coach body are built as a separate unit on jigs and then assembled on the underframe.

To illustrate his talk Gresley circulated a number of photographs, in this one capturing the production line layout introduced by Thompson at York in the early 1920s. (*RH*)

Although of poor quality Gresley used these pictures to illustrate the two methods of building carriages on the LNER. (Above) Sectional construction in wood. (Right) Tubular steel methodology in practice. It is probably true to say that Gresley had a preference for wood, perhaps on cost grounds alone, whilst Thompson was a strong advocate of an all metal finish. (*RH*)

'Some six or seven years ago I took up the question of electric cooking for railway carriages, and although difficulties were experienced in the early stages, on the whole the results had been so successful that shortly there would be in service on the LNER eighteen electrically operated dining cars . . . To the LNER belongs the credit for being the first railway in the world to fit these cars with electric cooking apparatus.

'Another notable development in the equipment of carriage stock was the abolition of dual brakes. The unification of brakes in this country was being proceeded with and in a few years' time there will only be one form of continuous brake in use on the rolling stock of Great Britain.

'The very latest development in railway carriage stock was the third-class sleeping car introduced on September 24th. It was a source of gratification to know that the cars, which had been built in the York carriage works, had been greatly appreciated by passengers and it is hoped that the introduction of this new type of coach would result in stimulating travel and help the railways to stay the inroads being made by road competitors.'

In the time available, Gresley could only briefly describe some of the developments taking place, though did include a slightly more detailed summary of his work with articulation. There were no references to individuals, but this tended to be the custom at the time. The CME was head and took the credit, but also shouldered the brickbats too. But there is little doubt that much of the credit must go to Thompson and the team he led. So, in a way, Gresley's paper became a sort of valedictory for Thompson's work. He probably deserved more, but he occupied a privileged position in a privileged world and his status in the company would suffice. But late in 1927, his career took an unusual turn, caused in part by the retirement of Frank Wintour and the series of staff moves sparked by his departure. And to London Thompson went to fill a post that looks remarkably like a step backwards to the casual observer.

The third of Gresley's A1 Pacifics, No. 1472 *Flying Scotsman*, with a rake of aging carriages, thunders by, reflecting the growing influence of its master on the LNER but also Britain's railways. By the end of the decade, his name was made and reputation was almost unassailable. Did Thompson look on with any trace of envy? (*PR/RH*)

CHAPTER 5

WAITING IN THE WINGS

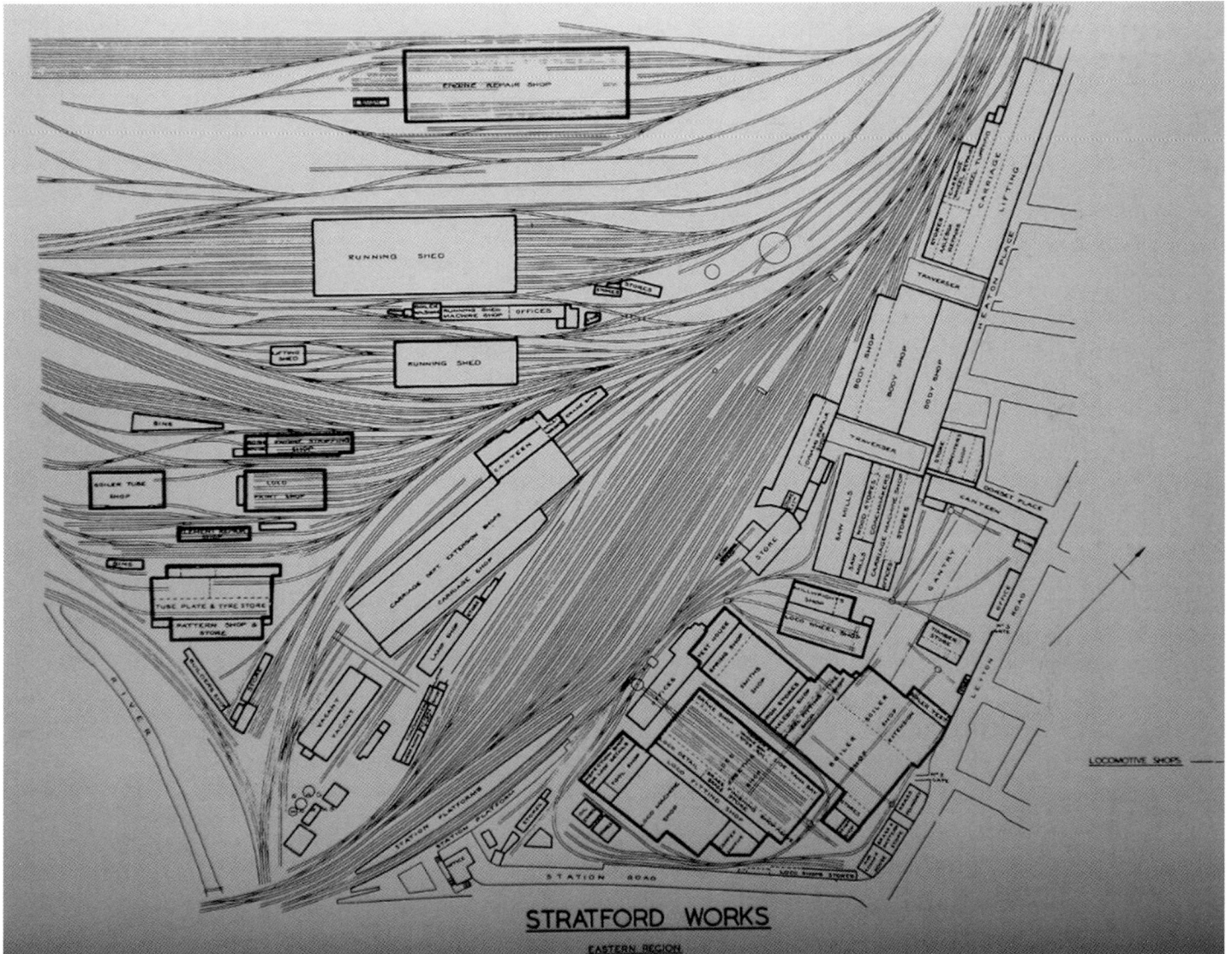

— Stratford Works as it appeared between the wars. It was an entirely self-contained business designed to meet all the construction and maintenance needs of the GER's locomotive, rolling stock and road vehicle fleet. There was also a test facility, a chemical laboratory, a drawing office, a power generating station, printing shop and a very active Mechanics Institute, nearby at West Ham, as an aid to education, amongst other things.

Stratford, like other well established Works absorbed by the LNER, no longer had the importance it once did as home of the Great Eastern Railway. Prior to 1923, it had an active locomotive and rolling stock construction programme guided by its CME Alfred Hill. But with amalgamation, and Hill's departure, it entered a period of decline,

seeing many of its tasks move to Doncaster and Darlington in the process. Nevertheless, it was still important to the company and its extensive facilities would continue to play a key role in the business for some considerable time.

Before the Great War, more than 6,000 people had been employed in an array of locomotive, carriage and wagon workshops that spread over a huge site to the east of Central London. Nearby sat the GER's main engine shed, which had an allocation of 500 or more locomotives, making it one of the largest in the country. With this fleet of engines, it served lines that ran from Liverpool Street Station to Cambridge and East Anglia, plus an expanding commuter network to the north and east of the City.

Although Hill, who was born in 1862, had proved to be a talented apprentice at Stratford, obtaining a highly prized Whitworth Scholarship in the process, opportunities to enhance his design credentials had been few and far between. In 1899, he became Works Manager at Stratford and then waited thirteen years to become Locomotive and Carriage and Wagon Superintendent. During this period, there was an active, though restrained engine building programme that was based on the work of his predecessors – T.W. Worsdell and James and Stephen Holden. So it was their S69 4-6-0s, E72 0-6-0s, G69 2-4-2Ts and Y14 0-6-0s that continued to be produced at Stratford. Then the war came, restricting Hill's opportunities to design new classes still further, although the scope for modifying existing types remained a constant theme.

By the end of his career, Hill was recognised as having managed the works effectively, but his locomotive legacy rested on his L77 0-6-2T engines, which began appearing in 1915. Production of these locomotives began at Stratford in 1915 and before work was transferred to Gorton ten years later, the East London Works had built twenty-two. So successful was the design that the LNER continued building them until 1928, by which time 134 were in service under the designation N7.

Thompson's appointment, though one of a number of moves resulting from Frank Wintour's retirement, was also caused by the gradual rationalisation of posts and places of production. With such a plethora of sites and facilities, duplication of effort was unavoidable and had to be dealt with if the benefits of amalgamation were to be realised. But, inevitably, old habits die hard as do old allegiances and there was resistance to change. Having brought greater efficiency to the carriage and wagon works in the North-East, Thompson's area management post was becoming redundant. To go back to York or take on a lesser post at Darlington would hardly be attractive to a man of ambition. But at the same time if he was to enhance his credentials for a top job he needed to broaden his experience. And here a Mechanical Engineer post at the increasingly prestigious Doncaster or Darlington would have offered him a suitable challenge and take him on another step towards becoming a CME. But with Arthur Stamer in charge at Darlington and Robert Thom proving the best candidate for the ever more demanding post at Doncaster, these key positions were unavailable.

The main office building at Stratford where Thompson would work for nearly six years. This photo was taken shortly before some rebuilding work commenced. (*RH*)

SOUTHERN AREA

TYPE J-68.

0-6-0   GOODS TANK ENGINES.

NEW ENGINES   BUILT   STRATFORD WORKS.

BOILER   HEATING SURFACE
BARREL Outs. Diaf. Max. 4'-2"   TUBES   909·4 sq.ft   CYLINDERS (2) 16½" dia'. x 22" stroke.
        Length   9'-1"   FIREBOX   86·77 "   DRIVING WHEELS 4'-0" dia'.
FIREBOX Outs. Length   5'-2⅙"   TOTAL.   996·17 sq.ft   WEIGHT ON DRIVERS 42 Tons 9 cwt.
GRATE AREA   14·5 sq.ft.
WORKING PRESSURE 180 lbs/sq.in.

Engine No.	Date sent into traffic	Superheater	Remarks
7031	6 · 10 · 23	Non - Super.	
7032	11 · 10 · 23	"	
7033	16 · 10 · 23	"	
7034	20 · 10 · 23	"	
7035	27 · 10 · 23	"	
7036	1 · 11 · 23	"	
7037	6 · 11 · 23	"	
7038	10 · 11 · 23	"	
7039	17 · 11 · 23	"	

Above and overleaf: Robert Thom throughout his career kept a number of albums that listed each new or modified locomotive in which he had some involvement. From 1923 to 1935, this covered the LNER and included references to the last new engines built at Stratford Works – the N7s and J68 0-6-0 tank engine. These were the last of 1,702 that rolled out of the sheds in the GER's long history. (*RT/THG*)

TYPE N-7.

O-6-2 PASSENGER TANK ENGINES.

NEW ENGINES

BUILT:- STRATFORD WORKS.

BOILER.

Barrel Outs. Dia. Max. 4'-9'
        Length.   9'-7'
Firebox Outs. Length 6'-0'
Grate Area   17·7 sq.ft.
Working Pressure. 180 lbs/sq.in.

HEATING SURFACE

Tubes small	626·9 sq.ft.
large	231·2 "
Firebox	110·2 "
Superheater	134·2 "
Total	1102·5 sq.ft.

Cylinders (2) 18"dia. x 24" stroke
Driving Wheels 4'-10' dia.
Weight on Drivers 49 Tons 15 cwt.
Total Weight in Working
     Order 62 Tons 5 cwt.

Engine No.	Date sent into traffic	Superheater	No. of Elements	Remarks.
7991	1 · 1 · 24	Robinson	18	
7992	1 · 1 · 24	"	"	
7993	8 · 1 · 24	"	"	
7994	16 · 1 · 24	"	"	
7995	23 · 1 · 24	"	"	
7996	31 · 1 · 24	"	"	
7997	16 · 2 · 24	"	"	
7998	21 · 2 · 24	"	"	
7999	19 · 3 · 24	"	"	

This left only Stratford or Cowlairs, in Northern Glasgow, as possible destinations for Thompson. Yet in each case, they had incumbents who were unlikely to move in the near future. Tom Heywood, having been Locomotive Superintendent of the Great North of Scotland Railway, then District Mechanical Engineer, succeeded Thom as ME of the Scottish area in 1927. At only 46, he wouldn't retire before 1940, so there was no immediate prospect of Thompson moving there to replace him. It was a similar position at Stratford, where Charles Glaze was Mechanical Engineer and had no immediate retirement plans either. But, at least, here there was another opening to attract Thompson. The ME was in need of an assistant to help push through change as well as take over many of his day to day tasks. Whoever took on this post would have the experienced Tom Wein as Works Manager, and William McDermid, the Chief Draughtsman, to support him. Both men were long term GER employees who knew the business inside and out.

Glaze, who would play an important part in Thompson's career over the next three years, might best be described as a locomotive man. He began work with the GER at Stratford in 1885 as a draughtsman and quickly took the opportunity of gaining extensive footplate experience. With his knowledge quickly amassing, he felt able to apply to become an inspector and then, in 1892, was appointed District Locomotive Superintendent at Doncaster. A move to Norwich followed and in 1899 he returned to Stratford, where he remained for the rest of his career. In 1912, Hill appointed him Works Manager, then in September 1921 Chief of the Running Section. Promotion to Mechanical Engineer followed in March 1923.

It seems he was well respected and was noted for taking an active interest in the work of the Mechanics Institute and in encouraging his young men to study and extend their qualifications. He was actively involved in the work of the British Standards Association, the Institution of Mechanical Engineers, Stratford Unemployment Committee, the Railway Clearing House and the Court of Referees run by Central Government. In recognition of all his efforts, particularly during the war years, he was awarded an OBE and earned the respect and trust of Gresley along the way. As a manager, he was noted as a moderniser with a deep interest in the health and welfare of those who served under him, and

Mr. C. W. L. Glaze.

sought improvements in labour relationships. This was still uncommon in the years after the war and occasionally put him in conflict with many management practices being adopted by the LNER in their drive for economy. This was nowhere more apparent than in 1927, when the company's senior management, in the aftermath of the General Strike, brought in short-time working in many of its lower profile establishments to save money. Morale was seriously damaged as a result, eliciting newspaper headlines that focussed on Stratford. It was in this mood of gloom that Thompson agreed to the transfer and took up the post as Glaze's assistant. Was it to broaden his skills or was it simply to toughen the management regime and increase the efficiency of operations? If the second of these, he was certainly a man who could review tasks and bring in changes where necessary.

Royal visits then, as they are now, were seen to be a way of boosting morale in difficult times. This was certainly the case in July 1927 when the king and queen journeyed to Stratford for the day. Whether this was adequate recompense for reduced hours and pay who can say? Although a few weeks away from transferring from Darlington to Stratford formally, Thompson was present for this high profile visit and can be seen to the left of Queen Mary (third along in the front row). Gresley stands to the king's right with the taller figure of Charles Glaze beside him. (LJ)

When recalling this period, Thompson said or wrote very little beyond that he was the 'Assistant Mechanical Engineer, LNER, at Stratford; directly responsible to the Mechanical Engineer; in charge of Company's Loco, Carriage and Wagon Shops'. But in his correspondence with Brian Reed in 1948, he did provide a very brief view of the problems he faced there and one success of which he was clearly proud:

'At Grouping, Stratford Works was awkwardly placed and out of date, split by the Loughton Branch and little in the way of wheel shop facilities. During my time we were able to achieve a good deal of modernisation. One result of this was that the shopping time for a heavy overhaul was reduced from 7 to 8 weeks to 23 days.'

Although locomotives were included in his brief, it seems likely that the main part of his duties focussed on the rolling stock side of business. Here the shops were more substantial in size than the engine side of business, had a higher work rate and were considerably more labour intensive. The scope for greater efficiencies was self-evident and ready for someone of his background and skill to consider. The loco workshops wouldn't be ignored, but, from the first, seem to have been of secondary importance in this modernisation programme.

If Thompson thought that moving to be assistant at Stratford was a retrograde step, he would soon have discovered that opportunities for advancement would grow exponentially. There was also the possibility, albeit not an immediate one, that he could replace Glaze, who was due to retire within a few years and this might move him closer to becoming Gresley's deputy or replacement. If he cared to look round the industry, he would have seen few other opportunities emerging. The GWR, LMS or Southern Railway still tended to promote from within and elsewhere in the industry competition was stiff, so the LNER still represented his best chance of promotion.

By late 1927, Thompson was well into his stride, understood the state of play in the workshops and was making progress in producing a modernisation plan. Judging by the documents that survive, he doesn't seem to have been someone who often put pen to paper, but in this case he seems to have made an exception. In December, he referred to his proposals in a short memo seeking approval from Gresley and Glaze to proceed with changes in the wagon works in Temple Way. Here, more than 800 people were employed in a cycle of work that saw 500 or more trucks go through routine maintenance each month, new trucks constructed and carriage frames built. With such a high turnover, an effective production line was essential and by mid-1928, changes had been implemented which achieved this, drawing Gresley's praise in the process.

As he settled into his place Thompson followed Glaze's example and became closely involved in staff training and education. Here the Mechanics Institute proved to be a focal point for his efforts. Up to this point in his career, it seems that his interest in further education was muted and there has been a suggestion that he resisted involvement in such things. If so, he seems to have had a change of heart and actively encouraged workers to seek better qualifications. His deeper interest may have been engendered in part by the emphasis Gresley and Whitelaw placed on such things and their support of the Directors' Scholarships, begun by the GER many years earlier. Nonetheless, he appears to have embraced all training schemes with some enthusiasm and over the next few years his involvement and interest is captured in a number of articles that appeared in the LNER's journal. The highlight of this seems to have been the annual awards ceremony in which he actively participated, taking obvious pleasure in the students' accomplishments. Yet despite this, stories of his increasingly erratic behaviour begin to unfold suggesting a man who wasn't at peace with himself or the world around him

In his biography of Thompson, Peter Grafton describes in great detail his rather austere, unpredictable approach to staff matters and even hints at neurosis. He quotes an incident where Thompson's concerns for his health, following a bout of jaundice, made him demand that the office temperature be maintained within certain limits. This led to thermometers being installed and their daily inspection by him. On a particular day, he found one registering too high or low a temperature and this led to a tantrum and a paperweight being thrown, which smashed a window in his office. He also describes Thompson stalking around the workshops, avoiding contact with employees and having something akin to a pathological aversion to repeating himself.

Elsewhere in the book he relates that Thompson took an almost obsessive interest in office layouts, rearranging whole sections to suit his own tastes and whims. Corridor panels were reduced in size and glazed so he could see what was going on, windowsills were rounded off so they wouldn't attract clutter and he was known to prowl around offices after work inspecting them. Here, it seems, was a difficult, troubled man whose sense of balance appears to have left him at times. And yet he was also noted for many acts of kindness and generosity, especially when it came to apprentices, ex-servicemen, health issues linked to the war and the many women he employed in offices and workshops. There are a number of surviving letters he wrote championing women's rights and also where he took action to alleviate problems men faced in the workplace.

The incidents of difficult, even unbalanced behaviour at times suggest an underlying emotional problem, which stress seems to have exacerbated. Here, if these and other reports are to be believed, is a man who found it difficult to control the extremes in his nature. Now we are more aware than ever of the serious impact war has on even the most rational of minds and post-traumatic stress disorder is recognised as a crippling condition that can only be dealt with effectively by psychiatric treatment, if it can be treated at all.

Its manifestations are many and varied and always disturbing for the individual concerned and those around them. After the Great War, those who suffered did so in silence. There was little help, except sectioning and incarceration in an institution, and little sympathy for those who suffered in an extreme way. Whilst most people never quite reached this state, they struggled through life as best they could. Thompson may well have been one of them, with his war record creating a fertile ground for this crippling illness. We shall never know for certain of course, but in trying to understand the man it is important to consider all elements of his personality and how it may have been moulded.

War weariness, shell shock, PTSD or any one of a number of other titles have been adopted to describe this phenomenon. But in each case, the symptoms and diagnosis are identical. The illness which is believed to be lifelong can express itself in many ways: poor reaction to stress; irrational, obsessive behaviour; lack of patience; a flash, often unexplained, temper; illogical and bitter mood swings; nightmares; flashbacks; suicidal thoughts; severe depression and much more. Whilst many of these

characteristics exist, to some extent, in all human beings, war had the power to bring them out in an extreme, barely understood way. A display of these traits in the work place would surely have had a manifestation in home life too. In Thompson's case, this could have been exacerbated by his wife's continuing ill-health and any marital difficulties that may have existed. In the circumstances a move to London could have proved very difficult.

Gwen seems to have had a strong affinity for life in Darlington, having lived there for so many years with her parents. A move to Doncaster following marriage had kept her sufficiently close to her family to make the move one of little consequence, but the upheaval of a move to London could have been quite another thing entirely. But several years earlier, her parents had

Thompson's home for 4 years – Chiltern Court in Baker Street. Construction was completed in 1929. It was 'a good address' and had many notable clients in its many luxury service flats, including the writers H.G. Wells and Arnold Bennett. In some literature of the time they were called bachelor apartments. (*THG*)

C.M.E. Supervisory Staff v. Locomotive Accountant's Staff Cricket Match, July 5th, 1933
Sitting left to right—H. C. L. Edwards, J. F. Wild, E. Thompson, D. Sayer, G. Reeves

Cricket remained Thompson's lifelong passion – as a player then as a spectator. Over the years, he was often pictured with different teams sponsored by the LNER. In each of these he appears unusually relaxed and smiling, the sport's therapeutic value only too evident. The Gresley Cricket Cup became an important event each year within the LNER and was hotly contested. The report for the match referred to in this photograph records that the CME's Supervisory Staff team 'led, for the first time in the history of these games, under the determined and energetic captaincy of the Mechanical Engineer, Stratford. The CME staff nearly achieved an ambition of 21 years standing, viz., that of lowering the colours of the Locomotive Accountant's office. An enjoyable game was played in a true cricket spirit but it was brought to an untimely end by bad light'. It seems that the ME was usually considered a non-playing captain, but it seems on this occasion that Thompson took off his jacket, rolled up his sleeves and joined in. (*LJ*)

decided to leave Yorkshire, where they had seemed to have become a permanent fixture, and moved to Nately Lodge to the west of Hook in Hampshire. This must, inevitably, have made her own move southwards more attractive, even highly desirable. And for a year she lived with them in Hook, whilst her husband occupied a flat near Stratford. But in 1929 they appear to have taken up residence together in Chiltern Court, a newly completed block of luxury apartments built above Baker Street tube station.

Here the attractions were obvious. A much sought after location, with Regent and Hyde Parks close by, an easy journey to Stratford and all the benefits of living in the capital. But although comfortable, this fully serviced apartment, as they were described when built, suggests a bachelor life or an occasional existence there.

With Hook only a short 40 mile drive or train ride away from Central London, it seems likely that wife and husband may have spent much time in the country with her parents. On the other hand, they may have chosen to live largely separate lives. One characteristic of PTSD is the pressing need for privacy or isolation and the Thompsons may well have chosen this option in the years that followed.

In some ways, his interest in the Mechanics Institute may have reflected a need for stronger human involvement beyond the call of duty, but his unpredictability at work and mood swings speak of a man in conflict. Yet the analytical side of his mind, which had proved so valuable in the war, allowed him to step back and focus on production issues and implement valid solutions. One thing is certain though, in the difficult years after the war he wouldn't have been alone in facing this turmoil. This may be why he sought out the company and friendship of Cecil Paget and Norman Raven, who, with their shared war experiences, could understand the lasting impact of that cancerous war. To be in a band of brothers was not simply a wartime need, for many it would become a necessary part of peace as well.

Sport still remained a passion and with Lords and the Oval close by he was able to enjoy Test Matches and county cricket. He was, it seems, a member of

Thompson was always a supporter of sport and actively urged participation amongst his work force. He also encouraged workers to attend sporting events. Coaches or charabancs could often be seen leaving with parties to attend events around London. On this occasion it is the 1928 Cup Final between Blackburn Rovers and Huddersfield Town at Wembley. It isn't known whether Thompson attended that year, but a brief diary entry suggests he did in 1930 when Arsenal won. Perhaps his days at Woolwich Arsenal created an affinity with this team. (*PR/RH*)

the MCC and in one of his albums he kept various match reports and programmes, most memorably the Australian tour of 1930 when Don Bradman scored 254 at Lords in 1930. Thompson also actively supported and encouraged works cricket teams and continued in his attempts to reduce an already healthy golf handicap, with his brother-in-law a regular partner. Around Hook there were several good clubs and at weekends Thompson played them, occasionally with Raven senior. And during his years at Stratford his interest in fly fishing increased, with several holidays to Scotland where he could pursue this interest, apparently meeting Robert Thom along the way.

With a settled home life of sorts, his efforts could be turned towards Stratford's pressing operational needs. Here Glaze's retirement in 1930 had a considerable effect. No record has survived to suggest whether Gresley considered any other candidates for the Mechanical Engineer post, but there may well have been a competition. Nevertheless, Thompson succeeded to the position and quickly established himself in this role.

There was certainly sufficient work to keep him fully occupied, but with Doncaster and Darlington becoming the main centres of activity, Stratford's role continued down a secondary route. Locomotive design work, in particular, was largely handled by Gresley's immediate team at King's Cross, where Bulleid and Spencer held sway, with the Chief Draughtsmen, Harry Broughton then Tom Street, at Doncaster. Of course, there were also Robert Thom and Arthur Stamer to make these ideas work in practice, a task at which they proved very adept. And alongside these tasks sat Gresley's active carriage and wagon development programmes.

Between 1926 and 1933, their joint efforts registered many notable successes, with new locomotives garnering accolades and headlines in equal measure. In this work Gresley had few equals, except, perhaps, the legendary Churchward, with whom his feats would most often be compared. If his time with the GNR had been noteworthy for its dynamism, his team's output now reached new heights of creativity and accomplishment. The J38 was taken to the next stage of development with

Thompson caught at an informal moment whilst fly fishing. (*ET/DN*)

the J39 0-6-0 goods engines, with production continuing until 1941, by which time 35 and 289, respectively, had been built. This was followed by seventy-six D49 4-4-0 passenger engines in 1927/28.

Meanwhile, work on the next generation of Pacifics continued apace, the classic A3 appearing in 1927 from Doncaster, with fifty-one A1s also being upgraded to the new standard. The first of seventy-three B17 4-6-0 passenger locomotives were turned out by North British in 1928, with later production being undertaken at Darlington and by Robert Stephenson & Co. Then there was the experimental 4-6-4 W1 compound four-cylinder high pressure locomotive which took to the rails in 1929. But this was only the tip of the iceberg. A new tank engine, the V1 2-6-2, appeared in 1930 with ninety-two being built over the next ten years. Longer term plans for a new 2-8-2 express locomotive were being formulated. And to all this could be added an already well established building programme that kept producing more and more engines – the Class 02 heavy goods engines, the N2 0-6-2T, the 2-6-0 K3s, the J50 0-6-0Ts and the N7s.

For Gresley, any development programme had to explore the potential of his ideas and his scientific curiosity drove him to consider many possibilities and new theories. Of course, many realised that steam technology had probably reached the limits of its developments, but in a country bankrupted by war and in a severe financial depression, alternatives were simply too costly to consider. So steam remained the primary, most cost effective option until better times arrived and to this end Gresley would constantly seek to improve their design, with streamlining gradually capturing his interest.

To those at Stratford, all this must have seemed to be happening on another planet, especially as it was once such an active place itself. But with no new locomotives to be built locally, only maintenance programmes remained to absorb the team in East London, although drawing office staff were known to be involved in some of the new projects in a support role. Yet there was some compensation for this omission. It was decided to modify some of the locomotives built by the GER in an effort to improve their performance. In some accounts it is suggested that this work coincided with Thompson's period in charge and credit is given to him for the conduct of the work. He certainly became involved but the task really began four years before his arrival.

During 1923, small numbers of James Holden designed D15 4-4-0s, D16 4-4-0s and J17 0-6-0s, plus Hill's J20 0-6-0 class locomotives underwent modification, according to Robert Thom's summary of activity. Year by year the programme continued, with numbers slowly growing, with Stephen Holden's B12 4-6-0s being added to the programme in 1926. By 1933, when Thompson departed the scene, this work had involved more than 180 locomotives, so represented a very sizeable task. But it was the B12 class which attracted most attention and drew Thompson into the project. This is significant because it seems to be the first recorded occasion in which he became involved in design to any great extent, albeit taking an established engine and modifying it. This isn't to say that he drew the plans or sketched out ideas, but there are indications that he expressed his thoughts, sought Gresley's approval to proceed and had regular input during reconstruction.

Gresley's modification of the B12s also included the ACFI (*Société l'Auxiliaire des Chemins de Fer et de Industrie*) feed water heating system. Fifty-one of the engines were fitted with this equipment at Stratford as an experiment, or so it seems. However, the expected benefits were not forthcoming – the maintenance costs were found to be greater than any savings achieved by lower fuel consumption. So, from 1932 onwards, they were gradually rebuilt. Gone was the ACFI equipment, which was unattractive to say the least, and the decorative framing around the main driving wheels. A longer round topped boiler with a 5ft 6in barrel, producing 180psi, with a marginally greater combined heating surface, was adopted in place of the Belpaire boiler. But there was another issue to be resolved, as H.C.B. Rogers recorded in his 1979 book about Thompson and Peppercorn:

'Trouble was experienced in 1932 with the B12, which had Lentz poppet valves, because the cylinders of this 1911 design were not standing up to the hammering of these valves and were beginning to crack. Thompson sought authority to rebuild them as piston valved engines and seized the opportunity to use a long valve travel.

'The design of the valve gear was entrusted to Albert English [Senior Technical Assistant to the ME and a man with considerable locomotive design experience]. Experiments were carried out on engine No. 8559, which had piston valves. These engines had Stephenson valve gear for their two inside cylinders,

New A3, No. 2596, appeared in February 1930 and is seen here pulling out of King's Cross. Thompson, it seems, took whatever opportunities that came his way to ride on the footplate and made a number of appearances on some of the highest profile trains, this one included. The photo above appears in one of his albums of the period, with some timings recorded on the back. He also kept a picture of engine No. 2544, *Lemberg*, which was a 1924 produced A1 that underwent modification to A3 standard in late 1927. (*ET/DN*)

Type D-15 (Part 1)

4-4-0   Express   Passenger   Tender   Engines.

REBUILT   STRATFORD   WORKS.

BOILER
BARREL Outs. Diaᵐ Max. 4'-9"
      Length   11'-9"
FIREBOX Outs. Length   7'-0"
GRATE AREA   21.6 sq.ft.
WORKING PRESSURE 180 lbs/sq.in.

HEATING SURFACE.
TUBES small   874.7 sq.ft
      flue   282.7 "
SUPERHEATER 154.8 "
FIREBOX   117.7 "
  TOTAL   1429.9 sq.ft.

CYLINDERS (2) 19"diaᵐ x 26"stroke
DRIVING WHEELS 7'-0" diaᵐ
WEIGHT ON DRIVERS 34 Tons 12 cwt.
TOTAL WEIGHT IN WORKING
      ORDER 52 Tons 4 cwt.

Engine Nos.	Date sent into traffic	Superheater	No. of Elements	Remarks.
8864	15·5·23	Robinson	18	Transferred from Type D-14. Belpaire Boiler fitted
8867	23·5·23	"	18	" "
8866	8·6·23	"	18	" "
8862	7·12·23	"	18	" "

Two examples of the continuing programme of rebuilding work carried out at Stratford under Glaze and Thompson's leadership. The modification work began in 1923 and ran on into the mid-1930s. The extent of Thompson's involvement in this work is far from clear and there are several apocryphal tales surrounding the programme that may or may not be true. Either way there is little or no surviving documentary evidence to confirm or deny these stories. (RT/THG)

137

SOUTHERN AREA.

TYPE D-16 (PART 2).

4-4-0 PASSENGER TENDER ENGINES

REBUILT :- STRATFORD WORKS.

BOILER		HEATING SURFACE	
BARREL Outs. Dia. Max.	5'-1⅛"	FIREBOX	128·2 SQ.FT.
Length.	11'-9"	TUBES	1035·2 "
FIREBOX Outs. Length	7'-0"	FLUES	344·5 "
GRATE AREA	21·6 SQ.FT.	SUPERHEATER	180·5 "
WORKING PRESSURE	180 LBS/SQ.IN.	TOTAL	1688·4 SQ.FT.

CYLINDERS (2) 19" dia. x 26" stroke.
DRIVING WHEELS 7'-0" dia.
WEIGHT ON DRIVERS 36 Tons 6 cwt.
TOTAL WEIGHT IN WORKING ORDER
(ENGINE) 54 Tons 18 cwt.

ENGINE Nº	DATE SENT INTO TRAFFIC	SUPERHEATER	Nº OF ELEMENTS	REMARKS.
8787	3 · 1 · 29	Robinson	21	Transferred from Type D-16. (Part 1).
8794	15 · 1 · 29	"	"	" " " D-15 (Part 1).
8841	80 · 1 · 29	"	"	" " " " "
8801	12 · 4 · 29	"	"	" " " " "
8826	15 · 4 · 29	"	"	" " " " "
8790	26 · 4 · 29	"	"	" " " " "
8845	13 · 5 · 29	"	"	" " " " "
8786	7 · 6 · 29	"	"	" " " D-16 (Part 1)
8784	10 · 6 · 29	"	"	" " " " "
8853	16 · 11 · 29	"	"	" " " " "
8898	20 · 11 · 29	"	"	" " " D-15 (Part 1)
8854	29 · 11 · 29	"	"	" " " " "

TYPE B-12 (PART 2).

4-6-0 EXPRESS PASSENGER TENDER ENGINE.

REBUILT:- STRATFORD WORKS.

BOILER
- BARREL Outs. Dia. Max. 5'-1⅛"
- Length. 12'-6"
- FIREBOX Outs. Length 8'-6"
- GRATE AREA 26·5 sq.ft.
- WORKING PRESSURE 180 lbs/sq.in.

HEATING SURFACE
- TUBES 1123·0 sq.ft.
- FLUES 366·1 "
- SUPERHEATER 201·6 "
- FIREBOX 143·5 "
- TOTAL 1834·2 sq.ft.

- CYLINDERS (2) 20"dia. x 28" stroke
- DRIVING WHEELS 6'-6" dia.
- WEIGHT ON DRIVERS 43 Tons 8 cwt.
- TOTAL WEIGHT IN WORKING ORDER 63 Tons.

Engine No.	Date sent into Traffic	Superheater	No. of Elements	Remarks.
8516	29·11·26	Robinson	21	Fitted with "Lentz" Poppet Valves. Transferred from Type B-12 (Part 1).

The first B12 undergoes modification. Only this engine would be worked on before Thompson arrived. From 1928 to 1933 at least 36 more are recorded by Thom as having been processed through the works at Stratford. The B12, which first appeared in 1911, was originally a class of 71 designed by S.D. Holden. Ten more would be added in 1928 to overcome a shortage of engines with this power rating, being built by Beyer, Peacock. (*RT/THG*)

Type B-12 (Part 3).

4-6-0 Express Passenger Tender Engines.

REBUILT :- Stratford Works.

BOILER
BARREL. Outs. Dia.* Max. 5'-6"
   Length. 12'-7½"
FIREBOX Outs. Length 10'-1½"
GRATE AREA 31 sq.ft.
WORKING PRESSURE. 180 lbs/sq.in.

HEATING SURFACE
FIREBOX 154 sq.ft
TUBES 979 "
FLUES 426 "
SUPERHEATER 315 "
TOTAL 1874 sq.ft.

CYLINDERS (2) 20"dia x 28"stroke
DRIVING WHEELS 6'-6" dia"
WEIGHT ON DRIVERS 48 tons 2 cwt.
TOTAL WT. OF ENGINE IN WORKING
ORDER 69 Tons 10 cwt.

ENGINE No	DATE SENT INTO TRAFFIC	SUPER HEATER	No OF ELEMENTS	REMARKS
8571	6 · 7 · 33	Robinson	24	Transferred from L.N.E. Type B-12 (Part 2)
8573	14 · 7 · 33	"	"	" " " " " "
8574	19 · 7 · 33	"	"	" " " " " "
8575	24 · 11 · 33	"	"	" " " " " "
8569	8 · 12 · 33	"	"	" " G.E. " "
8572	22 · 12 · 33	"	"	" " L.N.E " " (Part 2).

Fitted with Round top boiler
Long valve travel (6⅛") motion. 9½" dia. valves

The B12s begin their transformation at Stratford. (*RT/THG*)

and the valves being above the cylinders got their motion from a rocking lever pivoted at its centre. The valve travel was increased from the original 4/18in to 6 1/18in by moving the point of pivot so that the top arm of the lever was longer than the bottom arm. In the light of very encouraging results, English embarked on a thorough re-design of the gear. A full size mock-up was erected at Stratford and Thompson himself would turn the handle which operated it whilst English worked out the dimensions.

'When all was ready, one of the 1927 poppet valve engines was rebuilt with English's new valve gear. The engine was so successful that Gresley approved a large scale rebuilding . . . Thompson, of course, deserves full credit for his part in this programme.

'The success of the B12s led to an even more complete reconstruction of the "Claud Hamiltons". The B12s had been piston-valve engines from the start, but the "Clauds" had always had side valves. Rebuilding of these engines with larger boilers having round topped fireboxes and some with long travel piston valves began in 1932 under Thompson's supervision. Where the existing cylinders and slide valves were in good condition, however, they were retained. They were such good engines that, except where cylinders were in need of renewal, the extra cost of conversion was presumably not worthwhile.'

This programme would continue for a number of years, but it was no substitute for new locomotive work in many people's eyes at Stratford – especially those who had grown more used to tasks of greater substance in the past. One wonders whether Thompson looked longingly at the LNER's main centres of activity at King's Cross and Doncaster and actively sought a move to either place? If he did feel thwarted in his ambitions, there would have been some benefits to living in London to offset some of this frustration. He and his wife appear to have enjoyed a fairly settled existence in London and Hook, aided by the close proximity of the Raven family and Thompson's married sisters. Then there were his sporting activities in which he happily lost himself and membership of the University Club, which was only a short walk away from Baker Street. It was during these years that he joined two learned bodies. In 1929, backed and encouraged by Glaze, Gresley, Raven, Stamer and Sir Henry Fowler, the LMS's CME, with whom a friendship had begun to grow, he was elected a member of the Institution of Mechanical Engineers. Then there was the Royal Geographical Society of which he became a fellow, reflecting a lifelong interest, nurtured by his time at Marlborough. Alongside this his interest in history continued to flourish and he was known to visit sites of interest around London, with the Imperial War Museum, then in South Kensington, becoming a regular destination.

The IMechE was a natural progression for a man of science but also one of ambition. It was an ideal place to make contacts and learn of any new developments in engineering that might be used in other fields. It also contained an ever growing number of 'railwaymen', with some becoming President, including Raven (1925), Fowler (1927), Gresley (1936) and Stanier (1941), such was their influence. Thompson became a regular attendee over the years, but does not appear to have conducted any research or contributed any papers for fellow members to consider. Apart from the occasional comment on someone else's efforts, he appears to have contributed little to the life of the IMechE and chose not to join its sister organisation the Institution of Locomotive Engineers. From this it might be safe to assume that he favoured the IMechE for the contacts to be made, the social life it offered and its extensive library into which he often delved. As always, he was his own man and chose not to become a stereotyped establishment figure.

However, the comparative peace and order of his life in London came to an end in 1933. Arthur Stamer was due to retire in May and his prestigious post, based in Darlington but covering the north-east area, and included the works at York, Gateshead and Shildon, was open to competition. Once again, details of any selection process no longer appear to exist, but it resulted in Thompson being chosen to fill the vacancy. If Gresley had any reservations about his appointment none seem to have surfaced. This suggests that any personal differences that may have existed were of secondary importance when judging professional competence and in Thompson he had a sound, highly proficient manager.

TYPE D-16 (PART 3)

4-4-0 EXPRESS PASSENGER TENDER ENGINES.

REBUILT:- STRATFORD WORKS.

BOILER
BARREL Outs. Dia. Max. 5'-1⅛"
    Length 11'-9"
FIREBOX Outs. Length. 7'-0"
GRATE AREA 21·4 sq.ft.
WORKING PRESS. 180 lbs/sq.in.

HEATING SURFACE
FIREBOX 126 sq.ft
TUBES 957·1 "
FLUES 346·3 "
SUPER^HR 204·4 "
TOTAL 1633·8 sq.ft.

CYLINDERS (2) 19"dia. x 26" stroke
DRIVING WHEELS 7'-0' dia.
WEIGHT ON DRIVERS 36 Tons. 9 cwt.
TOTAL WEIGHT IN WORKING ORDER
    ENGINE :- 55 Tons. 18 cwt.

ENGINE No	DATE SENT INTO TRAFFIC	SUPERHEATER	No OF ELEMENTS	REMARKS.
8848	20·1·33	Robinson	21	Transferred from Type D-15 (Part 2).
8854	17·4·33	"	"	" " " " (" 2).
8802	24·4·33	"	"	" " " " (" 1).
8821	5·5·33	"		

The above engines have been fitted with round top boiler but retain existing slide valve cylinders

				Transferred from Type D-15 (Part 2).
8849	5·4·33	Robinson	21	" " " " (" 1).
8837	5·5·33	"	"	" " " " (" 1).
8809	22·6·33	"	"	

The above engines are fitted with:- Round top boiler
Piston valve cylinders, 8" dia. valves
Long valve travel motion - 5⅞" valve travel.

The D16s emerge in their new guise. (*RT/THG*)

Thompson's work in modernising workshops and increasing flow rates is often overlooked. He seems to have had a keen eye for detail and kept abreast of new developments which he could exploit to good effect. Here is just one small example of the automation he introduced, in this case in one of the carriage workshops. On this occasion it was an experiment that was later abandoned when tests showed the drive belt proved insufficient for the task. (LJ)

Gresley and his senior managers bid farewell to the greatly respected and much liked Arthur Stamer. Front row (left to right): Thompson, L. Farr, Stamer, Gresley and P. Liddell. Back row: Peppercorn, F.W. Carr, T.R. Grenside, E. Stephenson, H. Oxtoby, T.R. Turner, C.E. Page and W. Wells-Hood. (*LJ*)

The *LNER Journal* contained an article which summed up the man Thompson was replacing:

'It is no exaggeration to say that his retirement is an exceptional event, because he is one of the most popular and best liked officers the North-East Area ever had. A walk with him through the busy shops or running sheds is an inspiration. It is immediately evident that he not only has a keen eye for all the equipment he controls, but he also has an intimate knowledge of the staff.

'A man whose word is his bond, a tireless worker, trusted and respected by all the thousands of workmen he has controlled, ever ready to take the blame of others on his shoulders.'

Thompson must have been aware that if the NER had remained as an independent company Stamer would undoubtedly have succeeded Raven as CME in 1923 and he could conceivably have been Stamer's heir ten years later.

As often happens when someone of Stamer's skill and effectiveness retires, a review of workload takes place and there is some rebalancing of tasks. It was no different here. A notice published by Gresley records that 'R.A. Thom, ME Doncaster, to be ME Southern Area: Mr E. Thompson to be ME North-Eastern Area: Mr A.H. Peppercorn to be Assistant ME at Stratford'. Arthur Stamer had been in the Darlington post so long that he had acquired a broad range of duties, including acting as Gresley's Deputy CME at times. So his replacement didn't simply take on the post on a like for like basis, some duties being moved elsewhere. Nevertheless, Thompson's move was still a step up and would finally involve him in new construction tasks of some substance.

First, he had to sort out his domestic arrangements and it seems that Gwen decided to stay with her parents for a while. In the circumstances this proved to be a very sad and difficult time for her. Whilst holidaying in Felixstowe in December 1933, with her father and mother, Vincent Raven developed heart trouble. For such a robust, dynamic man this was probably a most unexpected event and clearly laid him very low. His condition was thought so poor as to make a return to Hook impossible and he lingered in a slowly deteriorating condition until 14 February, when he died.

In the months that followed, Gwen stayed with her mother whilst her husband found temporary accommodation in a company house called 'Ferndene' along Elton Parade within a short distance of Darlington Works. But with some of her father's £20,000 estate, she bought a substantial property, Old Hall, in the centre of Hurworth-on-Tees, not far from her sister Constance and her family, to which they moved. For some reason, she bought the house in her own name, a quite unusual step to take at the time and this may hint at the state of her marriage. Lady Raven also moved in and would spend the remainder of her life with the Thompsons there, with occasional sojourns to see her son Norman in London.

For someone in her condition, recent events must have proved most debilitating for Gwen. But in the countryside and in such a pleasant home, supported by a number of servants, and with her much loved mother and sister close by, there was a period of comparative peace as her husband got to grips with his new job in Darlington.

A visitor to Darlington would be hard pressed to find any trace of the huge railway workshops that existed in the 1930s when at their most active, employing some 3,000 plus people in the loco works alone. Perhaps the single most important structure remaining today to remind the casual observer of these great days is the old NER Stooperdale Headquarters that sits in Brinkburn Road. Most other buildings are now long gone with some of the land covered by a Morrison's supermarket,

one wall of which carries an old works clock. During the 1990s there was a small but significant steam revival when the A1 Locomotive Trust set up its business on the old Hopetown Carriage Works site. From here they produced their Pacific *Tornado* and their equally magnificent P2 *Prince of Wales*. If it wasn't for this group, the link between Darlington and its railway history would be tenuous to say the least.

Without more substantial reminders, it is hard to imagine the daunting task that Thompson faced when taking over from Arthur Stamer in 1933. Whilst the workshops hadn't been involved in Gresley's more glamorous locomotive projects, such as the A1 / A3 Pacifics, P2s and, between 1935 and '38, all 34 streamlined A4s, it had still actively participated in other important work. The J39s were mostly Darlington built and all seventy-six D49s were a product of the works there, with many continuing to be built under Thompson's leadership until 1935, as would the B17s. In addition to this, there was the conversion of Raven's 1913 Class H1 4-4-4T engines to 4-6-2 configuration and rather less extreme modification of his Class C7 4-4-2s. Bearing in mind Thompson's closeness to his father-in-law, and with his most recent death fresh in his thoughts, the new ME must have felt he was aiding the destruction of Raven's legacy. Nevertheless, his five A2 Pacifics were still running, and being maintained at Darlington, providing a testimony to his skill as an engineer, but this would soon change.

In 1936, their withdrawal from service was authorised by Gresley and by 1938 all of them had been cut up at Doncaster, the last shortly before Thompson replaced Thom there. For a man who may have been harbouring some antipathy towards Gresley, this might well have strengthened his feelings in that direction. But there is one interesting aside to this whole issue. In 1948, Thompson was interviewed by Brian Reed. The subject of the A2s was discussed. Whilst appearing not to dwell too long on the subject, Thompson alluded to a conversation he had had with Gresley about these engines when the subject of their future came up. He suggested to the CME that they be modified with two 21inch diameter cylinders replacing the existing three. The reference is brief but telling in two ways. It demonstrated Thompson's developing views on design and, perhaps more significantly, Gresley's opinion of the engines themselves. In 1948, Thompson simply recorded that the CME 'would have none of it'. One suspects that there may have been a depth of feeling, even resentment, behind these few words. Yet, at the same time, he went on to record that 'Gresley was the greatest locomotive engineer since Churchward', but quickly added, 'his only real failure was the conjugated gear'. It was by any standards a complex relationship.

In terms of new projects involving Thompson at this time, the most significant was probably the V2 2-6-2 heavy mixed traffic engine, which got underway in 1936. In time, 159 of the 184 built would be constructed at Darlington. In some eyes, it was arguably of greater importance to the company than the high-profile express locomotive programmes being built, primarily for its role during the Second World War. On top of this, the works played a prominent part in maintaining the LNER's large fleet of engines and had a role to play servicing carriages and wagons. So Thompson's workload was substantial and more focussed on locomotive work than at any time in his career. But there were wider production issues to consider and these would certainly have played to his strengths. At York and Stratford, such a clear thinking production man as Thompson couldn't fail to observe processes and seek greater efficiencies, which he did with great skill.

One of the reasons he was selected to be the ME at Darlington Works was undoubtedly to bring this expertise to bear on yet more shops in need of improvement. As the decade passed, the state of the LNER's finances had shown little sign of improvement, making savings still more important if any expansion plans were to be implemented. Gresley's locomotive development

The Old Hall Hurworth was built in the mid-eighteenth-century and modified a hundred years later and achieved listed status in 1952. No sign of the Thompsons' period of residence now exists, though the house and village are little changed. (*THG*)

During 1934, as Thompson settled into his new post at Darlington, Gresley's first P2, No. 2001, *Cock o' the North*, emerged at Doncaster. Rightly or wrongly, the fate of this class would rest in Thompson's hands and his later actions come to define his career and his apparent relationship with Gresley. (*DN*)

programme, though modest to some, was still a drain on resources so savings elsewhere were essential if it was to continue. It is reported that before Thompson arrived, some work had started, but this seems to have hardly scratched the surface of the problem and much remained to be done in all the shops.

No one person can manage all these tasks by themselves and Thompson was lucky enough to inherit many good people from Stamer. Inevitably, most names are now lost to time and so we will never know who really did what and have to accept a limitation on the way events and achievements are recorded. As a result, successes – and failures – tend to sit as an accessory to the leader's name. Nevertheless, in Thompson's case a few names have come to light which helps expand our understanding of what he and his team achieved.

Raven's legacy and Thompson's new Darlington empire as it appeared in the mid-1930s. This is the LNER's main North Road site and was located on the north-east side of the old Stockton and Darlington Railway. However, the ME's responsibility spread to other areas of the town – Faverdale, Stooperdale and Hopetown – and Shildon fifteen miles to the north-west of Darlington, plus York and Gateshead. (*PR/RH*)

Shortly before his arrival, Lionel Farr was promoted from Assistant Works Manager at Darlington to replace F.W. Carr who had transferred to Gorton. Farr remained in situ until May 1936 when he and Robert Smeddle, at Cowlairs, exchanged posts. Smeddle clearly impressed Thompson. When becoming CME in 1941, one of his first acts was to see his assistant promoted to be Mechanical Engineer at Darlington, succeeded in his old role by Lionel Reeves, who Thompson had also appointed. In 1945, the CME would authorise Reeves' promotion to be Mechanical Engineer Doncaster.

Elsewhere, Thompson had the very experienced W. Wells-Hood in charge of Faverdale and Shildon, whilst York fell under the control of William Brown, late of Doncaster. Meanwhile, Gateshead was run by George Caster who, until 1930, had worked for Thompson at Stratford. But there was one up and coming young engineer who was brought into the ME's sphere by Gresley himself. Thomas Cruddas had begun to make a name for himself at Doncaster, as Peter Grafton discovered. In the early 1930s, he joined the LNER where he became the foreman of the smithy shop. Gresley was an astute observer of people and had a good nose for sniffing out those with potential to rise higher and achieve more. In this he was probably helped by his senior managers, but he still had this considerable skill. Cruddas, by some means, came to his attention and in 1935, according to Grafton, accompanied Gresley on an inspection of Shildon, which by then was badly rundown. Thompson was in attendance and would have been party to the discussions that followed, which seem to have centred on the issue of closure or regeneration. Reconstruction was

The old North Eastern Region offices as they appear today in Stooperdale, Darlington. Several former members of Thompson's staff remembered the ME walking from here to the works in North Road (one used the phrase 'loping along'), where he would wander unaccompanied, inspecting all around him. From the few papers that remain, a tour would be followed by a number of short notes to the Works Manager containing observations and actions. (*THG*)

chosen and Cruddas, under Thompson and Wells-Hood, became the focus of these development plans. Such was their success that Shildon took on a new lease of life and Cruddas became Works Manager when Wells-Hood retired.

The NER had had its own Chief Locomotive Draughtsman, a post then inherited by the LNER. With amalgamation, it was always likely to be rationalised at some stage. From 1919, until his retirement in August 1932, the post was filled by R.J. Robson, a highly skilled designer, who had been promoted into the post by Vincent Raven and so would have known Thompson quite well. In this role, he was involved in the NER's electrification plans, but later, under Gresley, led on the W1 and D49 projects amongst other things. He was obviously a sick man when leaving in 1932 and survived only four months before dying on 6 January. If he had survived, he would undoubtedly have given the new ME much valuable support and advice. It wasn't to be, but the team he had built up, although subordinate to Harry Broughton, the Chief Draughtsman at Doncaster, would still offer much needed support to Thompson as he developed his ideas. Nevertheless, the scope of their work would always be in Gresley's gift, so likely to be muted with Doncaster in the ascendency.

If Thompson wished to improve his design credentials, to sit alongside his well-established reputation for production and organisational issues, there would still be some opportunities to do so. The sheer volume of work that he faced in running all these workshops would make this difficult at times. Nevertheless, he was closely involved in the production of the J39s, B17s, V2s and D49s, and had the opportunity to delve into other developments, building on the work he began at Stratford. But here he perhaps made the mistake of touching on an area of design that was very close to Gresley's heart, the conjugated valve gear.

The CME's development work in this field was a central theme in his life and so he guarded it jealously and displayed great sensitivity to any perceived criticism. Thompson, rightly or wrongly, saw flaws in Gresley's work which he strongly believed could and should be corrected. In many ways, it was an issue that came to define their relationship and reflected two strong willed men unable to find a compromise, but instead found cause for friction. Where the measured and diplomatic Bert Spencer understood his greatly respected CME and could suggest changes or modifications with a good chance of success, Thompson was in danger of falling foul of his obduracy. It seems to have been one thing for the ME, when at Stratford and Darlington, to seek Gresley's approval to modify the B12s or the B16s, but likely to be quite another matter when seeking to adjust the valve gear he had done so much to develop.

From his actions in the post-Gresley era, it is safe to assume that Thompson harboured doubts about the constant use of three cylinders when designing locomotives. There was also the question of Gresley's adherence to the idea of the three cylinders being operated by two sets of valve gear not three, by means of a '2 to 1' lever. It was a sound concept, mathematically at least, that had its origins in work undertaken and patented by David Joy in the latter part of the eighteenth century. This noted marine and locomotive engineer was constantly experimenting with valve gear and movement derived from a vertical link. His Joy Valve found its way into a number of locomotives, but didn't gain more widespread use. Subsequently, Harold Holcroft, a gifted young engineer who worked for the GWR and later the Southern Railway, evolved the concept for use in three-cylinder engines and patented his work in 1909, though allowed it to lapse a few years later.

The outbreak of war meant that he put any further design work on hold with the aim of resurrecting it later. By this time, though, a version designed by Gresley had been developed and patented (in 1915) and during 1918 had been fitted into a locomotive – a three cylinder 2-8-0 design numbered 461 – in prototype form. In the months that followed, it was tested extensively and successfully passed muster. Having proved its worth, the CME moved to apply the principle more broadly and the concept dominated his designs for years. In the process, he enlisted Holcroft's help to refine the idea still further, offering him a job as well, which he politely declined. So by any standards it was a key issue in Gresley's life and one on which he was sensitive to criticism. In the light of Holcroft's earlier work, and the suggestion of plagiarism, this is, perhaps, not surprising.

Over the years, there was a great deal of comment on his apparent rigid devotion to three cylinders and the

Type J-39 (Part 3).

0-6-0 Freight Tender Engines.

New Engines.   Built :- Darlington Works.

Boiler.   Heating Surface

Barrel Outs. Diaʳ Max. 5'-6"	Firebox	171·5 sq.ft
Length 11'-4⅝"	Tubes	871·75 "
Firebox Outs. Length Overˡ 8'-11⅞"	Flues	354·53 "
Grate Area 26 sq.ft.	Superheater 271·8 "
Working Pressure. 180 lbs/sq.in.	Total. 1669·58 sq.ft.

Cylinders (2). 20"diaʳ x 26"stroke.
Driving Wheels 5'-2"diaʳ.
Total Weight of Engine in
Working Order 57 Tons 17 Cwts

Engine Nº	Date Sent into Traffic	Superheater	Nº of Elements	Remarks.
1475	19·10·34	Robinson	24	
1476	24·10·34	"	"	
1477	29·10·34	"	"	Tenders second hand from Type A-2 engines
1478	14·11·34	"	"	
1479	7·12·34	"	"	

The construction of new locomotives at Darlington may not have been a substantial programme but it did, at least, provide regular work to top up all the maintenance tasks undertaken there. Here the appearance of new J39s and D49s are captured in Thom's records. Both types had long and valuable careers ahead and each class would see service well into the late 1950s, early 1960s. (RT/THG)

NORTH EASTERN AREA.

TYPE D-49 (PART 2).

4-4-0 EXPRESS PASSENGER TENDER ENGINES (3 CYL).

NEW ENGINES.   BUILT :- DARLINGTON WORKS.

BOILER   HEATING SURFACE
BARREL Outs. Dia. 5'-8"   FIREBOX   171·5 sq.ft   CYLINDERS (3) 17"dia x 26"stroke
     Length   11'-4⅝"   TUBES   871·75 "   DRIVING WHEELS 6'-8"dia.
FIREBOX Outs.Length 8'-11⅞"   FLUES   354·53 "   WEIGHT ON DRIVERS 41 Tons 10cwt.
GRATE AREA   26 sq.ft.   SUPER^HR 271·8 "   TOTAL WT. OF ENGINE IN WORKING
WORKING PRESS. 180 lbs/sq.in. TOTAL   1669·58 "   ORDER 64 Tons 10 cwt.

ENGINE No	DATE SENT INTO TRAFFIC	SUPERHEATER	No OF ELEMENTS	REMARKS.
283	19 · 8 · 33	Robinson	24	"The Middleton" (Fitted with Smith's Speed Recorder)
288	21 · 8 · 33	"	"	"The Percy"
292	23 · 8 · 33	"	"	"The Southwold"
297	30 · 8 · 33	"	"	"The Cottesmore"
298	1 · 9 · 33	"	"	"The Pytchley"

Fitted with "Woodard" Patent outside connecting rods
"Goodall" Patent Drawbar

conjugated valve gear. In response, Bert Spencer took the opportunity of defending Gresley's work when presenting a paper to the ILocoE in 1947 outlining the CME's ideas and achievements. He wrote:

'In adhering to a three-cylinder engine policy Gresley maintained that the clearly defined advantages of such an engine over a two-cylinder engine outweighed the complication introduced by a third cylinder. Fundamentally the nearer the variable crank effort of a reciprocating engine can be made to approach uniformity the greater will be the advantage derived for traction from a given adhesive weight. In this connection the superiority of the three-cylinder is apparent when the crank efforts of two, three and four cylinder engines of equal cylinder volume are compared.

'Whilst it can be urged that three independent sets of valve gear ensure a more accurate valve setting for the inside cylinder, the conjugated gear has the merit of simplicity and is not without advantages if due consideration is given to its inherent limitations.'

It isn't clear whether the diplomatic and faithful Spencer fully supported Gresley's ideas, but his final paragraph suggests he harboured some doubts. But the questions that followed his presentation in London, Doncaster and Newcastle were rather more clear cut when expressing reservations. E.S. Cox commented that:

'He always thought that Gresley's policy of applying the three-cylinder design to almost every type of locomotive was a little inconsistent. Where the power required was greater than could conveniently be provided by two cylinders, the three-cylinder arrangement was logical and suitable; but for medium and low powers it was difficult to see what advantage could be expected of it.'

A.F. Cook added to this by saying that:

'The only occasion on which Gresley produced figures in support of his claims for the three-cylinder locomotive was in 1925, when he compared the performances of the two-cylinder and three-cylinder

versions of the GN 2-8-0 and the NE 4-4-2 classes. As all the coal consumption quoted were about of the order of 4 1/2 -6½lb. per d.b.h.p hour this was hardly modern evidence of the superiority of the three-cylinder engine.'

When describing Gresley's conjugated valve gear there were references to 'the over-running of the valve spindle of the central cylinder', 'the arrangement suffering from inherent defects' and 'I find it difficult to accept that the conjugate valve had the merit of simplicity'. And, from this one question emerged, tabled by the Chairman, J. Hadfield:

'Whether the policy of the LNER is to continue to build the three-cylinder type locomotive, or had consideration been given to replacing the type with the more commonly used two-cylinder type? . . . I understand that the present policy of the LNER is to fit a third set of gear to drive the inside valve in three-cylinder engines.'

Bearing in mind that Spencer's paper was a eulogy for Gresley's work the comments, though highly complimentary, were muted and quite cutting at times. Spencer gamely supported his greatly admired leader, as one would expect from a man of his honesty and integrity, but this didn't fully overcome the message of disregard some felt for some of Gresley's ideas and methods. If these views were held in 1947, it stands to reason that they must have also been current in the 1920s and '30s as well and may underline why Thompson chose to seek improvements and, ultimately, question Gresley's approach to design.

Nevertheless, it doesn't seem to have been outright opposition to these ideas, but a gradual emergence of doubts about the performance of the conjugated valve gear. Here it is likely that Thompson relied upon his Works Managers and their staff for detailed assessments and advice. It is doubtful whether he would have known of any problems or reached any conclusions otherwise, especially on such a sensitive issue. He was an astute career orientated man, who wished to rise higher, so would only seek to question or challenge his leader in a measured, open way. And this is what he chose to do, or so it seems.

The start of Gresley's three cylinder conjugated valve dynasty. Engine No.461 emerges, painted grey, from the workshops at Doncaster on 1 May 1918. Gresley's promotion and frequent use of this valve gear was an issue that came to define his career, but also, in his reaction to its continual use, it did the same for Thompson. (*RT/THG*)

A common scene at Darlington in the 1930s showing Class D49s under construction. (*PR/RH*)

With the help of Cruddas, who had become something of an expert in welding during his days with Vickers-Armstrong and in ship building, Thompson was keen to exploit the potential of this process in the manufacture of rolling stock components. At the time, welding was slowly finding wider application in the railway industry as an alternative to forging.

Having discovered its potential, Thompson then sought to apply it in other areas of work. Concerns over the robustness of the rocking lever in the conjugated valve gear arose, with particular focus on the H-section's centre pin. Due to its position underneath the smokebox, ash contamination combined with leaked lubricant to increase wear in the pin and bearing; despite regular maintenance, this reduced its efficiency. By fabricating the valve motion in two half-box sections, welded at the seams one on top of the other, with a pressed in bush for the centre pin, Thompson hoped to reduce or remove the problem. Although a sound idea to explore, it hit one intractable problem. It proved impossible to check the stability of the weld without great difficulty and so the experiment was halted.

This early attempt at strengthening the design may or may not have been undertaken with Gresley's knowledge. But as it didn't seek to question the concept, only improve it, he was hardly likely to complain. The same thing happened again a few years later at Doncaster when Thompson's continued interest in the valve gear resulted in proposals for fabricating the equal motion levers. And in one of his last acts as CME, Gresley approved the drawings for this modification.

So, what does this tell us about their relationship? Clearly Thompson entertained concerns over Gresley's design and, as later events would show, believed the wholesale use of three-cylinders to be too inflexible as his advocacy of two-cylinders would later prove. But although recognising apparent flaws in the design, he chose an inclusive, measured approach in deference to his leader, probably being aware of Gresley's sensitivity on the subject. So he dealt with the issue and his CME in a mature, measured way, no matter what differences may have existed between them.

From the 1930s, a number of reports have emerged, often without accreditation, of Gresley's slightly prickly attitude towards Thompson. The gist of these is that there was a strong element of reproach and censure in their dealings which, on occasions, took on a public face. When writing on this subject H.C.B. Rogers drew heavily on letters written by John Harrison, who knew both men and observed their relationship over a period of time; Harrison was well placed to do so. He began as an apprentice to Gresley at Doncaster and rose quickly to become Assistant Works Manager at Gorton then Doncaster. After that, Thompson, as CME, promoted him to be Mechanical Engineer (Scotland) and during the 1950s his meteoric rise carried on under British Rail where he became Chief Mechanical Engineer. Of the differences between the two men he wrote in one of his letters:

'Gresley was not over-blessed with tact and did not spare Thompson in public, if he thought his ideas were poor. But criticism of him in front of others was something Thompson could never forgive. On locomotive policy, Gresley tended to discuss his ideas with Thom, Bulleid, Broughton, Street and Spencer but not Thompson, who felt out of it and brooded accordingly.'

In such a situation, apocryphal tales will often abound, but there is one that has gained more credence than others. In open meetings called by the CME, during which Thompson tended to say little, Gresley would turn to his ME, who had remained resolutely silent, and pointedly enquire whether 'Mr Thompson had anything to add' or 'What is Mr Thompson's opinion?'. If true, one can only surmise that it wasn't the most tactful thing to do and hardly likely to elicit a positive response from his ME. Private debate, even censure might be tolerated, public criticism or a display of irritation unlikely to be so.

To add wood to the fire, Peter Grafton tells the story of a visit by Gresley to Darlington to inspect a recently modified D20 locomotive. When discovering that Thompson had released details to the press without his approval, he not only made his feelings known on the subject in a forceful way to his deputy, but did so in front of some of Thompson's subordinates whilst inspecting the engine. If true, it is hard to imagine anything less likely to please even the most subservient of employees and Thompson

This picture appeared in the press during 1935 and captures dignitaries photographed in front of *Silver Link*. Thompson was known to have been on the footplate on several occasions that year and can be seen in the background, facing the camera in line with the cab wearing a grey trilby with dark band and a scarf tucked into his jacket to protect his shirt. He kept the article and photo in one of his albums. It seems he maintained an interest in this class for the remainder of his career, despite any antipathy there may have been between Gresley and himself. (*ET/LJ/DN*)

most certainly wasn't one of those. Strangely enough, during his visits to Darlington Gresley would often stay with the Thompsons and one wonders how the two men dealt with any perceived differences then. However, Gwen and her mother were both socially accomplished women and they may have smoothed over any rough edges in this relationship.

If Thompson felt peeved by Gresley's candour, he was quite good at doing this himself at times, as Harrison also records:

'ET was in many ways an extraordinary unpredictable character, who when he wished could charm a bird off the proverbial tree and yet at other times could be ruthless in his dealings with juniors.

'In my view Thompson was at his best when organising a department and thinking of reducing costs. He was a good picker of assistants, particularly where he knew he was weak – the control of staff and the handling of trade unions . . . I enjoyed working for him although it was a precarious business at times.'

In some ways, it seems to me that the relationship between Gresley and Thompson suffered because they both had strong, intransigent personalities. Both were born to lead not follow, each had robust views on many work related issues, design and production in particular. Yet for most of the time their experience and professionalism kept any disagreements in check and reduced rancour to an acceptable level. Through this they managed to work together, suggesting that there was an underlying respect, at least on a professional level.

After a deeply disturbing period in her life, Gwen must have found some peace of mind living in Hurworth. For her and her husband it was a time of adjustment that benefitted from the close friendship that developed with the Hall family, as Peter Grafton relates in his book. Though much younger than the Thompsons, Maurice Hall, who had been one of Vincent Raven's apprentices, and his wife Lilian, proved to be good friends. They were blessed with two children to whom Edward became close. In some ways they fulfilled the role of a surrogate family, which must have given him a glimpse of the joys of parenthood. The ease with which he related to children and the pleasure that he appeared to take in their company suggests that being a father would have added an extra, much needed dimension to his life. Sadly, though, this period of domestic calm didn't last.

In 1937, Gwen contracted scarlet fever. Clearly concerned by her condition, Edward took an extended period of leave to care for her, but also to meet strict quarantine regulations. During the weeks that followed, he passed the time by writing a history of England in a form suitable for children. Meanwhile, Lady Raven, whose health also seems to have been poor, decided to visit her son Norman in London whilst her daughter recuperated. While there, her condition gave cause for concern and she was admitted to a nursing home at 29 Devonshire Street, dying there on 2 August. One can only imagine Gwen's grief at losing a person who had cared and supported her for so long. The impact must have been devastating and her health which had never been good must have suffered as a consequence. A stress free period to recover from this trauma would have been beneficial, but this wasn't to be. Early in 1938, Robert Thom announced his intention of retiring and her husband was chosen by Gresley and the Board to replace him at Doncaster.

Whilst the ME posts at Doncaster and Darlington had equal responsibilities and rank, Doncaster had become pre-eminent within the organisation. It was where Gresley's most high profile projects had been developed and it was the old GNR's spiritual home. Thompson, as a disciple of Raven and Darlington, would have been only too aware of the significance of a posting there. And it was a message made clear in November 1937 when the hundredth Pacific was named *Sir Nigel Gresley* at a ceremony at Marylebone Station in honour of the CME and in front of the key members of the CME's team, past and present, including Thompson.

In a short speech William Whitelaw referred to this 'remarkable chapter in railway history represented by the hundredth Pacific designed by Sir Nigel who, I hope, has many more years of successful and happy association with the LNER, and particularly with his friends at Doncaster'. In response Gresley said:

'It is now 26 years since I was appointed Locomotive Superintendent of the former Great Northern Railway and have in that period of time been responsible for the design and construction of between 1,400 and 1,500 locomotives, which have cost upwards of £7,000,000. In this I was given great assistance at all times by the staff of my Department. It gives me particular pleasure on this occasion to have present my old friend Mr Wintour, who had helped him build my first Pacific, and Mr Thom, who did so much in the construction of the present locomotive and others of the streamlined class.'

He concluded with some words reflecting his debt to locomotive practice on the Continent and America and stressed the point that 'in all matters, co-operation is the best way to achieve results'.

In some ways it was a statement of legacy, as though the great days might be coming to an end. Now in his sixties, with increasingly poor health, he seems to have been dwelling on his achievements and would also have been aware of the 'gathering storm' in Europe. By 1938, the delusion of appeasement was at its height, but Gresley, for one, saw war ahead quite clearly. A view, it seems, he shared with Thompson, who knew only too well where German ambitions could lead. Added to this, and in a short period, Gresley had lost or would lose two of his most important lieutenants. Bulleid had just departed for the Southern Railway as CME and

A V2 on the production line at Darlington in 1937. It was the first major class of engine constructed in which Thompson played an active part. (*PR/RH*)

now Thom's dynamism and skill would also vanish. Gresley must have looked round and wondered who would replace them and the best available seemed to be Douglas Edge as his Principal Assistant at King's Cross and Thompson at Darlington.

These men do seem to have been strange choices, but for quite different reasons. Edge had a background in carriage and wagon work, with Thompson at Stratford for a time, so was unlikely to have provided the same technical input as Bulleid had once done. In addition, if the stories about Gresley and Thompson's difficult relationship are true, then his transfer to Doncaster might also be questioned. But it passed through without apparent difficulty, suggesting that they had made their peace or that Thompson was simply the best candidate available. And who could doubt this? He may have been

a difficult man to deal with, but he was also an expert in production methods and knew how to increase workshop output exponentially. In a commercial sense these were invaluable skills to have. With a war looming, which would require the marshalling of all industrial resources, such men would be at a premium. Design engineers would still have their part to play in the life of the railways, but it was giants of production who would hold sway in the years ahead.

The politics behind his move can only be guessed at, but the dynamics of Thompson's life at home are more easily read. But he was an ambitious man and probably sensed that a move to Doncaster might open the door to becoming CME. Thompson, being five years younger than Gresley, may have assumed that his leader would retire in the near future. In addition, he may have been aware that the older man's health was not good, witnessed by periods of absence due to ill-health and the presence of his son Roger during his visits and at formal functions. If his early departure became reality, then the man at Doncaster could become the natural successor. Certainly when looking around there were few other candidates to provide competition; they were either too young or inexperienced or, like Bulleid, happily ensconced elsewhere.

Thompson may also have had the backing of Ralph Wedgwood, who had known and worked with him for a very long time in the NER, the Department of Transportation during the war years and now on the LNER. It is unlikely that he would have been anything but an ally and a supporter of his cause. Thompson also had one other major qualification that would undoubtedly have appealed to a cost conscious Chief General Manager and the Board of Directors – he knew how to initiate and implement change at minimal cost. Doncaster, under Thom, had proved excellent at producing new locomotives and rolling stock in a remarkably short time when necessary. However, their general output across all functions, but primarily maintenance tasks, appears to

A special occasion marking the appearance of the 100th Pacific and celebrating Gresley's long career. The chairman William Whitelaw officiated. He would soon depart the scene. Following the death of his elder brother he 'found it impossible to continue to give adequate time to the affairs of the Company' and resigned in July 1938. He was replaced by Sir Ronald Matthews, who, unlike Whitelaw, had no background in the railway industry before joining the LNER's board in 1929. He was a product of Eton and was also a war veteran who subsequently held directorships in many industrial concerns. (*PR/RH*)

Sir Ronald Wilfred Matthews

Mr. C. H. Newton

In 1938, Whitelaw was succeeded by Matthews and a year later Ralph Wedgwood also departed, his replacement being Charles Henry Newton. He started his career as an administrator with the GWR before joining the GER and later became their and, later, the LNER's, Chief Accountant. From here he rose to become the Divisional General Manager at Liverpool Street Station in 1936. These two men would both play a leading role in shaping the last part of Thompson's career. They would both prove to be redoubtable allies. (*THG*)

have suffered from lack of someone with Thompson's skills to guide them. Thom was also a hands-on manager who took control in a direct way. Judging by the reams of notes, letters and instructions that appear in the files kept by the National Railway Museum, he took a very close interest in many matters that might have been better left to his senior staff to manage. In this he also became a post box for Gresley, taking many notes emanating from him at King's Cross adding a few words, and simply passing them on to the Works Manager, the Chief Draughtsman or their staff. To maintain control is essential but there is a

very narrow line between over-management and the exercise of effective delegation.

At Darlington, Thompson seems to have allowed his managers to manage, despite his often sharp manner. And the size of the task, other than new building or re-building of locomotives, was huge by any standards. Putting the servicing of carriages and wagons to one side, the locomotive works at North Road and Gateshead were responsible for the maintenance of more than 2,000 engines, plus a sizeable number of visiting engines which couldn't be managed elsewhere. Such was the extent of the work that,

One of Thompson's last acts as ME at Darlington was to supervise the construction of the K4 2-6-0 Class. They were designed specifically for use on the West Highland line. Once again it was a three-cylinder engine, the first of which appeared in January 1937. Five more were built in 1938/39. The second of the class, No.3442, survived into preservation and is captured in this photograph. (*THG*)

in 1934 alone, Darlington completed General Repairs on 620 or so locomotives, with many lesser routines and repairs added to this schedule. Other workshops would be hard-pressed to equal this work rate and then, of course, there were the rolling stock tasks to be added.

In such circumstances, Thompson's appointment would have made clear sense, but again the emphasis of his work would be on production methods rather than design. There might be greater involvement in this area of work but there would be no guarantee of this happening. So he agreed to go, but in so doing faced the problem of disrupting his wife's life at a difficult time. One can only imagine the discussions that would have taken place and the concerns she may have expressed. And in the weeks that followed before he replaced Thom, he agreed to occupy an official residence in

Thorne Road, where he and Gwen had lived before. Did she intend to accompany him on a permanent basis? We shall never know, but living in a company house didn't necessitate selling Old Hall and it would be there when her husband, now fast approaching 60, retired. So the change was probably one of short term expediency only.

As things turned out, she didn't make the move south. Lifelong illness and stress had weakened her sufficiently to make her future uncertain. By 1938, her doctor had certified that her mitral stenosis was in a chronic condition. In laymen's terms this meant that the mitral valve in her heart was now so badly scarred or damaged that it couldn't work properly. The symptoms of her decline would become only too obvious, quickly reducing her ability to cope with life. In the 1930s, surgery and drug treatment for such a condition were far in the future and so it was a case of rest and little else. In this state, there was a constant danger of relapse, particularly at times of great stress and strain.

On 22 May 1938, the breakdown finally happened. After a day in Doncaster preparing a house near the works for occupation, she returned to Old Hall and whilst in the garden a blood clot formed and passed into her head, causing a cerebral embolism. It seems that she was helped into the house whilst her sister Constance and brother-in-law, George Watson, were called, as well as her doctor, A.J. Thompson. A little later, with all three in attendance, she died, her husband unable to return in time from Doncaster, where he was taking over his new duties from Robert Thom. The following day, Watson registered her death, misspelling her name as Gwendolen in the process.

CHAPTER 6

A TROUBLED TIME

One can only imagine Edward's thoughts and feelings in the days and weeks that followed Gwen's death. Having lived for so long with a serious heart condition, her sudden demise may not have come as a complete surprise. But, even so, death will still be shocking and the cause of much grief and soul searching. There is also the contemplation of a future without a familiar figure beside you in the long years ahead. So, there would have been much sorrow and, perhaps, some guilt, especially if rumours of past indiscretions are to be believed.

In such tragic circumstances he was swiftly granted leave of absence by Gresley and Robert Thom agreed to remain at Doncaster until Thompson felt able to return to work. Gresley would have known only too well all that his colleague was going through, having lost his wife to cancer nine years earlier. He, by all accounts, bore the scars of this until the end of his life and in a short note to Thompson expressed his sympathies in a heartfelt way. If there were difficulties in their relationship, now was the time to put them to one side and allow shared experience and a sense of propriety to guide their actions.

There would have been much for Thompson to do in arranging Gwen's funeral and the disposal of her estate. She left no will, but then as now this creates no significant problems if the person is married, so all effects and assets would pass to the surviving partner without the need to pay estate duty, as it was called then. Probate still had to be sought, though in the circumstances this wouldn't have presented a significant problem, Edward being her sole legatee.

So, the funeral came and went with Edward supported by his family and by his brother-in-law Norman Raven. Theirs had been a very long friendship and in the months ahead they would travel to Corsica for a much-needed holiday. But first he had to take up the reins of his new post at Doncaster and allow the ever-friendly Robert Thom to take his much-anticipated retirement in North Yorkshire. At a dinner on 24 June at the Liverpool Street Hotel, Thompson sat alongside Gresley, Bulleid, Stamer and Peppercorn, amongst others, to celebrate the retirement of their old friend. Two days earlier, there had been a similar ceremony

An official photo of Thompson at the time of his posting to Doncaster, capturing the tired distressed state in which he found himself following the death of his wife. (*PR/RH*)

at Doncaster which Thompson had been unable to attend, but his new staff turned out in large numbers to say farewell to this greatly respected man. At the same time they must have wondered what might lie ahead.

It seems that most of the recorded stories emerging about Thompson's irascible, unpredictable and sometimes odd behaviour stem from his time at Doncaster as ME then CME. If this is the case, the loss of his wife coupled to the stress of taking on this new post may have contributed greatly to his troubled state of mind. Here was a man who, since the Great War, had displayed symptoms of PTSD and now had grief and loneliness added to that burden. The photograph that

Thompson's house in St Wilfrid's Road, Doncaster, as it appears today. It seems that he lived a rather lonely life here, following the death of his wife, from 1938 until his retirement in 1946 supported by a housekeeper, Rose Padfield, and a parlour maid, Ellin Ramsey. (*THG*)

heads this chapter was used to publicise his elevation to CME in 1941 but seems to have been taken three years earlier when becoming ME at Doncaster. In it we see a perfectly attired man, but one who looks distant and rather sad, any dynamism having given way to introspection. He was always an inward-looking person, but now his expression and demeanour speak of suffering, but an underlying sense of dignity and pride still exists. Much of what he felt would probably pass with time, but in this situation there is likely to be a residue of troubled emotion to undermine any peace of mind that may be found.

Although negative recollections of Thompson are well documented and may, of course, have become embroidered with time, there are other less caustic memories of him. One of the most important of these was written by Richard Hardy in his book *Steam In*

The Blood. In 1940, he was seeking to become a railway apprentice when studying at Marlborough College. His father had died shortly before making it necessary for Richard to begin a career as soon as possible. The LMS proved unhelpful and on the advice of his housemaster he contacted a retired Army officer in his acquaintance who suggested applying to the LNER instead:

'And so I did. By return I received a letter signed by Edward Thompson, the Mechanical Engineer at Doncaster. There were vacancies; my name would be entered but he advised me to start work as near the age of 17½ as possible. I was to attend his office for an interview. I remember so clearly my first impression of Mr Thompson. He was tall, elegant, and well dressed; he welcomed me kindly and interviewed me at some length. What were my ambitions, my home life, school, sport, interests, the lot? In October I was 17 years old; so I went back to school and counted the days until my railway life was to begin.'

He began his apprenticeship as planned and a little while later his widowed mother visited him for the first time. Worry and concern is a parent's natural lot, particularly when robbed of your partner. Being aware of this Thompson decided to become more directly involved as Hardy relates:

'. . . I shall never forget this first visit of my mother. She was arriving at about 5 o'clock on a Friday evening

and going straight from the station to my digs. About 4.30pm I was sent for by the foreman, who told me to report to Edward Thompson's office. He was still, of course, Mechanical Engineer, Doncaster. I was ushered into the presence, overalls, clogs and all; the great man simply said; "Go and meet your mother and bring her here to tea and you come too." So off to the western platform I went, met the train from King's Cross, and after my mother had finally recognised me under the grime I took her to his office, where we duly had tea, me still in my overalls and clogs. How Edward Thompson discovered that my mother was coming to see me I shall never know: I couldn't ask him and I never tried to find out,

On 3 July 1938, as Thompson replaced Robert Thom at Doncaster, the four month old A4 Pacific No. 4468, *Mallard*, made her world record run south of Grantham. Although probably having no direct involvement in this event, Thompson kept a number of photographs taken that day in his collection. These included this picture of the engine's driver and fireman (left Thomas Bray, right Joseph Duddington, and behind him Gresley's technical assistant Douglas Edge) in the dynamometer car used that day. Of note is the microphone hanging in the foreground. (*ET/DN*)

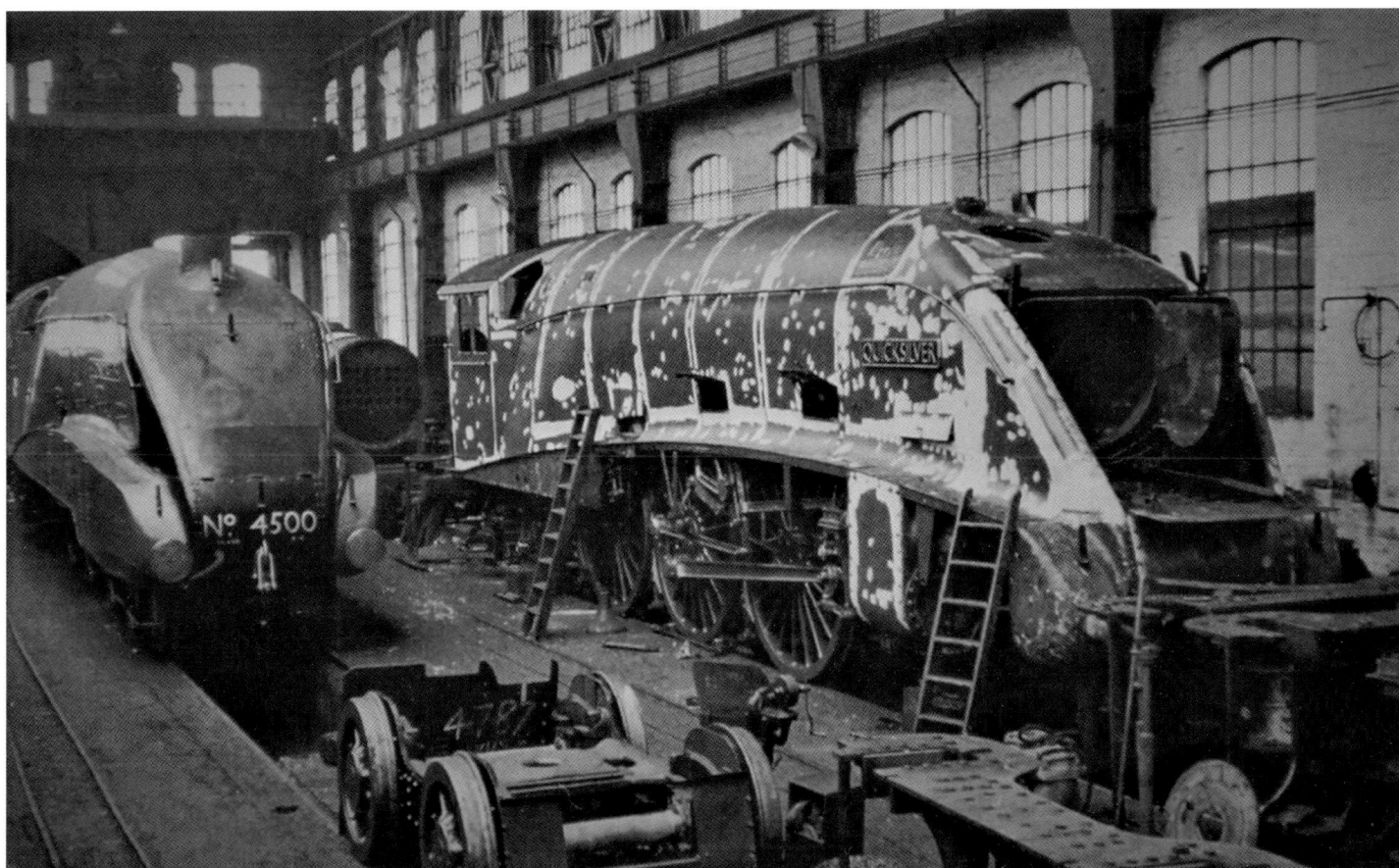

A scene that would become a familiar sight for Thompson - two A4s pass through the workshops at Doncaster. (*PR/RH*)

A4s continued to roll off the production line at Doncaster until July 1938, the last two – 4902 *Seagull* and 4903 *Peregrine* - under Thompson's supervision. A series of dynamometer car tests involving this class took place over the next couple of years in which he became closely involved. Not, apparently, on 3 July 1938 when 4468 *Mallard* produced her record breaking run. (*PR/RH*)

for it didn't do to advertise the fact that an apprentice had had tea in the boss's office. But it was very typical of the Thompson that I knew, and typical of him too in that he made me feel it as quite the natural thing for a 17-year-old boy to be eating sandwiches and drinking china tea in overalls in a very luxurious office.'

And later he added:

'Whereas his great predecessor could seemingly do no wrong, Thompson is sometimes portrayed as an ogre – but the truth is that both men wielded great power and like others of their generation used it quite arbitrarily when they thought fit. It has to be admitted that Gresley was a remarkable engineer though not necessarily a great administrator. On the other hand, Thompson was a competent engineer but a very fine administrator. Yet when they are both remembered it seems to me that Gresley's locomotives are treated as though they were all successes and Thompson's all failures. Most people seem to forget that some of Gresley's engines appeared to have octagonal wheels whilst others gave one a mauling when one sat down and a stitch whilst standing. So, if you choose to remember Edward Thompson for his work then judge him, as you would Gresley by his successes, which were many in times of great difficulty and hardship. But also look beyond the locomotives, which on the whole were commendable, and see the entirety of his achievement as an engineer and as an administrator, for this in itself is a rare gift and one easily overlooked.'

Over the next four years, Thompson would continue to play a role in Hardy's life and career. In time he would progress from apprenticeship to footplate and on to senior management positions in BR, so he was a very worthy witness of these events, as well as being a sound judge of character. But he isn't alone in his observations of Thompson. There are many other recorded instances of his kindness and thoughtfulness towards others in need of help. Peter Grafton highlighted another such case. Whilst at Stratford, Thompson took an interest in training schemes, the Director's Scholarship in particular. One 'scholar', believed to be R.J. Eldred, on reaching the end of his apprenticeship, and having

been a little older than the norm when starting his degree course, found that he would be without a job for his final year at university, so unable to support himself. It was standard policy amongst many companies for apprentices to be discharged at the end of their training and for them to seek employment where they could find it. It was this rule which affected Eldred. On being notified of the problem, Thompson, apparently without urging, tore up the man's dismissal notice and kept him on the company's books. In the 1920s, with austerity and poverty being the lot of many, this was an unusual act of generosity in a hard, often unyielding world.

These cases of subtle and reflective behaviour seem to demonstrate the way he understood human nature. He could empathise with those in difficulty, helping where he could to alleviate any problems or just simply be thoughtful and kind in his response. But is this a truer picture than the severe, austere, slightly pedantic figure described in other accounts? In truth, we are all a mixture of many different qualities with our response dictated by our nature and the problems life creates for us to solve. He faced much more than most and shouldered huge burdens in the process. He, like Gresley, Stanier, Bulleid and a few others, led organisations of huge size, dynamism and challenge. They were in positions where their every move could be scrutinised and condemned, where mistakes could cost millions and lead to the most critical press scrutiny. If they were difficult, demanding or truculent is it surprising, for they saw a bigger picture and had to manage much more than component parts. So it is small wonder that each of them could apply a strict autocracy when they thought necessary and lead with a harshness that appears unthinkable to modern eyes. It is also important to remember that they were Victorians brought up in the strict code of the age, where obedience was assumed and practised rigidly in an atmosphere of deference. In this environment, kindness or compassion were not commonly practised or expected. And each of them could be hard and unyielding and prove extremely difficult to deal with, even Gresley, as Henry Bulleid recalled in a story told to him by his father:

'Humanly, they sometimes discussed their wisdom, and sometimes the stupidity of others. Once Gresley took up his fireside position (in his office at King's Cross) quite indignantly, wanting to know how it

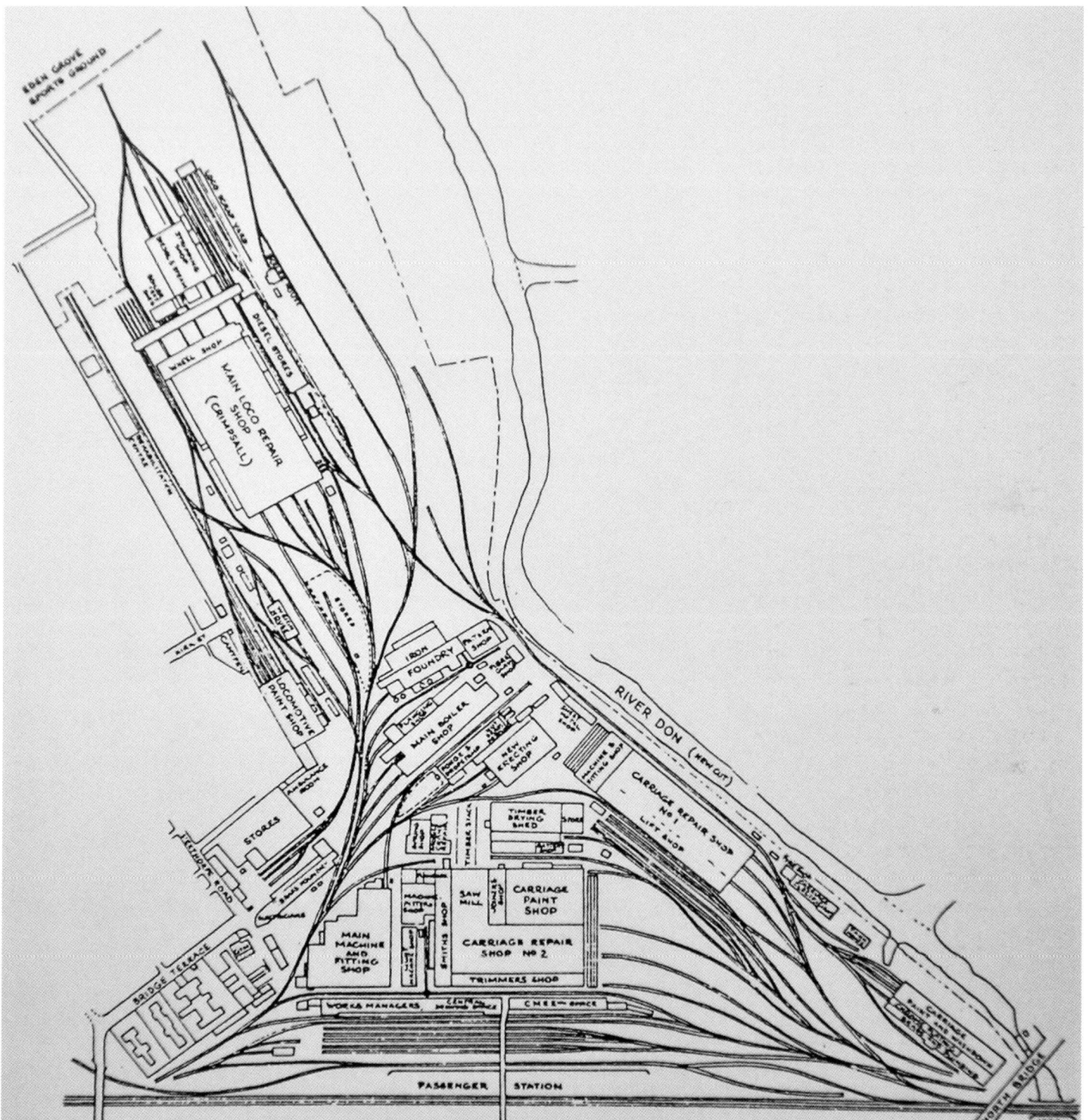

Doncaster as it appeared in the 1930s.

was that none of his assistants ever came up with any suggestions. "By the way," said Bulleid casually, "You remember that draughtsman you agreed to see last week?" "Of course I do the dam' fool." "Well there you are!" said Bulleid, "Do you think he'll ever come back with another suggestion?" Gresley was slightly penitent; each found it easier to see brusqueness in the other than in himself.'

Thompson collected a number of pictures of A4s, but this one seems to be of particular interest possibly because it captures engine No. 4902, one of the two A4s completed after he had taken over at Doncaster. Despite any concerns he may have had about aspects of Gresley's designs he appears to have had a genuine interest in this class, which is reflected in the photographs, papers and articles he collected. (*ET/DN*)

By the time Thompson took over at Doncaster the 2-8-2 P2s were all in service and receiving mixed reviews. The first two had been built with different front ends and sported smoke deflectors, but following the success of the A4s the other four P2s were built as streamliners. 2002 was converted to this shape in 1936 and 2001 followed suit in April 1938. It was a class with which Thompson would become closely associated when CME, but for all the wrong reasons. Nevertheless, he collected several photos of the class, of which this picture of engine No. 2004, *Mons Meg* is one, suggesting an interest in Gresley's iconic, but to some, flawed design. (*PR/RH*)

Another photo from Thompson's albums. *Mallard* heading north from King's Cross. During a series of dynamometer car trials involving A4s during 1938/39 he accompanied the trains on a number of occasions. (*ET/DN*)

Where Gresley and Bulleid differed from Thompson was in having greater self-confidence in public and to feel happy about expressing themselves more openly. They weren't shy men and could command by sheer force of personality, even with humour when necessary. For this reason, men such as this often appear more human and so are forgiven more easily for any transgression, coldness or capricious behaviour. Thompson, probably through shyness and introspection, rarely cut a sympathetic figure, but this isn't to say that his human qualities, as witnessed by many, were any less apparent or heartfelt. He avoided public utterances of any kind, or so it seems. He didn't make speeches or produce learned papers to be read in front of colleagues or fellow professionals. Not for him standing up at a Board meeting or, for that matter, local management committees to comment or make speeches, but, instead, he chose to

lead by example, by direct orders to individuals, personal negotiation or by the written word where necessary. Such people are naturally seen as remote even though they often manage more effectively than more gregarious, outgoing leaders.

There has been some speculation that he lacked confidence in public because he felt his voice was not commanding in nature. According to Richard Hardy, in a letter he wrote to me, he was 'softly spoken and carefully chose his words. He appeared to be most at ease when speaking to one person and not an audience. He had a stutter of which he seemed conscious and I wondered whether this might have accounted for this reticence in making speeches'. If this is so, one wonders whether this was a childhood condition or came about as the result of some later trauma, such as service in the war. Either way, there is no evidence to suggest that he received speech therapy to help manage the condition so would have relied on self-taught measures. Speaking slowly and softly was an obvious solution, and avoiding public speaking, which he did for most of his career.

It was a strange moment in time to take over at Doncaster. The works had been at the centre of so many of Gresley's greatest achievements and the latest of these was just coming to the end of their construction programme. By July 1938, the last A4 Pacifics had just left the production line, neatly coinciding with the end of Thom's career. It was, by any standards, a class which had set the railway world alight and would reach the pinnacle of their record breaking ways that year with Thompson firmly in charge at Doncaster. Although playing no part in their development, he seems to have been interested in the class and was noted riding on the footplate of a number of these engines from their earliest days in 1935.

In some ways, their completion marked the end of a particularly creative period in the LNER's short history and the years that followed, though they didn't know it at the time, would prove far less productive. Of course, the war must bear some responsibility for this, but it seems likely that Gresley's increasing age and deteriorating health also played a part. For such a strong, capable man, any signs of declining powers would be difficult to accept. But when he died in 1941, it emerged that heart problems had plagued him for some time and that vascular dementia was probably upon him. In his last few years, he would spend more time working from a home he shared with his daughter Violet in Watton-at-Stone, Hertfordshire. Here Bert Spencer and his Chief Clerk, Harold Harper, would occasionally assemble to help him complete his work. And when attending any formal function, it had become increasingly common for the CME to be escorted by his son Roger, who appears to have had no other reason to attend but to ensure his father's wellbeing.

A picture of A4 No.4493 *Woodcock* shortly after she appeared in July 1937 and on which Thompson rode in October that year, if the brief comment on the reverse of this print is anything to go by. (*ET/DN*)

On 7 March 1939, senior LNER officers gathered together to celebrate Ralph Wedgwood's departure. Gresley and Wedgwood are standing to the left of the table. Gresley made an unusually short speech and was accompanied on this occasion by his son Roger (sitting to his immediate left). He was a late addition and a seat was found for him next to his father. Thompson, who can be seen in the top right hand corner of the table, gave up his seat to allow this to happen, perhaps aware of some personal difficulty his CME was facing. Arthur Peppercorn can be seen in the right foreground near the camera. (*PR/RH*)

Roger's regular presence is captured in many reports of the time, but three of these are of particular note. In 1938, he accompanied his father to South Africa to look at and study electrification projects there. He also chaperoned his father on a trip to Scotland when the ILocoE entertained a party of German engineers. A few months later, in March 1939, when Ralph Wedgwood was leaving the company, he was entertained to lunch by his senior officers at the Great Eastern Hotel in London. The seating plan reveals that Thompson should have been sitting next to Gresley, but gave up his place to allow his son to sit beside him instead. In photographs of the occasion these changes are only too apparent.

Thompson's new domain didn't simply cover locomotive tasks and the Carriage and Wagon Works at Doncaster, but also included the Locomotive Works at Gorton and the Carriage and Wagon Works at Dukinfield in the Manchester area. His authority also extended over the LNER's two Chief Draughtsmen, Tom Street (Locomotives) and A. Willitts (Carriages and Wagons), who were both based at Doncaster. In such a

situation, it was natural to assume that Thompson had become Gresley's deputy and the strength of his position was made even stronger by the CME's slow, but inexorable decline. But if such an arrangement existed it was an informal one. Yet in the months that followed Thompson's appointment, he regularly visited the CME in London. Here Eric Bannister, a junior member of Gresley's HQ team, captured a flavour of his CME's reactions to these visits when he wrote:

'The only time that he (Gresley) was likely to be solemn and silent was when a certain engineer was visiting and Harper would warn us "Don't go near Gresley – Thompson is coming!"'

In contrast, Gresley toured less as his mobility seemed to decline, although some accounts of this period suggest that a degree of dynamism still existed. This seems to have reassured both Matthews and Newton that all was well, even though they may well have harboured doubts about his fitness to continue. But with Thompson and many other effective managers in place, there was probably little to concern them when it came to the overall efficiency of the CME's department.

It is sad to think of this great man in decline when still comparatively young and one wonders whether he gradually became a figurehead only in the last two years of his life; a fate almost unbearable for one so gifted and active. In the background, peace was giving way to war, with its corrosive effects spreading over all aspects of life in Britain. The Munich Agreement was signed in September 1938, with Czechoslovakia virtually handed to Hitler on a plate. In short order, the Nazi leader violated this naïve agreement, annexed Bohemia and Moravia-Silesia in March 1939, then signed a non-aggression pact with the USSR which opened the door to the invasion and annihilation of Poland. With Britain and France guaranteeing to fight if and when this attack

took place, the path to war was set. And so, the sword of Damocles, which had been hovering overhead as Hitler rose to power, finally fell in September.

With so much happening, it is small wonder that in the months before war was declared that locomotive design tasks and the glamour of streamlining projects faded into the background. By early 1939, with appeasement having failed, industries all over the country were being placed on a war footing. This was particularly so with the big railway companies, where huge numbers of craftsmen were employed and where extra manufacturing capacity might be unlocked if required.

All these things would have been very clear to Thompson, for whom the last world war had been an event of such significance. Sitting in Doncaster and being of astute mind, he would have seen the signs of war approaching and thought about what might lie ahead.

Gresley's great experiment transformed and as captured in one of Thompson's albums. The W1 4-6-4 with its high-pressure water tubed boiler ran in its original form from 1929 to 1935, when the CME decided that the experiment was unlikely to yield any further benefits. Throughout her life she was maintained at Darlington and Thompson seems to have taken an active interest in the engine whilst in his charge there and rode on her footplate according to notes he left. In 1937 she was rebuilt into a more conventional form, albeit with streamlining, at Doncaster. In this condition Thompson again accompanied her on at least one run. (*ET/DN*)

Invasion hadn't been a realistic option in the last war with such a strong navy to guard our shores but it might be so this time with Britain's armed forces depleted by two decades of austerity and cutbacks. There were also the added threats of gas or chemical attacks or mass bombing from the air. These he had experienced first-hand in the trenches and they were generally expected to be deployed on the battlefield again or, worse still, against targets on the homeland.

Knowing the outcome of this war, we tend to ignore or underplay the true impact of its threat. But looking through the eyes of many in 1938 and '39, it seemed that a holocaust would soon descend and independence and democracy be forfeited, with subjugation and genocide to follow. Ignorant hope can only last so long in the face of such a threat and as 1939 dawned, so Britain's leaders finally thought in terms of re-armament and not

conciliation. It was towards this end that the country's industrial might would have to be directed, with the railways playing an essential role in keeping the whole enterprise supplied and moving. If it were to succeed, this creaking infrastructure would have to meet huge demands and its personnel have to work wonders to keep it going in the face of near impossible demands. It was a role for which Thompson was ideally suited, no matter what may have been his state of mind. A man such as he – tenacious, uncompromising and a highly skilled production engineer, with an understanding of military matters – would have all the attributes needed for this task. In good health, Gresley could have coped with this load, but a man in such poor condition would have found it impossible to sustain such an effort for long and would probably have been broken by the burden.

A strangely peaceful pre-war scene as engine No. 2743 *Felstead* ambles past the photographer. Within a short while the sidings in the background will be filled with a plethora of trucks hauling loads in support of the war. *Felstead* was the first of Gresley's A3 Pacifics, having been turned out by Doncaster in August 1928. Initially she appeared with a corridor type tender (No.5330) but this was changed to the old GNR type with coal rails in 1929 (No.5255) with which she ran until 1957. (*PR/RH*)

In mid-1938 some of these things were only just being glimpsed and the day to day work of running such a large organisation would soon have absorbed Thompson. There were systems and working practices to study and understand. There were people to assess and performances to measure. And there were improvements to be sought and changes made if the works under his control didn't meet his high production standards or match his expectations. He is reported as saying that Thom's way of working was somewhat out of date and inefficient. True or not, it is something a man as uncompromising and disciplined as Thompson would think. With such a long-established and apparently successful regime in place at Doncaster, Gorton and Dukinfield, any dissenting voices would soon find expression and strong views would be expressed. But as most would soon realise, he was unlikely to relent in any way, especially with war fast approaching.

When interviewed by Brian Reed after the war, Thompson hinted at some of the problems he faced at Doncaster, in terms of the workshop layout and the pressing need to increase productivity:

'The Works had an awkward layout and not much could be done to improve it unless the carriage works was taken away and a new layout planned. When I became Mechanical Engineer I put in hand preliminary plans for a completely new works on this basis, which would have provided for new construction of 12 locomotives a week. In conjunction with a standardisation programme for no more than ten locomotive classes, the re-planned Doncaster Works could have undertaken all LNER new construction, except perhaps the shunting locomotives, which I envisaged would be diesels.'

Such an ambitious plan was unlikely to be approved or reach fruition with the war so close. But his proposals do shine a light on the way he thought and the views forming in his mind about the way the LNER should rationalise, modernise and intensify its operations. Greater efficiency, economy of effort and spending to save were concepts he believed in and implemented throughout his career. If the war hadn't intervened, it is interesting to wonder where he might have taken the LNER with his plans for modernisation.

By late 1938, the LNER's locomotive building programme seemed to be hitting a flat spot; hardly surprising after so many busy years. The bulk of these new tasks fell equally between Darlington and Doncaster. Thompson's old stamping ground was still producing J39 0-6-0s and would build a final group of eighteen in 1941. In addition, the V2 programme still had some years to run and would only complete in 1944. However, Doncaster did build two batches of ten each in 1939/40 and 1941/42, plus complete construction of V1 and V3 2-6-2 passenger tank engines between 1938 and 1940. To this would be added twenty-five Class O2 2-8-0 locomotives in 1942/43 and Gresley's final design – the 2-6-2 V4 mixed traffic locomotive – in 1941. Meanwhile, Gorton produced a final group of J50 tank engines, thus ending a production run begun at Doncaster during 1913.

In addition to this, some modification of existing types continued, though here the work was probably reducing in scale. Of these, the B16 4-6-0s were probably most noteworthy. In 1938, one engine, No. 2364, received new cylinders with two sets of Walschaerts valve gear on the outside and derived gear for the inside cylinder. Six more followed suit when the trial engine had proved itself. Other programmes of note saw the N7s receiving round topped boilers and a continuation of work on the B12s which Thompson had helped set in motion many years earlier at Stratford.

Electrification was also back on the agenda as war approached. It had been nearly seventeen years since Raven's ambitious plans had been shelved in the aftermath of the Great War and amalgamation. But it was a programme that hadn't been forgotten. In the interwar years, ideas had been floated and assessed, but real progress had been dogged by lack of funding. London's underground system, some Southern Railway commuter lines, plus the Manchester to Altrincham and the Wirral lines were the exceptions, but little else happened of any consequence although planning for other lines continued. This changed in 1935, when a new Railway Act came into being. This was one of a number of measures introduced at the time to help alleviate unemployment, partly through funding from central government. This allowed the LNER to progress electrification of its Liverpool Street to Shenfield commuter line and the cross-country route from Wath and Sheffield to Manchester. When war was declared, some progress

The first LNER Class EM1 Bo-Bo (0-4-4-0), No.6701, electric locomotive with most equipment installed and awaiting final assembly at Doncaster during 1941. As a prototype its gestation was a long one with work beginning in 1939. But this is often the case with research and development projects. A period of testing followed on the Manchester to Altrincham line before she was accepted 'into stock' on 20 September 1941. Following this she was placed in store, the work on the line for which she was intended having stopped. (*PR/RH*)

had been made but any further developments were suspended 'for the duration', or in this case to 1949 and 1954 respectively when the lines were finally completed.

The design work for the A6M electric multiple units for the Shenfield Line and the Class EM1 Bo-Bo locos for the Sheffield-Manchester line was undertaken at Doncaster. But when the projects were temporarily shelved, only one Bo-Bo had been completed under Thompson's supervision at Doncaster, whilst the EMUs had progressed little further. However, it is believed that six units were built and placed in store until some unspecified time in the future. Both classes would eventually play an important part in the evolution of Britain's railways and Thompson was able to participate in this development in a small way at least. To Gresley must go the lion's share of the credit, with Henry Richards under him as Electrical Engineer leading on many of these developments. Richards had been recruited by the CME from the Southern Railway in 1924 and would go

on to supervise and extend this work post-war with the LNER and then BR.

Even though the war effectively put paid to electrification projects, the Electrical Engineer and his staff didn't pass under the control of Thompson when he became CME in 1941. Instead, Richards was promoted to Chief Electrical Engineer and ran his team as an autonomous group. The reasons for this change aren't known, or the politics that underpinned it for that matter. Did it happen with Thompson's agreement or did he feel it was a criticism of his abilities and leadership? There has been some speculation that he resented the change, but there seems to be no hard evidence to prove this either way. Certainly, he would have been aware of the kudos attached to the projects, especially in the light of his late father-in-law's advocacy of electrification. But in 1941, with the country still facing defeat and a huge task before him, it was unlikely that he could have given these projects the attention they deserved.

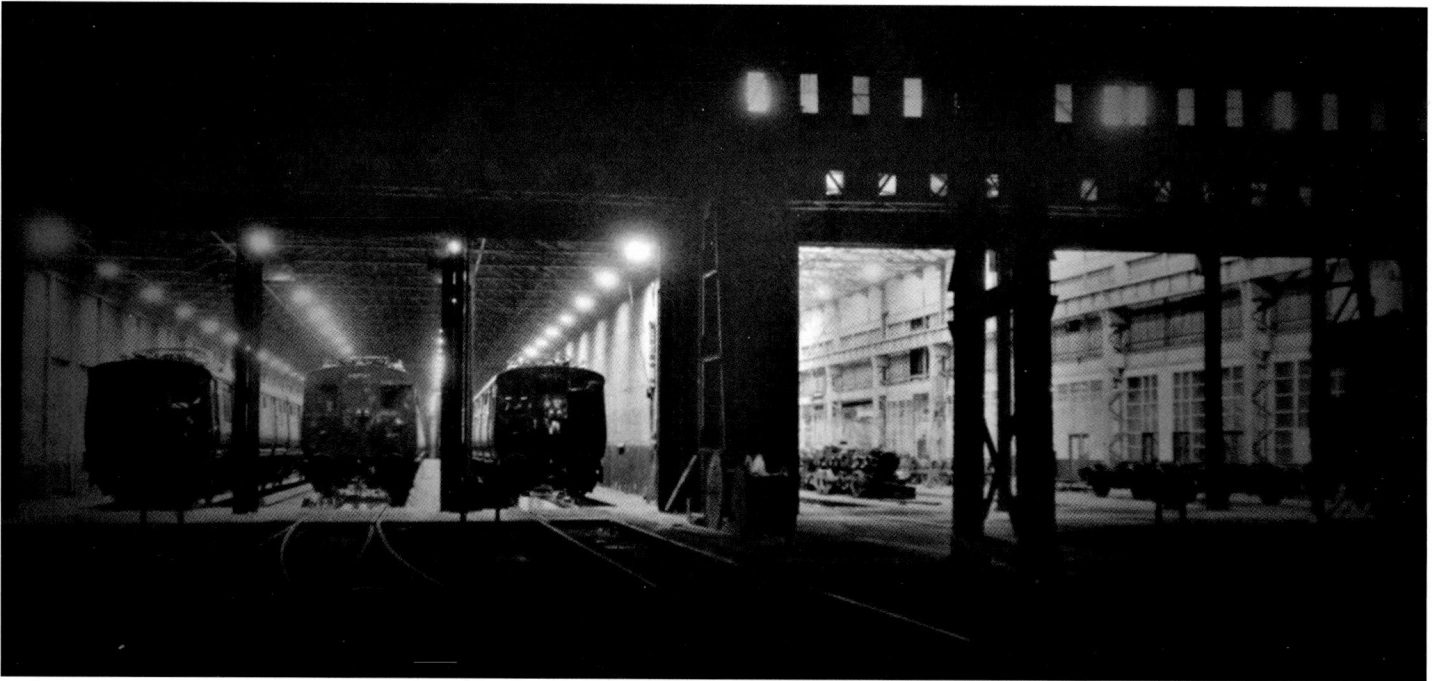

A post-war view of Class A6M EMUs on shed at Ilford ready for duty on the Liverpool Street to Shenfield Line. These units were powered by 210hp Crompton Parkinson traction motors. The Birmingham Railway Carriage and Wagon Company built the driving trailers and Metropolitan Cammell the other units. Whilst researching this book I came across a reference to 'the bogies being based on a Thompson design'. I couldn't find any mention of this elsewhere so assume it is either an error or was another Thompson employed by the LNER. Of course, it isn't beyond the realms of possibility that he was involved, in which case he may simply have suggested a design that could be adopted. (*PR/RH*)

So, he probably gave the matter only a passing thought and then moved on. As it turned out, the path to electrification on the LNER and then BR was an exceptionally slow one and wouldn't see any real progress in his lifetime, let alone before he retired.

By the time war was declared in September 1939, the country had already undergone months of preparation. Evacuation of children had begun, rationing was soon implemented, gas masks were issued, black out measures had become a daily ritual and Anderson Shelters slowly sprang up in peoples' gardens. But few would have expected the air raid sirens to sound across London so soon after Chamberlain's gloom laden broadcast announcing that the conflict had begun. However, bombers didn't appear overhead and the population quickly returned to the routine of their daily lives to ponder what lay ahead. At Doncaster, the Prime Minister's speech was broadcast around the works, as it was in many other factories, shops and homes across Britain. For those who had served in the Great War it must have seemed as though all their sacrifices had been in vain.

And for those who had been too young to experience its tragedies there lay the fear of the unknown.

Most men working on the railways were given reserved status, just as they had been in 1914-18. For those under forty, this didn't remove the issue of conscience though. Many men felt the need to sign up and fight and regarded a life at home, no matter how useful, as unacceptable. So, from the beginning of the war, the railway companies had to absorb a steady loss of highly skilled men. Finding suitable replacements would prove difficult and each company began employing women in ever increasing numbers to fill the gaps, before conscription directed many men and women into industry. As a strong advocate of a mixed industrial workforce, Thompson embraced this need very quickly and soon the shops under his control had made the transition.

As an ex-serviceman himself, he knew the trials his men faced when joining the forces and interviewed many of them before they left, offering whatever support he could. Inevitably, losses soon followed, each name being recorded in the LNER's *Journal*. When informed that one of his young men had been killed, Thompson wrote to the family offering his condolences. By the end of the war, these letters would number in their tens if not their hundreds. And he knew full well that those who survived would return some day and be faced with a difficult period of adjustment.

Richard Hardy was one young man who experienced this crisis of conscience and felt a pressing need to serve in the forces and so sought release from the LNER:

'I decided I must join the RAF. We could not get release for anything other than flying duties. So I went to Mr Thompson and explained that I wanted to go, and he gave permission. I had my medicals and examinations and was told by the RAF that I would be on my way within a month, or possibly less. The month came and went and nothing happened. And it never came: and I have a feeling that it was Edward Thompson who put a stopper on it. Maybe he was right, I don't know. If I had left and joined the services, I would have forfeited my premium and might have ended my railway service. But my mother had paid my premium, and helped me to exist, and this she could ill afford to do. So I stayed.'

By the end of the Great War industry had absorbed many thousands of women to replace men who were serving 'at the front'. With this lesson in mind Thompson quickly instituted a similar plan in 1939/40, building on a policy he had advocated in peace time. By 1941, when this picture was taken at Doncaster, an even higher percentage of the workforce were female and they worked in all the workshops, alongside men, which had been a rarity in the Great War. In time the government instituted conscription to support industry and both men and women were directed into factory work. (*ET/DN*)

Many of the LNER's workshops would be heavily involved in armaments production. Dukinfield was one of the first (seen here in 1941) and would spend the war producing ammunition, in one form or another, for the Army and Royal Navy. Other workshops would build heavy calibre guns for use on land and sea, repair or build aircraft and their component parts, and support the production or refitting of military vehicles, including tanks. All this to be managed at the same time as maintaining 6,500 locomotives, 18,000 plus carriages and a quarter of a million trucks. (*ET/DN*)

He could have added 'and this kept me alive'. Flying duties, whether with Bomber or Fighter Command, were a lethal business with the chance of survival occasionally worse than those on the Somme in 1916. Thompson would have known this and realised that combat service, though noble, came a poor second to keeping the railways going. By this stage of the war the haemorrhage of experienced men, and in Hardy's case trained footplate crew, had risen alarmingly, placing a huge burden on those who remained. This led to maintenance standards falling and made it more difficult for the workshops to meet armament

production targets set by the Ministry of Supply. So, one life saved meant a slight easing of the manning problem and one less grieving parent for Thompson to deal with. In the face of a strong desire to 'do his bit', Hardy probably didn't appreciate this at the time and later wrote in a letter that 'it took me a long time to fully understand that his involvement was well meant and based on the mature judgement of someone with great experience of these matters and was best in the long run'.

Robert Thom's son, also called Robert, was another man who benefitted from Thompson's help and support.

Very few V2s were named, but in the lead up to war newly built engine No. 4844, was christened *Coldstreamer* at Platform 1 at King's Cross. Ronald Matthews led the ceremony which was attended by Major-General Sir Cecil Pereira and a large crowd including Gresley and Edward Thompson, whilst the band of the Coldstream Guards played a medley of well-known tunes. (*PR/RH*)

Like his father, he was a mechanical engineer who began his career at Gorton and when war was declared was serving at Shildon. Thom and Thompson were, of course, old colleagues but also old friends. And in this dual role, the new CME advised the 36-year-old to join the Royal Engineers, which he did. Late in 1946, when facing the uncertainty of demobilisation, Thompson quickly arranged a post for him at West Hartlepool, then Doncaster. It was an act of kindness to Robert junior which his father greatly appreciated and was reflected in two personal letters to the CME.

With war came the same level of government control over railway companies that had been exercised twenty years earlier. During 1938, the Railway Executive Committee was re- formed with its first chairman, Ralph Wedgwood, being appointed shortly after his retirement from the LNER. In the months ahead, the Committee gradually absorbed more members from the key companies – Charles Newton from the LNER, James Milne of the GWR, William Wood from the LMS, Gilbert Szlumper of the Southern Railway and Frank Pick for the London Passenger Transport Board.

On 1 September, this body and the railway companies came under the direct control of the Minister of Transport. This ended all autonomy and kept each company in check, so stifling any activity that wasn't war related. It was a necessary evil, but it ended a golden age of development. For a time, all the glamorous express engines produced by Gresley, Stanier and the rest, which had been a key feature of pre-war life, were in danger of being decommissioned. In the utilitarian world ushered in by war, sturdy, economic workhorses were finding favour over these thoroughbreds. It was a restriction that soon passed when wiser minds realised the size of the task they faced, but for a time their fate did hang in the balance. Over the next six years they would be tested to their limits, with maintenance often reduced to the barest minimum making life for all concerned in their operation exceptionally difficult.

For a healthy Gresley this would have been a daunting task, but with illness advancing it would have been impossible, so it would fall to men such as Thompson, Peppercorn and the Works Managers to ensure that the LNER's locomotives and rolling stock fleet could meet all essential demands. The conditions under which they operated would soon deteriorate as Britain's Allies fell away in the face of a seemingly unstoppable Nazi onslaught. The evacuation from Dunkirk was swiftly followed by the Battle of Britain and a prolonged bombing war in which the LNER's east coast lines and facilities became targets, albeit most often at night when accurate bombing was difficult. For this reason, the Luftwaffe tended to target cities and large towns, with London bearing the brunt of most attacks.

Doncaster would occasionally find bombers overhead, possibly seeking the railway workshops. But it wasn't until December 1940 that the town was hit, though little damage was done on these occasions. All this changed on 9 May 1941, when a raid caused sixteen deaths, seventy-three injuries and much damage to property, but the railway remained unscathed, as it did the following September when a number of aerial mines fell on the town centre killing two people.

King's Cross Locomotive Depot late 1940. Even when buildings or track were severely damaged or demolished by bombs, the trains kept running. Large teams of men became very adept at repairing all the damage. But if the Germans had managed to keep up this war of attrition, the prospects of survival may have evaporated despite their best endeavours. By turning east to attack the Soviet Union, Hitler gave Britain, and its railways, a chance to recover. (*PR/RH*)

In the blackout, Doncaster's substantial workshops were difficult to find and would have required much more intensive attacks if they were to be seriously damaged. But the raids did have a debilitating effect on those whose sleep was disturbed and could seriously undermine morale as well as cause production in the workshops to shut down each time the alarms sounded.

Strangely enough, the only damage the works suffered at this time seems to have resulted from an accident, though rumours of 'fifth columnists' at work did circulate for a while. Whilst German bombers were operating in the area on 21 December 1940, with Sheffield their main target, a fire caught hold in the carriage body shop severely damaging it and other buildings and rolling stock nearby before being brought under control. Thompson convened an immediate board of inquiry to try and establish the cause, with help from the fire brigade and police. There appeared to be no evidence of bomb damage or deliberate fire raising. So, the general consensus seems to have been that the fire may have started spontaneously or have been caused by a carelessly discarded cigarette or match.

Workshops are notorious places for cast off material of all types to gather in bins or sit loose on the ground. In this case, Thompson established that felt offcuts of weatherproofing material were in evidence and the samples examined had become contaminated with linseed oil, so were a fire risk. This theory seemed to satisfy all concerned and would inevitably have led to a tightening up of inspections and site cleanliness. But the works could ill afford to lose these buildings and their production capacity at such a crucial time.

However, production rates didn't suffer at Doncaster, and across industry, solely due to enemy action or accidents. During the 1920s and '30s, industrial disputes had become commonplace as workers began to insist on improved rights or for that matter any rights at all. These disagreements grew in severity and culminated in the

Middlesbrough Station after a raid on 2 August 1942. One bomb from a Dornier 217 exploded in front of the engine blowing in one cylinder, whilst the second bomb in the stick demolished the station and this rake of empty carriages. (*PR/RH*)

Workshop staff at Doncaster turned their hands to many tasks in support of the war effort, including building armoured vans for service on many RAF airfields. As the conflict deepened the railway companies would absorb many other tasks. They would prove remarkably successful in this role even though it was of secondary importance to keeping the country running. (*PR/RH*)

General Strike of 1926. Once this Pandora's box had been opened, the nature of industrial relations soured considerably. For those who had sacrificed all in the Great War, old restrictive practices became increasingly unacceptable and so strife became part of life. This was none more so than in the workshops that came under Thompson's control and his approach when dealing with trades unions, as John Harrison recorded, could create ripples:

> 'He knew that his autocratic bearing irritated them before a discussion even started, and many is the time that one had to have another meeting after he had gone to straighten things out and smooth down ruffled feathers.'

Such an approach may appear counter-productive, but when dealing with trades unions it is a sound, well-established tactic that they themselves use on many occasions. Brinkmanship and appearing intractable sends out a very clear message – this is where I stand and this is as far as I go, so negotiate and settle and avoid strife and strikes. It seems that Thompson was a past master at doing this and the strike rate at the shops he managed appear to have been considerably less than other places in peace or war.

Although Thompson could be a tough negotiator with local trades union representatives, he had the ability to forge a worthwhile relationship with one of their leaders – ASLEF's William Allen, who in 1940 became the union's General Secretary. He had joined the GNR

Above and overleaf: An ASLEF certificate Thompson kept amongst his possessions and the union's General Secretary, W.P. Allen, with whom Thompson became friendly. (*ET/DN/RH*)

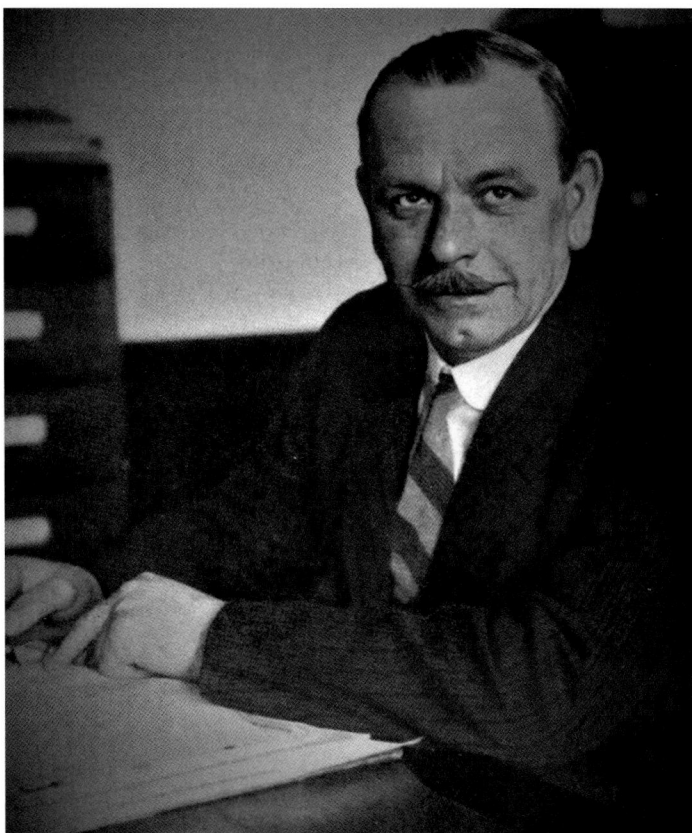

as a loco cleaner before the Great War at Hornsey in North London, becoming a fireman then driver during the conflict. But more importantly, he had been encouraged to become a local union negotiator, quickly gaining a reputation for hard bargaining on behalf of his members. When Thompson moved to Stratford in 1927, he and Allen, having now risen through ASLEF's ranks, worked together and seem to have forged an effective working relationship. But it wasn't until 1941 that Allen's influence became a significant factor in the work of the railways. This was partially due to a strong socialist element being recruited to Britain's War Cabinet, most notably Clement Attlee and Ernest Bevin. Through them, strong and effective management of the work force was exercised. Here Allen proved his worth by successfully negotiating a retrospective pay deal with the Railway Executive that reflected his members' huge contribution to the war effort. At the same time, he sought and won improvements to working conditions, which included new and better canteens, hostels, showers and toilets. These were all measures that Thompson helped implement as ME Doncaster and then CME, many in advance of the national agreement. From this

it is safe to assume that a good rapport existed between the two men, a flavour of which is hinted in a note Allen wrote to Thompson in August 1946. He thanked him 'for lunch at the University Club' and added 'I wish you a long and productive retirement'.

Allen's rise continued in the post-war years when the Labour Government implemented its nationalisation plans. In setting up BR a management team, entitled the Railway Executive Committee, was established to drive through these changes. This had seven members, chaired by Sir Eustace Missenden, and included Bill Allen, now CBE, who resigned his position with ASLEF to become the executive responsible for Staff and Labour Negotiations and Welfare. In recognition of all his hard work the first new A1 Pacific, initiated by Thompson and completed by Peppercorn, No. 60114, was given his name. It is believed that Thompson attended the naming ceremony in October 1948.

In many ways, Thompson was a fair man when it came to workers' rights and has been recorded as being a believer in the principle of 'a fair day's pay for a fair day's work', introducing productivity schemes linked to earnings along the way. This was an attitude most likely forged in his mind during the Great War having witnessed suffering and sacrifice on an unmanageable scale. But he chose to exercise it with caution, because it was his responsibility to maintain production at all costs, balance the books and ensure that any changes were affordable. So, he tended to be hardnosed in public and allow his managers some freedom to negotiate. Having an apparently remote, immoveable and difficult person in charge, to whom everything must be referred, can be a sobering reminder that a higher authority exists and settlement at a junior level is far better. This seems to have been the case when he was a Mechanical Engineer and then CME.

As the war slowly progressed and its impact became only too apparent, the railways began to creak under the strain of the increased workload. On the LNER alone, locomotive failures that had run at slightly over 1,300 in 1938 were now beginning to exceed 2,000 a year and the position with rolling stock was similar in a war of attrition. In peacetime, the companies had flexibility to expand or contract to meet their customer needs, but now they had to make do and mend and tackle an ever-increasing workload with a diminishing resource. To help them do this, they needed strong leadership, but on 5 April 1941, the LNER lost its kingpin when Gresley died.

Although illness appears to have stripped him of much of his energy and power, he was still a man of great repute and a commanding presence within the LNER. But, sadly, by 1941 he seems to have become a figurehead incapable of exercising the authority he had once wielded with such skill and assurance. Power had begun to pass to others and Thompson in particular and even though he was only five years younger than the CME, he appeared fit and ready to continue the battle.

There has been much speculation about the process which Matthews and Newton employed to find Gresley's successor, some of it seeming to be coloured by prejudice towards Thompson himself. For this reason, it is hard to establish exactly what happened and who may or may not have been considered in the process and to be frank, there is no reliable evidence that they considered or approached anyone else. All that can be said with any certainty is that Thompson was formally appointed on 28 April, though had undoubtedly filled the post on a temporary basis for a while before that due to Gresley's declining health. Was he a good choice? By experience and training most certainly. With his knowledge and skill of production techniques, coupled to an ability to drive an organisation towards difficult goals, he was best placed to manage in a war where new, sleek, headline grabbing designs would have no place. Peacetime perhaps less so, but in 1941 this seemed a distant possibility and, with defeat staring Britain in the face, an unlikely one. Sir Richard Matthews summed this up best in late April when he wrote of Thompson:

'His outstanding qualities as an efficient organiser have been amply testified by the improvements he has effected in the methods of production and the progressive systems of repairs he has introduced at the various works with which he has been connected,

As the war progressed and the risk of bombing increased much of the LNER's HQ team evacuated to Lord Hampden's country house, near Welwyn (above). With Gresley tending to work from his home this left only a skeleton staff at King's Cross. When Thompson succeeded to the post he remained at Doncaster, being joined there by a few members of staff from London, including Bert Spencer and Douglas Edge. Nevertheless, Thompson would still spend considerable time in London and at the new HQ in Hertfordshire. (PR/RH)

which have contributed in no small measure to the high efficiency and fine quality of workmanship to be found in our modern locomotives and rolling stock built in these works.'

When taking up the reins Thompson called his senior managers together and is reported as saying to them, 'I have a lot to do, gentlemen, and little time to do it in'.

This has been interpreted by detractors as meaning that he planned to undo Gresley's legacy. But fair-minded people tend to see in his words an expression of intent relating to the war, which at that time could still have ended in defeat or, at least, be expected to last for many more years. Whatever interpretation is placed on his words, there was little doubt that he and his department faced a daunting task. 'Cometh the hour, cometh the man'

may not be a sentiment some might apply to Thompson, but his time had finally arrived and he wouldn't shirk from doing his duty, no matter how painful it might be.

If he needed any reminder of just how serious this war had become, the message was forced home in June when he heard that Gwen's nephew, Michael Watson, a Squadron Leader with 82 Squadron, had been killed on active service. Whilst flying a Bristol Blenheim on a bombing mission over the Aegean Sea fate overtook him and his crew. In unexplained circumstances he crashed leaving another young wife and parents to grieve.

Thompson wrote to his mother shortly afterwards, 'Words cannot express the sadness I feel that Michael has gone. It is small compensation that he lost his life doing his duty in a worthy cause. You and George must miss him terribly as do I . . .'

Thompson kept a number of photographs of bomb damage inflicted on the LNER. In this case it is King's Cross Station following a raid on 11 May 1941 when two 1,000lb bombs from a stick did serious damage to the west side of the buildings. Part of the roof was brought down on this N2 tank engine which lived to fight another day, not so twelve people who lost their lives, whilst many more were injured. The casualty list could have included Gresley's HQ staff if most hadn't been evacuated; the company's general offices having taken the brunt of the damage. Thompson visited the station shortly afterwards to view the damage and, presumably, discuss repairs. After two years on the Western Front he was used to such things and his experience would have proven invaluable. (PR/RH)

CHAPTER 7

TO BE THE LEADER

How the LNER appeared when Thompson became CME. An array of different types of engines, many of them inherited in 1923 from the constituent companies, with little standardisation due to a policy of building different classes to meet different local needs. This and concerns about the performance and rising maintenance costs of Gresley's three cylinder engines with conjugated valve gear were two issues that taxed Thompson. He would seek answers to both questions when the war gave him time to do so. (PR/RH)

When announcing Thompson's promotion, Ronald Matthews drafted a press release in which he wrote:

'There is a general feeling of satisfaction that the directors have chosen for this very important post one who has been associated with the activities of the CME's Department since amalgamation, and who is fitted by training and ability to carry out the tradition of progress created by his predecessor, having had, at one time or another, charge of the company's locomotive, carriage and wagon works in England.

'His new responsibilities, covering as they do locomotive, carriage and wagon work, road motor engineering and docks machinery, together with the Chief Chemist's Department, come at a time of considerable difficulty, but he is assured of the loyal support and co-operation of the staff under him who wish him good health so that his energies may be unimpaired by the strenuous task he has been called upon to undertake.'

With the bombing war still raging and London regularly 'blitzed', the decision was taken that Thompson would remain at Doncaster, rather than move south to the LNER's wartime HQ near Welwyn. But with such a large empire to manage, spread across the UK, where he sat was largely immaterial. To lead effectively and ensure that production kept pace with need, he would have to make regular visits to a number of places, Welwyn and London included. The wisdom of the move from central London was reinforced only two weeks after his appointment, when King's Cross was bombed and severely damaged.

Very early in his tenure, Thompson would have been briefed by Matthews and Newton on what they expected of him. They also confirmed that Henry Richards would be detached from the CME's Department and become Chief Electrical Engineer, with an enlarged team around him. Thompson's reaction to this change is difficult to gauge as he seems to have expressed no view on the subject.

In many ways, this re-assignment of work did make sense. Having observed Gresley struggling with failing health, Newton probably realised that the burden on the CME was far too great and didn't wish to make the same mistake with his aging successor. There was also the possibility that electrification, which stood little chance of being developed whilst the war lasted, might prove to be an unnecessary distraction. For anyone interested in the future, and Thompson showed every sign of being so, the temptation to dabble might be too great, especially at a time when all his energies had to be directed towards supporting the war effort.

In recalling the instructions he received on becoming CME Thompson said little but simply stated that Matthews and Newton made it known that 'the war precluded the introduction of new designs, but I had freedom to build more engines of existing classes should the need arise'. Whilst accepting that such a limitation must apply, he did, early in his tenure, feel moved to highlight the worsening condition of engines with three-cylinder conjugated valve gear and the increasing costs of maintaining them. To emphasize such a point, he then suggested that things might only get worse, increasing the amount of time these engines would spend out of service. By 1941, the Divisional General Managers were expressing their concerns about poor availability and time under maintenance of the Gresley engines. And judging by the files that remain it was an issue that the running department raised with Gresley himself. He, according to Thompson:

'had come to realise that an improvement was needed, but in the end simply admitted that he could not make any better of it. I remember that on the cover of

one report about the performance of the 600 odd locomotives fitted with this type of motion Gresley had written "the performance of these engines is shown to be inferior"!'

Was this a case of Thompson being disingenuous with the facts when recalling his actions in seeking to eliminate one of Gresley's key developments? Or was he genuinely responding to growing concerns about poor availability and performance expressed to him by the Divisional Managers, through Newton? If so, these were criticisms the CME could ill afford to ignore if he wished to keep his job.

Inevitably, many have translated his actions as being prompted by a desire to eradicate his predecessor's work for reasons of spite or malice. Others, of course, believe that a good engineer, when faced with evidence of poor performance, seeks improvements and this is where Thompson seems to place himself.

As this is still a contentious issue in the LNER's history it cannot be treated lightly and any worthwhile description of Thompson's work must seek to unravel such a complex issue if justice is to be done to do both men. But it is a story that unwinds slowly as the war intervenes and pressure grew on the new CME to find solutions. Here one can't underestimate the burden that fell on his shoulders, or the problems involved in ensuring there were enough locomotives and rolling stock to meet so many pressing needs. There would be times when demand would exceed supply, so failures in service could be ill-afforded and poor performance judged very harshly.

One thing is certain, though, Thompson couldn't have managed such a load by himself and needed a good team around him if he were to succeed. Here history has played him ill at times, with suggestions that he displayed a vindictive, uncaring attitude to some of the men who had served Gresley. Yet in this one sided assessment it is hard to separate fact from fiction.

In reality, Douglas Edge continued to be the CME's personal assistant, though being a carriage and rolling stock expert meant that his contribution to the locomotive side of business was slight. But so was James Blair who replaced Norman Newsome, as Carriage and Waggon assistant, a little later, Newsome preferring to stay in London and not move to Doncaster.

The once shining and chic A4s soon deteriorated under wartime conditions. With lower standards of maintenance becoming the norm problems would soon emerge on this and other classes of engines, but the A4's underlying strength kept them going. Considering they were thoroughbreds, their time undergoing repairs and servicing would compare favourably with the other Pacifics. And they remained fairly economical when it came to fuel consumption whilst, at the same time, pulling far larger loads than the pre-war high speed trains for which they were designed. By the end of the war they would all be tired and in need of major maintenance, but so would all the other engines in the LNER's fleet. The rolling stock and the company's infrastructure was little better. (*ET/DN*)

Tom Street, the Chief Locomotive Draughtsman, was moved sideways by Newton to be CD for Richards on electrification projects and so continued work he had begun under Gresley. He was replaced by D.D. Gray under the talented Edward Windle as Chief Draughtsman. Perhaps most significantly, he brought in Peppercorn to become ME at Doncaster, making him Assistant CME and his heir apparent at the same time. Having had recent experience of Gresley, who seemed loath to have a deputy after Stamer retired in 1933, this action shows great presence of mind.

The LNER's *Journal* highlighted other changes Thompson introduced:

'In future there will be five Mechanical Engineers. In addition to Mr Peppercorn at Doncaster, who will also supervise the 'outdoor' carriage and wagon work on the Great Northern Section and the Great Central Section between Sheffield and Marylebone, there will be an ME to supervise Gorton locomotive works, who will report directly to the CME. Mr T. Heywood will continue to be styled ME (Scotland). Mr F.W. Carr remains in charge at Stratford. Mr R.A. Smeddle becomes ME Darlington (on promotion from Locomotive Works Manager at Darlington), to replace Mr Peppercorn. Mr J.F. Harrison has been appointed to the new post of ME at Gorton.

'Mr Harper will remain in charge of the HQ Office with the title of Assistant to the CME (Clerical). Mr Windle will be in charge of both locomotive and carriage/wagon drawing offices. Mr F. Day will continue as Head Carriage Draughtsman and

Shortly after Thompson took office as CME the works at Doncaster received a visit from King George VI and Queen Elizabeth. The CME, assisted by Charles Newton and Arthur Peppercorn, escorted them around the main buildings where they met many workers. Such events provided an immense boost to moral and Thompson displays a relaxed demeanour clearly enjoying such a prestigious occasion. He, apparently, made no attempt to select people to be presented to the King. Instead he let the visit flow without any restriction as witnessed by the photo on page 183 in which one of the 'local characters' (possibly a smithy) regales the Queen with some now long forgotten tale. (ET/DN)

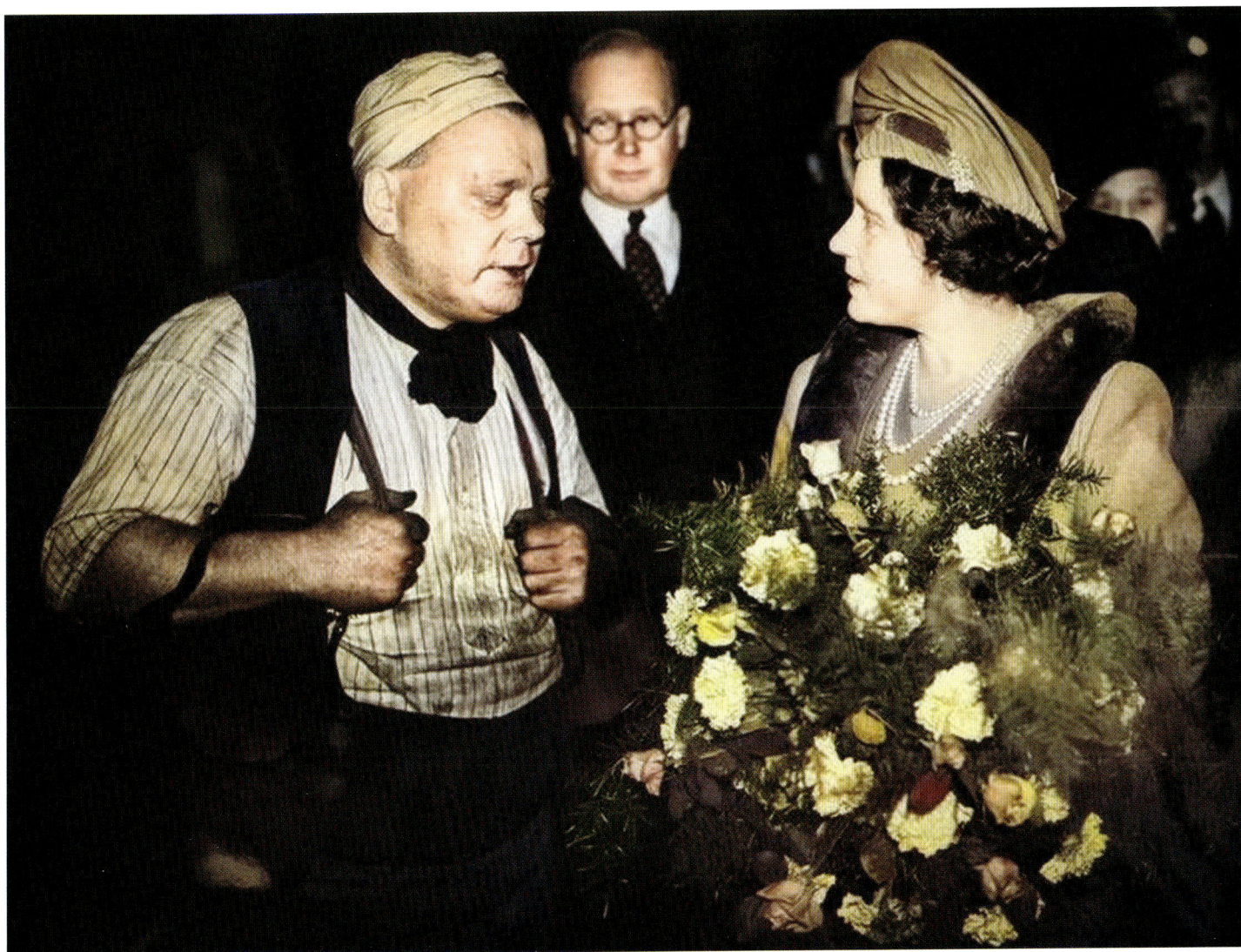

Mr D.D. Gray has been appointed Head Locomotive Draughtsman.'

Thompson, it seems with Harper's assistance, wrote up these changes but it was the CME who added a final, telling paragraph:

'It will be appreciated that something like a revolution has been made in the methods of conducting work of the department, but there is every reason to think that the departures from the old-established practice will put fresh vigour into the establishment which Sir Nigel Gresley has built up since 1923. He left a great example to his successor and the object of all the arrangements described above is to revitalise the mechanical engineering branch of our railway work and keep the LNER in the forefront as an exponent of modern development, calculated to secure economy and efficiency.'

The one name missing from this list was Bert Spencer. He had faithfully served Gresley for nearly twenty years and probably knew him as well as anyone. But more importantly, he knew the CME's way of working and could take the great man's concepts and develop them in a way that captured the essence of Gresley's ideas. He had proved perfectly suited to this role by training and temperament and had undoubtedly proved to be a great support as the CME's health declined. Yet now Thompson seems to have had no place for this gifted engineer. In some quarters, this has been portrayed as an act of pettiness at best or vindictiveness at worst. As is often the case the truth probably lies elsewhere.

Mr. A. H. Peppercorn

Mr. T. E. Heywood,

Mr. J. H. Smeddle, O.B.E., T.D.

Mr. F. W. Carr.

Thompson's five Mechanical Engineers. All experienced men who served him well for his five years as CME. Only John Harrison (top right hand corner) seems to have recorded any memories of this period. (*LJ*)

Spencer, whilst assisting Gresley, either worked at the CME's home in Watton or King's Cross in the rapidly emptying offices there, whilst living in Barnet. But post-May 1941, there was little reason for him to stay in London as he recalled in a letter written in 1962:

'Just after Sir Nigel died Mr Thompson sought me out and thanked me very courteously for all my hard work. He wanted to discuss my future and told me that he would be based at Doncaster so wouldn't need an assistant in London. He suggested that I could be posted to Stratford as assistant to the Mechanical Engineer instead. Being concerned about my wife's safety I didn't wish to remain in London and he proposed that I move to Doncaster or Darlington instead.

'He went on to explain that he would have less need for personal technical assistants and because of the pressing need for rolling stock and wartime production he preferred men with this background. He added that the Chief General Manager was of the opinion that there would be little scope for new locomotives whilst the war lasted so my current task would lapse for the duration.

'After some consideration, having listened courteously to my views, he suggested that I could be employed in another role in his Headquarters assisting the new Mechanical Engineer there. This suited my wife and I, especially as we both came from the North-East of England.

'I was initially employed in planning workshop tasks across the LNER with Cyril Elwell ensuring that all ran smoothly. However, Mr Thompson suggested that I maintain Sir Nigel's papers and continue working on the ideas he had pursued regarding steam locomotives, but with an emphasis on alternative cylinder arrangements. Later on, in 1943, I was called to the CME's office and it was agreed that I would work full time on standardisation proposals and new designs. Over the next 2½ years I did much personal work for the CME and sat near him in his office at Doncaster.'

Bert Spencer seems to have been a charming, unassuming man by nature as well as an engineer of some standing, but wasn't a man to court controversy. Gresley had recognised his strengths when still young and helped him flourish. However, it seems likely that Spencer wasn't suited to very senior rank and found his forte in being a good personal assistant or deputy, quietly going about his work influencing events by the cleverness of his ideas and great diplomacy. He was a pragmatist and a realist and always did the job to which he was directed. Such a man is worth his weight in gold and served Gresley and those who followed with skill and equanimity. If Thompson felt unable to employ him, initially at least, in the same capacity as Gresley, he changed his mind when it became apparent that locomotive design was again on the agenda and he needed support. However, Spencer never achieved the same

The ever faithful and talented Bert Spencer (centre of the group in the foreground with the light coloured hat) on 1 June 1934, when Gresley's first P2 was launched at King's Cross. This unassuming man rarely, if ever, sought the limelight and supported his greatly respected CME for nearly twenty years. Gresley's death, as Spencer later wrote, 'came as a great personal blow to me'. Thompson is often seen as a villain in casting Gresley's trusted assistant into obscurity for purely vindictive reasons. But the truth, as is often the case, was rather different as Spencer himself recorded not long before his death when living in retirement in Shaldon, Devon. (BS)

level of influence he enjoyed pre-1941, no matter who was in charge, but his skills were recognised and, as the war allowed, he re-entered the world of locomotive design where his true calling undoubtedly lay. When Peppercorn succeeded Thompson in 1946 the new CME continued with this relationship.

Many years later, Newsome added an interesting footnote to this story:

'Shortly after Sir Nigel's death most of his staff were transferred to Doncaster. After many years in London I was loath to leave, Bert Spencer less so. To accommodate our family's needs Thompson interviewed us and offered both of us posts at Stratford. After a few days Bert declined the offer and transferred to Doncaster, but I went there [Stratford] as Assistant Works Manager of the Carriage and Wagon Works. I must say that Thompson was quite decent with me, not though with some people – I can't complain at my treatment. Thompson was a very good engineer, but he had a reputation for upsetting a lot of people.'

All these staff changes took effect very quickly and the men he chose could all conceivably be called Gresley's men, the late CME having been part of their selection and development when in office. If there was anyone who believed that he might wish to strip away reminders of their late chief, they may have been pleasantly surprised. If he did bear any ill will or sought to eradicate any memory of his illustrious predecessor, he either hid it well, was wise enough to know that these were good men who had all the requisite skills or it simply wasn't an issue with him. In addition, there is no evidence that any of the men he chose to be his senior managers were disadvantaged because of it, each remaining secure in their positions with some being promoted further during their careers.

Whilst these changes were being made, Thompson, ever conscious of the needs of war and poor availability of locomotives, created a new central management group which he announced in the LNER *Journal* in early 1942:

'Readers will be interested to learn that Mr C.H.M. Elwell, Locomotive Running Superintendent (Eastern Section), has been seconded for special duties to the CME's Department, with the title of Assistant Mechanical Engineer (Outdoors). The change is as a result of the setting up of a special organisation for dealing with the maintenance and repair of engines.'

Cyril Elwell had spent all of his career at Stratford on the running side and would have been known to Thompson during his time there. Although working for the Southern Area Divisional General Manager, the CME seems to have negotiated his release and set up an office at Doncaster for him and his new progress chasing team. It would be Elwell who would lead on assessing any problems with locomotives and highlighting ways of solving any one of a number of issues that arose. The fact that he was an experienced engineer as well as a Running Superintendent gave him great insight into the problems likely to emerge and the solutions available. In this role, he would play an increasingly important part in directing his CME along certain lines.

Through Elwell, the three General Managers would bring their influence to bear on locomotive policy as users have every right to do. It had been this way since amalgamation, when the running department was taken away from the CME. But Gresley, by sheer force of personality and by being successful most of the time, bestrode the narrow world of the LNER like a colossus, to slightly misquote some of Shakespeare's most famous words. With such a display of dominance, few, if any, felt able to challenge his ideas or leadership, so his position was a strong one indeed. Consequently, the impact the running department's senior managers had on design or maintenance programmes was far less than it might have been. Thompson would never achieve the same level of pre-eminence and would always be held by the authority of Charles Newton and work under the influence of the different incumbents of these Divisional posts.

During his time as CME, there would be five men occupying these three key positions and each had the power to demand action from Thompson on issues over which they felt strongly. In the Southern Area there were George Mills (1941 to 1945) then Victor Barrington-Ward (1945 to 1947). The North-East was covered by Charles Jenkin-Jones (1936 to 1947) and Scotland by Robert Inglis (1941 to 1944) then Thomas Cameron (1944 to 1947). Of these, Barrington-Ward, Jenkin-Jones and Inglis were university educated with degrees in Engineering, Mathematics with Engineering and Civil Engineering respectively. Mills began his career in 1895 as a trainee auditor with the North British Railway, advanced to become an accountant before rising to be Ralph Wedgwood's Principal

With the drain on men for the armed forces continuing as the war dragged on, the LNER, like many industries, faced a huge man-power and skills shortage. Under Thompson, this problem reached its peak and threatened to overwhelm the company, even with overtime and shift working. By careful and astute management, he quickly overcame the problem recruiting several thousand women in the process ensuring they received appropriate training. Their work covered many functions, including the specialist skills required to operate successfully on the shop floor as well as the Drawing Office as both these photos taken at Doncaster reveal. By all accounts, the CME closely involved himself with these tasks and was a strong advocate of women in the workplace. (*ET/DN*)

Mr. George Mills, F.R.S.S., M.Inst.T.,

Mr. T. F. Cameron

Four of the LNER's key General Divisional Managers with whom Thompson worked. Victor Barrington-Ward (top left) and Robert Inglis (top right) would both be knighted after the war for their services to the LNER and the communities in which they lived. Each of these men could exercise great influence over the CME if they so wished, but seem to have forged a fairly good working relationship with him. But it was they who would have highlighted failings in service of the engines or rolling stock and looked to the CME to sort out the problems. (*LJ/RH/DN*)

Adviser on financial matters. But he wished to broaden his experience and transferred to the operational side of the LNER to become the General Manager(Scotland) then DGM in 1941. Last but not least, there was Cameron who had risen to prominence from being a traffic apprentice with the North Eastern Railway. In the Great War, Barrington-Ward, Mills and Cameron saw distinguished service with the Royal Engineers and each ended up as officers working alongside Thompson for the Director General of Military Railways.

Despite their different backgrounds and educational attainments, they were all men of substance who had proved their worth to the LNER. Each had also had dealings with Thompson over many years so were familiar with him, possibly making wartime working a little less fraught. Inevitably, they would have looked to the CME to sort out any problems that reduced availability of locomotives and rolling stock, or caused failures in service. As the war progressed, maintenance standards couldn't be sustained at peacetime levels and complaints would soon have been wending their way to Doncaster with the request to sort things out. The term 'rock and a hard place' is apposite in this situation. But one thing is certain; the pressure on all of the men involved was extreme and liable to affect their health. In fact, Elwell died suddenly from a heart attack in May 1943 caused, if rumours are to be believed, by the stress of work. Thompson, moved deeply by his passing, attended the funeral and wrote an obituary which said much about his friend and colleague and revealed some things about himself as well:

'Born in Dublin on 6th October 1889 and educated at Haileybury in Hertfordshire, he went to the Stratford Works of the old Great Eastern Railway in 1906 to learn his calling. He learnt it thoroughly. Of practical work he was a master; of the theoretical side he was a Bachelor of Science. Perhaps he will be best remembered so far as his work is concerned by what he did in the Locomotive Running Department, where in 1938 he became Superintendent of the Eastern Section. Then in December 1941 he came to my Department as Mechanical Engineer when the decision was taken to add the duties in connection with the Mechanical Supervision of the Locomotives at the Sheds of that Department. He spent 18 months

at this during perhaps the most difficult period through which this service has passed and is passing. He was invaluable.

'We shall miss his very real knowledge and experience. We shall miss his charming personality, his gay humour. We have lost a grand colleague and a very dear friend.'

In a very short period, Elwell did much to sort out problems with production programmes and flow rates through the workshops. And it was he who, in early 1942, began giving substance to increasing concerns about the state of locomotives with conjugated valve gear, the availability of the P2s and many other issues, including the lack of suitable freight engines. These were all issues passed to him by the General Managers and the Works Managers, who would have gathered information as engines passed through the workshops for maintenance and repair. All of this material was collated, analysed and compared, resulting in a summary that would have made difficult reading for a CME struggling to make sure the railway had sufficient working engines. With so many people involved in this process, the picture that emerged would probably have been a balanced one, with little opportunity for spin or manipulation to suit any preconceived notion or bias.

Yet it is here that the main debate on Thompson's apparent trashing of Gresley's legacy rests. Rumour and conjecture suggest that the CME, even though armed with a wealth of information and analysis, and struggling to meet so many wartime commitments, took this opportunity to mount or continue a vendetta against all things Gresley. Anything is possible, of course, and great men and women can as easily be as vindictive as

Cyril Elwell, Thompson's friend and faithful and effective assistant at probably the most challenging time of his career. (RH)

anyone else, but it is probably more sensible to assume that this was neither the time nor place for such pettiness. And even if it had been, Ronald Matthews and Charles Newton would surely have brought some common sense to bear.

It seems much more likely that Thompson was simply responding to issues raised by the General Managers and reinforced by Newton, as their Chief. After all, he was a man who knew where his duty lay, as witnessed by his wartime service and the many senior positions held since the early twentieth century. It is very doubtful he would have lasted so long or been so successful in high pressure jobs if it were otherwise.

As Richard Hardy, a balanced, informed and astute observer of these events, wrote to me:

'The CME was unlikely to have carried a grievance, if indeed he had one, to such petty lengths. He would have had better things to do with his time in the war. It is said that Edward Thompson had a vindictive streak that relentlessly drove him to reverse some of Gresley's policies. I doubt if that was so, but he certainly had his own ideas and was determined to use them, which was a perfectly laudable ambition. Perhaps the policies he pursued were a shade too drastic for comfort and were pushed through by powerful men against the advice of subordinates who were by no means always right in their judgement. But Gresley wasn't above taking the same line when it suited his purpose.'

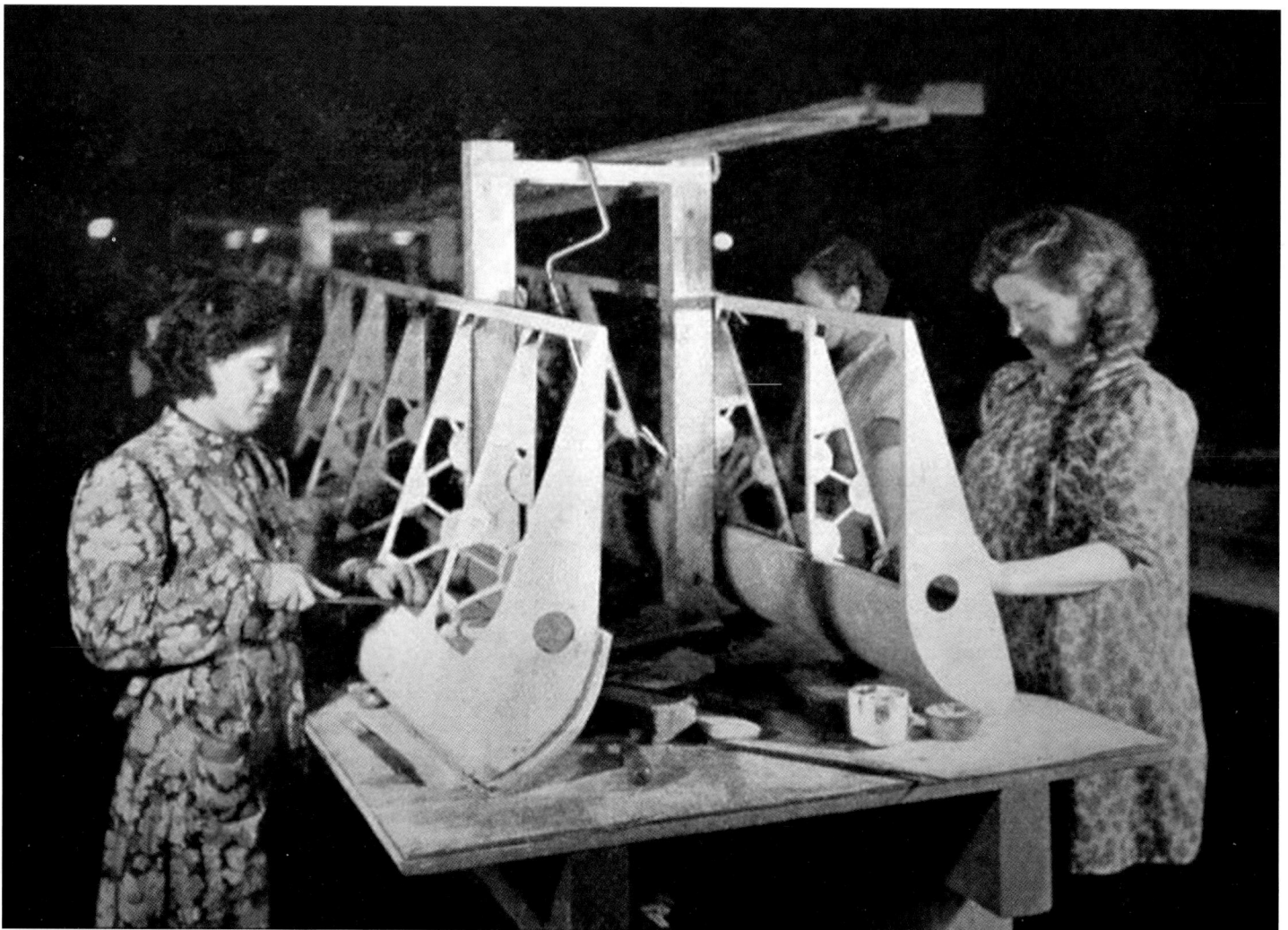

Above and opposite: Wartime scenes on the LNER displaying the variety of additional tasks that fell to the CME to manage and control, ensuring all the time that their primary tasks weren't forgotten. *(PR/RH/DN)*

Whatever the cause or the politics involved, it was clear to many that there was a growing concern over the condition of all the locomotives under the LNER's control as overuse took its toll. Whilst recruitment kept pace with departures to the forces (estimated to be more than 27,000 during the war) the replacements were unlikely to have the same skill levels and this would have added to the slow decline in maintenance standards.

The size of the task the company faced was probably summed up best by Ronald Matthews in a speech he made in March 1946:

'During those years, special trains with troops, stores, ammunition and other Government traffic numbered 127,000 apart from the vast tonnage of traffic and innumerable passenger journeys by ordinary services on Government account. There was also the part played by the LNER in connection with the Bomber Offensive. With more than three quarters of the Nation's bomber aerodromes on its system, the LNER bore the brunt of the vast movement necessary to build them, staff them and service them. The building of the aerodromes in East Anglia alone involved 1,700 special trains in the transport of 750,000 tons of slag and tarmac: the movement of aerodrome personnel called for 460 special trains and every raid of 1,000 bombers meant the running of 28 trains of petrol and 8 trains of bombs over our system. Without efficient rail transport the Bomber Offensive as planned would have been impossible.

'The LNER's workshops also contributed largely to armament production, manufacturing aircraft components, parts for tanks, guns and shells, Bailey and Inglis bridges, and complete motor dinghies and Balsa rafts for battleships. All this was carried out in the face of very heavy air attack, resulting in a greater amount of damage than in the case of any other Railway Company, and, it is sad to record, the death of 303 members of staff.

'And so what is the effect of all this stress and strain? How do we stand now for the future? Those six gruelling years of abnormal traffic, during which time heavy arrears of maintenance accumulated have had their effect on the physical assets of our undertaking. Many locomotives are in need of thorough repair, and an inability to undertake new construction during the war years has meant that many are still at work long after they ought to have been scrapped; carriages are six years older and our stock needs renovation and replacements denied to us since 1939.

'During this time there was an acute shortage of skilled labour and here I pay great tribute to the

P2 No. 2006, *Wolf of Badenoch* as it appeared during the early years of the war. There were concerns about these engines' coal consumption and problems with damaged driving crank axles due to overheating big-ends. In addition, reduced maintenance standards, as reports soon revealed, meant that wear in the conjugated valve gear was becoming excessive reducing these engines' efficiency and availability. For these reasons they would soon feature in Thompson's modernisation plans. (*ET/DN*)

On 23 July 1941, A4 No.4462 was renamed *William Whitelaw* in a ceremony at York, after the last company chairman. Up until then she had been called *Great Snipe*, but whilst under general repair at Doncaster, during June and July, it was decided that the engine would be re-titled. At the same time, she also lost part of her side valancing in the hope that this would make maintenance easier in wartime and reduce a perceived problem of overheating. However, the front section was retained. It is reported that this was a measure that Thompson himself recommended for the A4s, and the two streamlined B17s, soon after taking over as CME. The front section of skirting remained for only a short period. When No.4462, which had been based at Heaton, was transferred to Haymarket in Edinburgh, it seems that the shedmaster, T.C.B. Miller, decided to remove the remaining pieces forward of the outside cylinders following several incidents of the panels opening whilst the locomotive was moving. This was the second engine to be unskirted; No.4487 having preceded 4462 by a matter of days. This photo shows two directors, plus William Whitelaw and Edward Thompson (second from the right) enjoying a lighter moment as the Scottish Saltire is pulled back by some unseen hand or simply swept aside by a gust of wind. It is interesting to note that when Thompson authorised the removal of the valancing over the driving wheels, he followed the pattern set when the P2s were streamlined. The design of their front ends created a shape which curved round the cylinders for aerodynamic effect. Did Thompson recognise this as a valid solution and was happy to keep it intact? (*ET/DN*)

magnificent work performed by all during the war which inevitably involved great mental strain and physical fatigue.'

Towards the end of his presentation, Matthews produced a few statistics to show how greatly the war had increased the volume of traffic the LNER carried. He focussed on wagon loads and concluded that in 1938 they covered 5,726 million net ton miles and in 1945 this had risen to 7,410 million (a 22 per cent increase), all this being achieved with virtually the same number of engines (6,533 in 1938, 6,356 in 1945).

To bring the company back to its pre-war position he concluded by saying that:

'The aim in the next five years is to build in the Company's shops, or by contract, 1,000 locomotives, 5,500 carriages and 70,000 freight wagons. It is encouraging to hear that the first of the 300 locomotives of the medium mixed traffic type should be at work very shortly.'

Although no mention is made of any individual, it is clear that much of the success for these achievements could be laid at Thompson's feet and the team he led. As Richard Hardy concluded, would such a man have found time or have the will to pursue a feud? Most probably not. In truth, if Gresley had lived and had been able to work throughout the war there is every likelihood that he might have struggled to achieve all that Thompson did in keeping the railway running. They were men of quite different talents and in a war of attrition, Thompson was possibly better suited to the post than someone with Gresley's design skills.

When Matthews stood up to speak he had the certainty of knowing the war had been fought to a successful conclusion. In the first two years of Thompson's tenure, defeat was a strong possibility and every effort was being made to produce a workable fleet of engines in the face of their rapidly deteriorating condition. Added to this, all the evidence collected by Elwell pointed to the fact that it was the most modern locomotives that were causing most concern. And these appeared to be those with three cylinders and conjugated valve gear designed by Gresley and his team.

This wasn't solely a matter for the LNER to sort out. In 1941, the Minister of Transport set up a committee to oversee the use being made of all the railway workshops. This body, under the chairmanship of Sir Alan Mount, the Chief Inspecting Officer of Railways, had as its primary target 'to sort out the extreme unevenness of work being undertaken in support of the war' and identify any significant problems. All the CMEs were members, as were representatives of various government ministries and the Admiralty. At the same time, the Mechanical and Electrical Sub-Committee of the Railway Executive, formed early in the war, came under the chairmanship of William Stanier. Its brief was

similar to the Mount Committee and in this role could wield considerable power and influence over individual railway companies.

Ernest Cox, who was Stanier's Personal and Technical Assistant, and would later rise to senior rank in BR, observed the workings of both committees and wrote:

'The Mount Committee waged a ceaseless war of nerves on the CMEs and Sir Alan used techniques of his former enquiries into train accidents to conduct inquisitions into everything which prevented or delayed increase in Government work in railway shops (both committees gathered fortnightly for meetings throughout the war).'

Here Cox underlined the effect of Mount's continuous campaign on at least one of the CMEs, in this case Frederick Hawksworth of the GWR:

'Hawksworth's "Gethsemanes" were the Mount meetings where his spirit groaned aloud in the frustration of being alternatively bullied and coaxed to produce, to him, quite meaningless data.'

If the experienced Hawksworth felt this way, then Thompson, whose position was probably not as secure, having only recently been appointed, would surely have felt equally exposed and pressured to come up with answers and solutions. The tenacious Mount continued to be unrelenting in his approach:

'By March 1942 the first rumbles were heard of shortages of locomotives to cope with the enormously increasing war traffic and the REC had to report that it was 500 locomotives short to deal even with the traffic in hand, to say nothing of what was to come. Now all our activities were thrown into reverse and within a month or two Mount and committee were exerting as much pressure to get all war work out of the workshops which could in any way impede production of locomotives and wagons. The companies were only permitted to build mixed traffic or freight engines.'

In such a judicious and critical environment, any significant maintenance and availability problems

The Luftwaffe's Baedeker Raids of 1942 were deemed to be in response to RAF attacks on German cities, some of them of historic interest. Bath, York, Exeter, Canterbury and Norwich were chosen and came under direct attack. Even though the Luftwaffe couldn't hope to equal the massive weight of bombs dropped by the RAF, they could still cause considerable damage. On the night of 28/29 April, York was raided, seventy-nine people were killed, with many more injured, and many properties were damaged including the North Sheds which was stabling A4 No.4469 *Sir Ralph Wedgwood* overnight whilst away from her parent shed at Gateshead. She was lifted and stripped down for assessment, removed to Doncaster, presumably on a slow tow, where she was deemed beyond economic repair and condemned in June that year. According to notes kept at the time, Thompson visited York on the 29th to inspect the damage, so following a pattern set early in his career when regularly visiting the scenes of accidents.(*PR/ET/DN*)

would have been identified and scrutinised closely. So the issue of the Gresley engines that had been kicking around in the LNER for many months was finally brought to their attention. We do not know who engineered this or why and there has been speculation over the years that it was Thompson who was chief culprit, unable to get Newton to move on the subject. But the end result was that the CME engaged Stanier, as chairman of the M & E Sub-committee, in the debate and sought his advice and opinion on the subject.

Over the years, the two men had developed a certain warmth towards each other, if their surviving correspondence is anything to go by. This may have been a result of their membership of IMechE or simply represented a meeting of minds. Despite many classic locomotives with his name prefixed to their title – Stanier's Black Fives or Coronations for example – the part he played in the fine detail of their creation was slight by comparison to that of his Chief Draughtsmen, Herbert Chambers and Tom Coleman. In fact, Eric Langridge, one of Stanier's senior draughtsmen at Derby, gave more substance to this view by claiming, in his book *Under Ten CMEs*, that 'he (Stanier) was no designer as such' adding the telling words 'but then, how many CMEs were?' In truth, he had a clever, analytical mind, but was essentially an exceptional production engineer who, like Thompson, understood

Doncaster in wartime with skylight shutters and ventilators open during the day to improve working conditions. By night all would be closed down under the tightest blackout conditions. To meet ever more pressing demands for locomotives, rolling stock and armaments the workshops were often on 24-hour shift working, but even this did not halt the decline in the condition of many hard worked engines. The locomotive undergoing maintenance appears to be a Robinson Atlantic and has received a coat of black paint. Though reaching the end of their lives, shortages meant that these engines carried on working, some into the early 1950s. (*ET/DN*)

Pre-war express services soon gave way to more utilitarian work for the A4s and Gresley's other celebrated engines. Here engine No. 4468 *Mallard* still looks the thoroughbred she was even in wartime colours, though pulling a far less glamorous load. (*PR/RH*)

As the war progressed, and as maintenance schedules allowed, engines were painted black and LNER was shortened to NE. Here engine No.4466 is turned out in the new scheme. After 4469 was destroyed in a bombing raid the name *Sir Ralph Wedgwood* was eventually transferred to 4466, which had formerly been *Herring Gull. (PR/RH/DN)*

and managed programmes and outputs with great skill and dexterity. On top of this, there was also the matter of personality traits. Stanier shared some elements of Thompson's shyness and was himself noted as being a man of few words. But he was more successful than the LNER man in overcoming this natural reserve when speaking in public and became a well-known figure in the process.

Through their membership of these two government-sponsored committees the issue of engine failure rates and maintenance problems would have come to the fore. Stanier agreed to study the reports Thompson's team had prepared and provide some independent analysis. To do this, he suggested that the experienced Cox undertake the 'leg work' and prepare a report. To underpin his impartiality in this matter, one can point to the fact that Gresley and Stanier had been friends and were great admirers of each other's work. So, in such circumstances it was most unlikely that he would have allowed any element of personal antipathy or antagonism to enter the debate. Undoubtedly, he would have been critical of Thompson if he'd thought this to be the case and refused to participate. He would also have ensured that his assistant did the same. However, there was one key difference between Stanier and Gresley in the matter of cylinders. The LMS man tended to vary the

number used, with two, three or four not being uncommon. But where three were used they were each fitted with independent sets of motion.

Cox left behind a brief account of these events and added an interesting description of Thompson:

'He was a most imposing figure, tall, aristocratic looking, immaculately dressed, whose wont at the beginning of a meeting was to set out on the table before him an assortment of pencils, chains, watches and other symbols of wellbeing. Although he played a full part in all that was going on, another part of his mind was clearly occupied by thoughts of the locomotives he was going to design…He had a considerable admiration for Stanier and used to discuss with him the various projects he had in mind.

'This association led to an intensely interesting diversion in 1942 when he arranged with Stanier for me to visit and prepare a report on the 2 to 1 valve gear….It was an unassailable fact that unit play at each of the eight pin joints was multiplied by eleven by the time it reached the middle valve, and in fully rundown condition the lost motion could amount to 3/8th. This resulted in reduced power at low speeds due to insufficient port opening, while at high speeds the combined effect of overtravel of the valve,

Two unidentified locomotives, the nearest one a V2, rest in the gloom of an unidentified shed on an unrecorded date. Peacetime working conditions were poor, but in wartime, with blackout restrictions in place, they grew considerably worse. (*THG*)

plus whip in the combining levers, could produce up to 50 per cent more power in the middle cylinder than in either of the outside. There was also a spate of hot inside big-ends, ten times as many in the inside position as at the outside, six times as many as the LM experienced with the inside big-ends on a comparable number of its own three-cylinder engines. The high speed engines of the 4-6-2 class suffered the highest proportion of failures, the 2-6-2 and 2-8-2 types also being high. A certain lack of stiffness in the marine big-end arrangement also appeared to contribute to this result.'

One thing that is clear from Cox's writings, which appeared after Stanier's death in 1965, is that he was no great fan of Thompson. Phrases such as 'Machiavellian campaign he was conducting against all things Gresley', 'correcting the mistakes of his predecessor' and 'Thompson's many internal wars' are scattered through his memoirs. Underlying all these negative words is an accusation that he manipulated Stanier and himself in this matter for a dishonourable purpose. From this, one is left to ponder the nature and accuracy of these views and whether Stanier shared them in any way. If he did, it is highly unlikely that he would have wished to become embroiled in Thompson's 'turf war', no matter what central role he played for the Railway Executive Committee. I think it more likely that Cox did find evidence of problems with Gresley's engines and produced a fair assessment which Stanier duly scrutinised, felt honour bound to report and signed off without any apparent disquiet.

It is strange that, having confirmed the existence of these problems and the probable causes, that Cox should later accuse Thompson of sharp practice in the way the problem was highlighted and managed. In doing so,

Cox seems to paint him, rather crudely, as 'villain' with the sole aim of trying to wreak havoc on his predecessor's work. Whilst there is little doubt that Thompson could be ruthless when necessary, this is a quality inevitably stitched into the DNA of anyone who reaches very senior rank in any organisation. Without this trait, it is impossible to command especially in the middle of a shooting war. But there are degrees of ruthlessness and some will get the balance wrong, exerting pressure when there is no need to do so and, perhaps, enjoying the trappings of power too much in the process. Despite what Cox infers, the indications are that Thompson generally did what was necessary and no more to meet the heavy demands placed on him. Richard Hardy, once again, caught a flavour of this:

'I can remember some of Thompson's changes. The Crimpsall Repair Shop, in Doncaster Works, that deafening, rough, raucous hive of activity, was ruled for many years by Rupert Vereker or "Little Bob". An Irishman who used superheated language under the slightest provocation and held sway during the hard

times when he had delegated power to sack men as he walked down the shop on a Saturday morning. Times had changed by 1941 and Thompson, who had responsibility for the Main Works through the Works Manager, took note of the problems he was causing at such a difficult time and arranged his transfer to Mexborough where he took charge of the Running Shed . . . Thompson's apparently brutal move was totally justified.'

In the absence of any words from Thompson, it is difficult to judge where the truth might lie in all these assertions about his attitudes and motivation. A generous person would say that he was doing the best he could in difficult circumstances and within the limits set by his own personality and the powers that commanded him. But a more cynical person might see something completely different. Long after the event, and with such contradictory views expressed by those who lived through those times, it is almost impossible to reach any firm conclusion. He was, and remains, something of an enigma and someone who became all things to all people. But along

Gresley' second P2, *Earl Marischal*, in final streamlined form. Although only running approximately 35,000 miles a year she spent nearly a quarter of her time in wartime undergoing repairs and maintenance. A4s running 60,000 miles plus a year would average10 per cent and burn considerably less coal (estimates vary but 50 per cent has been quoted). With pressing wartime demands it is, perhaps, not surprising that their future was placed in doubt, despite their great pulling power. (*ET/DN/RH*)

the way he did much good work and I believe that his analysis of the problems he faced led him towards logical conclusions and, more often than not, valid solutions. It also seems clear that he saw no need to court popularity, but followed a course he thought valid and remained his own man, adhering to principles he valued.

With all this happening in the background, and stripped of any real power to develop new locomotives, unless specifically related to the war effort, Thompson could only pick around the edges of the design issues Gresley had been able to explore with greater freedom. He could follow the REC's directives and consider proposals for freight or mixed traffic engines, although gaining approval for any new construction could prove challenging. He could also address the modification of existing types where their performance fell far short of requirements. He could consider the LNER's post-war requirements and pursue his ideas on standardisation, drawing inspiration from Stanier's work with the LMS. But in 1942 and early 1943, all the signs seemed to be pointing to a war lasting many years more, with the most stringent restrictions likely to remain in place for an indeterminate period. So, his freedom to explore ideas remained limited and the pressure to keep producing a fully working fleet and meet other wartime production targets overrode all other considerations.

Inevitably, any changes he could make would be achieved by stealth and strongly reasoned arguments. The level of support he needed to achieve even part of the changes he thought necessary was significant, both inside and outside the LNER. This is where the Stanier/Cox paper was so important. Realising this, neither man rushed to any conclusions and appear to have assessed evidence objectively, without any obvious bias. Their report was finally released by Stanier on 8 June 1942 to Newton and Thompson concurrently, and, judging by the address list, copies were also circulated to Sir Alan Mount and other members of Stanier's Committee. It was a fairly brief three and half page submission, but it pulled few punches and would have left Charles Newton in no doubt about the scale of the problem. The remit which Thompson had set Stanier and Cox, with the Chief General Manager's approval, was straightforward and unambiguous:

'There are 652 three-cylinder locomotives on the LNER on which the inside valve is driven by an arrangement of rocking levers known as the "Gresley" or "2 to 1"

valve gear. Mechanical trouble has been experienced with these engines, and I have been asked to give considered opinion on the merits or demerits of this gear and its influence on mechanical failures.'

Cox was given complete freedom to examine locomotives, speak to users and maintenance staff, study reports of failures and servicing records. It seems that no door remained closed to him during this review or obstacles put in his way. In addition, Cox makes no mention of meeting Thompson or receiving any other instructions from him. So, it would seem that the conclusions he reached were not affected by undue pressure or manipulation, but were simply the result of an experienced well-trained locomotive engineer reviewing facts and making an independent assessment. At the end of the report, he and Stanier listed three conclusions and recommendations:

'The "2 to 1" valve gear although theoretically correct is, in practice, incapable of being made into a sound mechanical job, and rapid wear of the pins, and incorrect steam distribution, are the inevitable results of its use. In view of its inherent defects and the discontinuance of its use throughout the world, a good case can be made for not perpetuating it in any future design.

'It is certain that with this arrangement of valve gear it will be necessary to give the engines a frequent overhaul in the Shops and even then it is not possible to eliminate the effect of lost motion due to running clearance required in the pin joints and the effect of expansion of the outside valve spindle on the inside valve.

'It is a matter of consideration, therefore, as to whether certain of the classes should not be fitted with an independent inside valve gear.

'The excessive inside big end trouble experienced is, in my opinion, due mainly to the design of the big end. The alternative designs already developed by the LNER should alone bring about considerable improvements. The use of higher grade white metal and the elimination of the brass strip across the bearing are also, in my view, worthy of consideration in view of extensive experience with three-cylinder engines on the LMS.'

Unfortunately, any words on this subject by Thompson are few and far between and in their absence, conjecture and rumour have tended to fill the vacuum. However, when being interviewed by Brian Reed, he did allude to some of these events:

'My first appreciation of the problems led me to conclude that the locomotive fleet was in dire need of standardisation. This was particularly noticeable in the case of boilers, as the 1942 replacement programme contained no fewer than 81 different types. Even in wartime I intended making a start on reducing this number by preparing a plan containing a minimum number of standard locomotives and boiler types leading to a programme which could be initiated in the war years and expedited in the post-war period.'

On the question of new designs and the continued use of three-cylinders and Gresley's conjugated valve gear he added:

'I refused to do this and after considerable discussion (with Ronald Matthews) agreed that an independent report should be submitted on the working of all engines on the LNER with this motion.

The resulting report led to a fundamental change of direction of LNER locomotive policy'.

Finally, he offered a partial defence of his views on this subject by saying:

'the cumulative effect of wear in the 27 pin joints in the two outside sets of motion added to the inertia effect of the main conjugating lever which led to over travel of the centre valve after about 8,000-10,000 miles. This over travel forced Gresley to restrict cut-off to a maximum of 65 per cent which in turn led to difficulties in starting heavy trains'.

Hardly a detailed argument to justify such a large programme of work, but his case was backed by Stanier and Cox's report. However, there would undoubtedly have been other papers circulating within the LNER to support his proposals; such is the way in any large business then or now. Thompson then went on to describe a particular issue involving his plans for the P2s:

'This conversion was instigated chiefly by troubles with the conjugated gear, although tyre wear and

The first P2 to be rebuilt. Her record card shows her progress towards an 'act of vandalism' or essential change, depending on your viewpoint. The complete failure of her crank axle in 1939, which could have resulted in a serious accident, and similar incidents with the other members of the class, hastened reconstruction. (*ET/DN/RH*)

performance were also contributory factors. The availability of the engines for the 12 months prior to rebuilding had been more than 47 per cent and on one occasion, three of the six were under repair at Doncaster [engine Numbers 2003, 2005 and 2006 all between September and October 1941].'

With problems appearing to increase with this class, Thompson recorded that he contemplated rebuilding one of them to Pacific configuration as a means of eradicating the problems, rather than tweak the existing design. But he also believed that this would 'extend their range of operations in Scotland by making the engines less wasteful of coal'. To test this theory, he submitted a scheme to the company's Locomotive Committee in late 1942, seeking permission to modify the engines. He later reported that his:

'original proposal was at first opposed by Andrew McCosh, the Chairman, who eventually [presumably under pressure from Thompson in early 1943] said "Well, rebuild one". A few months later, having received favourable reports from every driver he had spoken to, insisted on all six examples being rebuilt.'

McCosh, who had made a name for himself in coal, iron and steel industries, and Thompson attended Cambridge together and were awarded their Mechanical Sciences degree at exactly the same time. So, there is a good chance they were known to each other when McCosh was appointed Chairman of the LNER's Locomotive Committee in October 1942, after having been Deputy Controller at the Ministry of Supply for three years. Whether this link proved of any value is hard to say, but McCosh would play an important part in approving Thompson's proposals for locomotives in the final years of his career. But McCosh wasn't known for being easily swayed or having an acquiescent personality, quite the opposite in fact. So, he would probably have questioned Thompson closely on need, expected benefits and performance when new or modified locomotives were being contemplated or were in service.

Nevertheless, and despite the rigours of the process, Thompson went through in seeking improvements to engines, his actions were later criticised and condemned by some. But how fair are these assertions and what evidence exists, beyond personal opinion, to take the argument in either direction? Here, the case of the P2s is apposite. They were the first of Gresley's most iconic

classes to undergo a Thompson makeover, if you discount the minor changes made to the A4s' valances.

For the two-year period from January 1941 to December 1942, some maintenance records for the P2s still exist. More would have been available but for BR's policy of weeding and destroying records no longer required for accounting purposes in the 1950s and '60s. Those that remain show that the six engines were out of service in the main workshops for 109, 166, 175, 213, 91 and 182 days respectively, whilst running an average mileage of approximately 35,500 a year. But these figures, which include weekends, take no account of time out of service at sheds due to breakdowns or other daily maintenance tasks for which records no longer exist.

However, in his book *Steam Was My Calling*, E.S. Beavor, a pre-war Doncaster apprentice who would rise to become a Locomotive Shed Master, hinted at significant and unquantified problems in the running department with the valve gear and maintenance:

'After the first year of the chaotically deteriorated maintenance following the outbreak of war, Gresley's 2-to-1 conjugated valve was running about on many locomotives with so much wear that steam distribution was seriously inefficient. This condition had led to so many over-loaded middle big ends that even Gresley in his later days was significantly worried about it. To a notable degree it was due to his own gross lack of concern for repair facilities in the running sheds [over which he had no day to day control]; King's Cross "Top Shed" in particular was a disgrace of a place…

'None of the sheds were provided with even the simplest equipment which would have enabled local staff to overhaul a 2-to-1 gear. Instead, the parts had to be sent away by stores van to the main works, and the engine itself was then immobilized for a week or longer before the material came back again.'

However, the 'lost' days that can be identified show downtime running at 15 per cent for engine No. 2001, 22.7 per cent for 2002, 23.9 per cent for 2003, 29 per cent for 2004, 12.4 per cent for 2005 and 24 per cent for 2006. In contrast, when the first P2 (2005) rebuilt re-entered service she lost 114 days to maintenance between 18 January 1943 and 31 December 1945, or approximately 15.5 per cent when running

It is hard to deny that the P2s were powerful, impressive looking engines and speculation about the design and their rebuilding will continue as two 'new ones' appear to grace the twenty-first century. One wonders what might have happened if the class had been used on the London to Edinburgh route rather than north to Aberdeen for which such an engine seemed unsuited, though designed for this purpose? On face value it seems reasonable to conclude that they might have been better employed south of the border.

under wartime conditions. This is hardly the ringing endorsement Thompson may have sought. But she had been the best of the class when running as a 2-8-2, in terms of lost days, so may not have been the best choice if the CME was seeking to validate his ideas. With their much higher totals, 2002, 03, 04 and 06 would have fitted the bill better. However, this is only one way of measuring performance and other areas tend to provide clearer justification. Here the words of those who worked these engines in service are of value.

Norman McKillop, a Haymarket driver, had long experience of the P2s as built. In 1955 he recalled overheating axleboxes, coupling- rod bushes 'cutting' to such an extent that there was a broad line of 'gold' from the nave of the wheel to the rim where the brass and oil had run from the bush. He also reported the four coupled drivers being 'too close together for some of the curves I knew so well' between Edinburgh and Aberdeen. To this he added,

'I knew this was a Gresley near miss and was disappointed.'

'The *Cock o' the North* became something of a star attraction to all except the lads who had to fire her. During a railway exhibition in Fife one gentleman, with a retinue of followers, put the following question "They tell me she is excessively heavy on coal. Is this the case?" [he turned out to be George Mills who had just been appointed General Manager for Scotland] . . . I told him how the engine could haul any two trains if you cared to tie them together . . . but no matter how a driver tried to economise she swallowed a hundredweight of coal to the mile [other unofficial estimates place this much lower], where a Gresley Pacific was doing her job on anything from 28 to 35 pounds [trials in 1948 with the A4 show they burnt coal at the rate of 40 to 42 lbs per mile, with the A3s slightly higher than this] on the same road with a slightly smaller train. I tried every trick in the pack (to reduce consumption) – it was no use.

'That gentleman knew the language all right. I tried to answer his questions with a simple yes or no. As a driver it wasn't my place to suggest what was wrong, but his questions were real problems.'

Of course, George Mills would become the Chief General Manager for the Southern Area in 1941 and sit beside Thompson at Doncaster while debates on the future of the class were underway. Clearly, if McKillop's words are to be believed, Mills would have brought his knowledge of the type, and any reservations he had about the class, with him. And he was a man who could wield considerable influence and demand change when necessary if he wanted to.

But how does the P2 compare to Gresley's other iconic design, the A4, which if Thompson was truly trying to dismember his predecessor's legacy would have been a far bigger and better target? Their downtime during the same two years of war fell between 8 per cent and 12 per cent, whilst running an average mileage in excess of 60,000 a year in the process. During post-war Locomotive Exchange Trials, in which Bert Spencer took a leading role, it was demonstrated that the A4s would burn an average of 3.06lb. of coal and 24.32lb. of water per dbhp-hr without lighting up consumption deducted. This was less than the other classes of express locomotives participating in the trials (the LMS Coronation and Royal Scot, the GWR King and the SR's Merchant Navy Pacific).

Bert Spencer's undated summary of results of trials between A3 and the P2 Classes. Hopefully the report of which this was a part may appear and throw new light on comparable performance. *(BS/RH)*

Sadly, a direct comparison between the A4s and P2s based on official figures seems impossible, as no comparable tests were run, as was often the case between classes of locomotives over similar routes. However, in February 1935, trials on the Paris-Orleans Railway with engine No. 2001 produced an average of 3.62lb. per dbhp-hr in the process. This was achieved when running with a brake load at 44.7mph, 52.924 mph and 67.977mph respectively and before coal usage in lighting up was deducted. Of course these figures, and McKillop's comments, relate to the first engine and not the rest of the class which were much modified and so may been more economical. But even so any reduction may have been a small one.

Perhaps of greater significance are the results of trials run between an A3, No.2001 as built and a modified P2 sometime in the mid to late 1930s, a summary of which Bert Spencer kept amongst his papers. Sadly, only two undated pages appear to have survived,

one with broad averages, the other with more detailed figures. Nevertheless, they contain many pertinent facts and figures. Perhaps the most interesting of these is coal consumption per mile. Over a range of cut-offs, presumably with comparable loads and over similar lines, the A3 used on average 44lbs of coal by comparison to 66lbs for No. 2001 and 52lbs for the other P2.

Running costs will inevitably play an important role in quantifying success no matter how an engine might perform in other respects. When required, the P2s could pull huge loads over difficult terrain. But with more time in the workshops, the P2s would probably have been more expensive to repair and maintain without achieving the mileage or availability of the A4s, other Pacifics or the V2s. Yet as Thompson later commented, 'In all, 683 locomotives had the conjugated gear and a dozen sets were always under repair at Doncaster. Another 12 sets were always in the Darlington shops and six or so at Cowlairs.'

Thane of Fife's sheared off crank axle during examination at Doncaster. Excessive working stresses caused metal fatigue and subsequent fracture. It was a problem that afflicted the P2s and Bulleid's Merchant Navy Pacifics as built. The photo of 35020's failed crank axle in 1953 could be inserted here, it being virtually identical. The LNER were very lucky that these failures didn't lead to a serious accident and fatalities. (*ET/RH*)

So it is likely that this element of cost may have been spread fairly evenly amongst all these locomotives and not just the P2s or A4s. However, high speed express locomotives may have been more prone to these problems especially when servicing standards fell during the war. But the absence of maintenance records allows no firm conclusions to be drawn either way.

In terms of breakdowns, there is a little more evidence to suggest that the P2s could present problems at times. On 25 July 1935, Bulleid rang staff at the Drawing Office in Doncaster according to a surviving loose minute:

'Arrange for Mr Windle to go to Cowlairs at once as the pony truck casting of engine No.2001 has cracked ... When he has inspected the casting on No.2001 he should go and look at the casting on engine No. 2002 [then at Dundee] to see if this is alright.'

A handwritten note confirms that the same problem existed, with urgent action to remedy the fault being taken. But it seems, from the limited information available, that the problem was never entirely entirely resolved. And to this can be added a more complete record of problems caused by the nature of the line from Edinburgh to Aberdeen itself and the 2-8-2 configuration. The stresses applied by the curvature of the track were thought responsible for a number of incidents of crank axle failure. On 18 July 1939, engine No. 2005 suffered such a breakdown, requiring repair at Doncaster. This was followed by *Mons Meg* on 27 May 1942 and *Lord President* on 29 July 1944. There are also suggestions, not confirmed by the surviving records, that there were other failures. Undoubtedly, Thompson would have been only too aware of this problem and it would have featured large in his thoughts when contemplating future policy.

This was an almost identical problem to the one faced by another class of engine with which Bulleid was closely related, the SR Pacifics. On 24 April 1953, when passing through Crewkerne, Merchant Navy No. 35020, *Bibby Line*, suffered a catastrophic failure of the crank axle resulting in damage to the locomotive and station building, but no fatalities. Investigations later revealed the problem had been caused by metal fatigue; the cyclic stress range having exceeded the endurance limit of the axle. On this occasion, BR withdrew the whole class for evaluation and found the problem to be widespread, resulting in redesign, component replacement and

regular ultrasound inspections. Complete rebuilding of the class began three years later, the failure in April '53 being deemed to be a contributory factor. The LNER were lucky that a P2 axle failure didn't result in a similar accident or worse. If it had, Thompson would probably have been condemned for not taking the action he did.

It has been suggested that the issues of wear and failures on the line north of Edinburgh might have been resolved by employing the P2s on the straighter main line between King's Cross and York. It is a valid point, especially at a time when greater wartime demands could have been met more effectively by utilising their phenomenal pulling power. But even if Thompson had argued this case, and there seems to be no evidence that he did, he could only recommend, not action it. Such a decision would have fallen to the two General Managers, George Mills and Robert Inglis, and Charles Newton to consider and approve. As Mills, from the earliest, doesn't appear to have been a fan of the class, he is unlikely to have wanted this responsibility and so they remained north of the border.

In 1947, Oliver Bulleid, who had played a leading role in the design, construction and testing of the P2s, was moved to speak on this issue. Following Bert Spencer's address to the ILocoE, in which he presented a precis of Gresley's work, Bulleid was recorded as saying:

'When tested on the open road between Orleans and Tours she (No. 2001) developed a very high horsepower, of the order of 2,800, and again showed herself to be an efficient engine from the point of view of coal consumed per DBHP. In service, however, she was an extravagant engine. The fundamental reason why she was an extravagant engine in service was that she wasn't properly used; she was not put to the use for which she was designed. Instead of working trains well within her capacity over long runs, she was employed on a service such as Edinburgh to Dundee, went to Aberdeen and hung about there, and did very poor mileage per day, with the result that she showed a heavy coal consumption, most of the coal being burnt through misuse rather than in working trains.'

There is much more to be uncovered and written on this subject, but it seems to me, from what is available, that Thompson approached the problems reported to him in a measured way. He didn't simply launch into a

No longer clean and working glamorous express trains, but dirty, unkempt and pulling excessive loads in an attempt to meet wartime demands. An unidentified Gresley Pacific does her duty in the most difficult circumstances. (*PR/RH*)

rebuilding programme seeking to undermine Gresley's legacy, but considered the evidence of poor availability, failures in service, maintenance costs, standardisation and more. He sought reputable independent assessments from very skilled engineers to confirm these views and, at the same time, found no dissenting voices amongst his colleagues in the LNER; though Bulleid would undoubtedly have said something if he had still been with the company. Put simply, he was responding to a serious operational and safety issue presented to him by those charged with day to day running of the railway. There would also have been input from the LNER's Locomotive Committee and two major external bodies (run by Mount and the REC) eager to enforce Government policy and ensure maximum availability. In the face of all this, Thompson, I believe, managed effectively. However, this isn't to say that his solutions to the problem were right or successful, but more on this later.

However, there is one issue that continues to puzzle me. In all the words written criticising or condemning Thompson for his work on Gresley engines, it seems to be forgotten that the A4s remained largely untouched. Perhaps, because of their fame and prestige, they were untouchable but this seems unlikely in the face of Thompson's strength of character and sense of independence. It is more likely that he thought them effective and may even have admired the class considerably; if the reports of his many trips on their footplates are to be believed and the number of photographs of them in his albums. He didn't even pursue a policy of defrocking them or the two B17s or the rebuilt W1, as the LMS did its streamlined Coronations. The exigencies of war may have been responsible for this, but it was hardly a major item of work and one that could have easily been added during a period of heavy general repair when the locomotives were stripped down

The most significant part of Gresley's legacy, the A4s, seemed to be safe in Thompson's hands. Apart from the removal of the side valances they remained untouched during his period in office. If his purpose was to question, even denigrate Gresley's achievements these engines would surely have gone the same way as the P2s. Here, in 1941, *Sea Eagle* still has a semblance of peacetime glamour with a shine to her paintwork, but having recently lost valances. In 1947 No. 4487 would be renamed *Walter K. Whigham* in honour of the LNER's new deputy chairman. *(PR/RH)*

A publicity photo used by the LNER during the war reported to have been taken on *Flying Scotsman*'s footplate in March 1941. Clichéd but nonetheless effective. *(PR/RH)*

to their component parts. And the benefits derived from easier access and maintenance were lauded by Stanier for one. It seems to me that the CME ignored the many practical issues that his production and output driven mind usually focussed on because he admired the A4s considerably.

In many ways, Thompson's first nineteen months in office were dominated by the extreme effort needed to keep the railway running. His chairman had made it clear that the freedom Gresley had enjoyed to design and build locomotives and rolling stock had come to an end, for the duration at least. As it turned out though, there was some leeway as long as projects could be linked to the war effort. Thompson, whilst working effectively within these parameters, kept one eye to the future, as good leaders do, recognising that the pressing demands of war would eventually ease and normality return. He clearly wanted to prepare the locomotive and rolling stock fleet for war and peace. So, 1941 and '42 were about 'manning the pumps' but, at the same time, trying to prepare the company for peacetime and establishing future policy. The war still had a long way to run, and there would be many disasters and pitfalls along the way, but as the Allied cause slowly improved, Thompson found time to begin fleshing out his ideas and moving the company towards a new reality before retirement.

CHAPTER 8

DESIGN AMBITIONS

The Second World War was the most barbaric conflict in history. For those living under its shadow there was no escape from its effects. It was a total war in which everyone across Britain participated, whether serving in the forces or industry or simply suffering the ravages of bombing at home. It had been very different in the Great War when stress on civilians had been huge, but they hadn't been pursued in their own homes by an enemy intent on their destruction. There were a few pin prick raids, but these caused minimal damage and few casualties along the east coast and in London, where Zeppelins and Gotha bombers occasionally ventured. This time there was little respite and from 1940 to '45, the enemy inflicted bombing, rockets, 'Doodle Bugs' and great hardship on an increasingly jaded population. For those who had served in the trenches it must have rekindled unpleasant memories of suffering and loss, yet they were a generation who seemed best suited to rise to the challenge again. None more so than Thompson himself.

His experiences on the Western Front had clearly marked him in many ways, as it did all survivors, but it also gave many who survived this torment great inner steel. And in his five years as CME, this proved essential in helping him manage successfully in such a pressured environment. But it came at a huge personal cost and at times the cracks in his personality were exposed, with displays of odd, even manic behaviour so typical of scarred veterans of the Western Front. The most obvious signs were there for all to see; working endless hours, even to the extent of sleeping on a bed made up in a small annexe to his office; rarely if ever taking a break; contacting his senior managers at night when they were at home with queries; altering offices to make staff more visible; taking to 'prowling the workshops'; taking on extra duties such as standing fire watch shifts; becoming increasingly fastidious about his appearance and more. And yet, despite the strain, he carried on when men half his age and with a fraction of his responsibilities would have buckled. Here was the dedicated and brave Lt Colonel of 1917-18 again letting nothing stand in the way of his duty.

By 1943 the strain of managing in war was becoming only too apparent as this picture of Thompson suggests. He still looks sharp and business like but there is a weariness in his bearing. (*PR/RH/DN*)

It must have been a lonely existence, with only a large, quiet house, a housekeeper, a parlour maid and the occasional cleaner to keep him company when absences from work were possible. Yet, even allowing for this, he was still capable of many acts of kindness and generosity to his friends and those at work in need of help. Richard Hardy's memories do not reflect isolated incidents.

There was, of course, the other Thompson – the one who ran his department with ruthless efficiency, ensuring that production rates were maintained or even exceeded. To some in his employ these could be bruising, never to be forgotten encounters. He didn't suffer fools gladly, but to fight a total war means that there

Thompson was a keen supporter of the National Savings scheme during the war and actively encouraged his workers to contribute. Sales drives, like this at Doncaster, were part of regular life across his department. (*ET/DN*)

will be many victims and leaders have to drive and fight more vehemently than the enemy's leaders if victory is to be secured. For those who had survived the Great War and all the defeats of 1939 to 1942, this was only too clear.

No man or women can go on for ever under such pressure, though. For Thompson, there were the occasional breaks and distractions. By this stage in the war, the Hall family had moved to live near Wrexham. Although a difficult place to visit in wartime, the CME regularly journeyed there for a weekend break. Here he would find some measure of peace walking in the hills around Brymbo and occasionally fishing for trout and salmon in the Alum and Clwyd Rivers to supplement

wartime rations. Horse riding also seemed to play a part in his life there, as a photo taken by the Halls of him wearing riding gear bears witness.

When time allowed, he also enjoyed holidays in Cornwall and on the south coast of Sussex, though this became more difficult as the war went on and the area was gradually submerged by the massive build-up of men and arms for D Day. But work contacts also provided some welcome breaks and a close friendship grew up between Ronald Matthews, his wife and Thompson. Lady Matthews seems to have taken the lonely CME under her wing shortly after her husband became chairman in 1938. In the years that followed, he became a regular house guest at their homes in Doncaster and

Sir Ronald Matthews (left) and Lady Vera Matthews (centre with bouquet) photographed during 1946 when the *Waverley* paddle steamer, which was built for the LNER to replace a ship of the same name lost at Dunkirk, was launched on the Clyde. The couple would both have an influence on Thompson's life, through professional patronage and friendship. Lady Matthews was known to campaign actively for women's rights and on welfare topics and found in the CME a willing advocate of these issues. Peter Grafton recalls in his book the time when she, on one of her visits to Doncaster Works, noticed that some female workers, when removing grease and other agents from locomotive frames, risked serious chemical contamination. Trichloroethane was generally used for this purpose and the workers were adding it to sawdust, coating the metal and then removing it by scraping. A chemical such as this can cause severe health problems by ingestion through the skin or inhalation and Lady Matthews suggested that it could be removed by hosing down instead. Thompson agreed and quickly implemented changes. Also attending the launch ceremony were Andrew McCosh, T.F. Cameron, Divisional General Manager, and Thompson, at the invitation of Lady Matthews. Throughout his life he seems to have been interested in maritime history and shipping. (*LJ/RH*)

Letwell, being remembered with much affection by one of their children, Prudence, who called him Uncle Ned.

Work would undoubtedly have been a subject discussed by both men on these occasions, as would their ideas and plans for the future. In any large organisation, conversations 'in the margins', so to speak, are often as productive as reams of development papers and discussions at committees and Management Board meetings. One by-product of these conversations may well have been Matthews' decision to select Thompson as CME and not any other potential candidate. But there also seems to have been a strong social element to these visits, something that had been missing from Thompson's life since being widowed in 1938.

His rapport with the perceptive and unreserved Vera Matthews would seem to have been beneficial in many ways, in his personal as well as his working life.

So we see a man in the most difficult and pressured situation taking on a crippling workload yet coping, although signs of stress were only too apparent, partly assuaged by brief breaks. Of all the tasks facing him, though, planning for a future beyond the war and the development of locomotives probably took second place to simply keeping the fleet going and producing armaments. So any ambitions Thompson may have had to branch out into the world of design would always be arrested by the straightjacket of time and the lack of opportunity. By comparison, the only external constraint that Gresley seemed to face, once the Great War was over, was a financial one, which as history shows didn't stop him experimenting and producing many new locomotives.

As Thompson approached the end of his career, did he wish to be remembered for more than simply being an excellent production engineer and manager? Although an admirable achievement, he would have realised that it was the name that prefixed a class of locomotive that provided a more recognisable measure of success. But by 1942 he had done little to build up such a legacy, beyond some modifications to existing classes. Yet it appears to be something that was important to him, judging by the material he approved for publication when retiring in 1946.

Here we see a curriculum vitae carefully drawn up to mark the results of a professional life where design work takes precedence. It presents an interesting summary, but many have argued that the precis it contains may be too bold and, perhaps, undeserved. There is a consensus amongst some that in claiming a legacy, he destroyed a legacy, or so the story goes. So where does the truth lie? To judge this issue fairly you need to strip away a great deal of conjecture, cast aside the politics and the normal manoeuvrings that go with senior management and consider only the facts and the practical limitations under which he worked between 1938 to 1946. There were, of course, a few indications before then of his interest in design and the sort of ideas he was capable of developing. At Stratford, he had worked on the B12 4-6-0s. At Darlington, there had been his attempts, using welding techniques, to fabricate the rocking lever in Gresley's conjugated valve gear and his involvement in rebuilding Raven's B16s and Worsdell's D20s. He would

have gone further and modified his father-in-law's Pacifics by converting them into two-cylinder locomotives, but was thwarted in this ambition by Gresley who had them scrapped instead. And behind all this work he was directly responsible for the production of new V2s, D49s and the first K4, though not their design. But it was at Doncaster that his ideas were allowed to flourish and his design credentials finally take shape.

In 1939, with his experience of running railways on the Western Front, Thompson raised the issue of the LNER's Class 04 2-8-0s again being supplied to the War Department with Gresley. These engines, designed by John Robinson for the Great Central Railway, had proved of great worth in the Great War and Thompson believed they could do so again. Surviving correspondence, in late 1939, reveal his plans for modifying 300 engines and the general acceptance of this idea. These changes, including the fitting of Westinghouse brake gear and steam heating, were well underway and, by November 1939, forty were reported as ready for despatch with work on the others proceeding with haste. But with the Phoney War causing stagnation on the new Western Front and with no imminent attack by the German Army predicted, the order was postponed. The invasion of France and the British Army's evacuation in the summer of 1940 was too swift to allow the plan to be revived and it was held in abeyance until late 1941.

By this time, the whole issue of locomotives for front line service had been reviewed by the Ministry of Supply and the question of the 04s was swept up in this strategy. Now, as CME, Thompson was directed to re-activate the plan and he issued an order for the preparation of fifty engines at Gorton. He added, in a general instruction on 6 September 'the engines chosen for modification work must not have a mileage exceeding 20,000 since last General' and 'be despatched to Glasgow, Greenock, Birkenhead, Cardiff and Swansea for shipment overseas between 16th and 29th September'. Very quickly, this programme was extended with another forty-two locomotives being added for service in the Middle East. It seems that the CME visited John Harrison at the works during this period to personally superintend the work and ensure that the deadlines were met. Harrison recorded his memories of these encounters:

'It was my regular job to meet him every weekend at Chester and bring him by car to Gorton for the day

A Class 04 (ex-LNER No. 6185) converted for war use and oil burning, operating in Egypt in 1943. In two world wars these locomotives proved of immense use, but were superseded by newer designs – the LMS 8Fs and by War Department-ordered Austerity 2-8-0s and 2-10-0s. (*ET/DN*)

[probably after he had spent time with the Hall family in nearby Brymbo]. These journeys were the occasions when he opened up and told me a good deal of what he wanted to do and why. He had a mind full of ideas, some of which seemed quite impractical to me. When he told me to carry out some of the wilder ones I pretended acquiescence and hoped he would eventually forget all about them, which he generally did. He had a very active mind that was often effected by the severe stress entailed in running his department in war. This made him difficult at times and woe betide anyone who argued with him. Yet at other times he was open to debate and appreciated our contribution provided that it was presented in a diplomatic way.'

As the war progressed, Thompson would turn his attention to the Class 04s that remained with the LNER and the way they might be improved or replaced, but more about this shortly.

Whilst this work was going on, the development of other locomotives for military service was being considered by the War Office and the Ministry of Supply. These plans included the growing needs of the railway companies themselves. With its fine record of success, William Stanier's 2-8-0 Class 8F was chosen to augment the programme. By 1939, 126 had been built and another 726 would be added during the war. To meet these demands, many of these engines were constructed not only by the LMS, the Southern Railway and the GWR, but also the LNER at Doncaster and Darlington between 1944 and '46. Tom Coleman, the LMS's Chief Draughtsman and leader in designing the 8Fs, was seconded to each company and got to know each CME. Shortly after Thompson died, he wrote:

'He impressed me as a man and an engineer. I met Thompson a number of times, in company with Stanier on two occasions. Both men enjoyed an easy

Some of the LNER team responsible for constructing LMS 8Fs at Doncaster and Darlington as recorded in a photo retained by Tom Coleman 'the LMS's Chief Draughtsman' following a short period of secondment. Thompson is recorded as being in this picture. If so, the only figure that looks like him is standing second from the left front row wearing a double-breasted suit (which he seems to have favoured) and a dark fedora hat. (*TC/ML*)

relationship and discussed locomotive design and seemed to share many views and opinions. When the 8Fs were being built at Doncaster and Darlington I helped oversee the work and found the CME to be co-operative and interested in all aspects of their construction. The class seemed to appeal to him and he absorbed much technical information we had gathered since they first appeared in 1935. Having studied this material and, by all accounts, ridden on their footplate a number of times, he felt that they might have been improved by the addition of an LNER boiler. We discussed alternatives in a spirited way, as we did the benefits of streamlining and several other issues including the question of standardisation. Here he expressed great admiration of the progress made by Sir William.

'He also seemed to be very impressed with the LMS Class Fives. These became a topic of conversation between us as did the issue of smoke deflectors and the related research work undertaken by Frederick Johansen at Teddington and Derby in the '20s and '30s. He had attended a presentation given by Johansen to the Institution of Mechanical Engineers on the effects of air resistance in 1935 and had retained many papers on the subject. He had also attended a presentation given by Harold Holcroft in London in September 1941 which drew on Johansen's work. Thompson was clearly intrigued by the subject and seemed to see merit in it. I found him approachable and thoughtful . . . He was no hidebound traditionalist in the matter of design, which was refreshing. Unfortunately, there were many who were.'

In due course, the Class 04s and 8Fs would be overtaken in number, if not quality, by two 'austerity' engines designed specifically for war use – a 2-8-0 and 2-10-0. These began appearing in the early months of 1943 and by the end of the war, 935 and 150, respectively, had been built. Unlike the 8Fs, the LNER played no part in their construction, but under Thompson's guiding hand, judging by surviving correspondence, they purchased 200 of the 2-8-0s to supplement its tired and ageing fleet in 1946.

The needs of war also played a part in Thompson's development of another Robinson designed Great

Central Railway class of locomotive – the two-cylinder Q4 0-8-0 tender engines which first appeared in 1902. By 1911, eighty-nine had been built. With ever increasing freight needs dominating day to day activity, there was a growing pressure for more tank engines to undertake heavy shunting duties. The Q4s were deemed to be nearing the end of their lives during the mid to late 1930s and by 1941, only forty or so remained in service with the rest due to be scrapped. The pressure of war and the restrictions on new construction meant that these engines had to continue in service. The CME is credited with seeing the potential contained in this class if rebuilt and set in motion a plan to modify all of the class into 0-8-0 tank engines.

As tender engines, the Q4s had a role but as tank engines they had a more valuable specialist task to fulfil. With this in mind, he obtained permission to convert an initial batch of locomotives and in late 1941 the drawing office was set to work. The brief called for the retention of as much of the old engines as possible. This included the cylinders, motion, the boiler, although these would be cut down in length to accommodate an enclosed cab, a 4½ ton capacity coal bunker and frames, though these were altered at the rear to support the buffer beam and draw gear. Side tanks were fitted capable of holding 1,500 gallons, but this proved insufficient in service and some were upgraded to 2,000 gallons. By adopting these frugal measures, there was a minimal requirement for new castings at a time of great shortages and ate up far less workshop time than a new construction would.

The first of the new class, designated Q1, made its appearance in June 1942 and twelve more followed. A proposal to build the others remained on the table, but the war ended before this could come to fruition. The engines that saw service seemed to have been reasonably successful, remaining in service until 1959, and led Thompson to include such a type in his standardisation plans.

Above and overleaf: Before, as designed and the result. A soon to be redundant Q4 is translated, at minimal cost, into the Q1, in which guise it found a useful role until the late 1950s. (*ET/DN/RH*)

HEATING SURFACE—										
TUBES	...	...	...	...	...	...	1,068 SQ. FT.
FIREBOX	...	...	...	...	...	...	141 "
TOTAL	...	...	...	...	...	...	1,209 "
NO SUPERHEATER							

TUBES ...	...	...	228—1¾ IN. DIA. OUTS. { 10 FT. 2½ IN. BET. TUBEPLATES
GRATE AREA ...	...	...	...	...	...	23·62 SQ. FT.
TRACTIVE EFFORT (AT 85 PER CENT. B.P.)	...	...	25,644 LB.

"Q1" Class

The way this project was developed seems to sum up Thompson's approach to engineering; strong on practicalities and economy of effort, but there was more to it than this. He had been taught at Marlborough and Cambridge to approach any technical issue in a structured way and to carefully analyse all aspects of a subject before reaching conclusions and taking action. It was a lesson strongly reinforced by his experiences with the NER, GNR and LNER. The basis of this work is identification of an emerging need or problems with an existing design. Quantification, analysis, modelling, testing and construction of a prototype, if necessary, to assist evaluation, with no sudden rush to set in hand a programme of work until the way ahead is clear, a benefit can be demonstrated and an action justified. It was a process to which the term measured response can best be applied and Thompson's approach seems to have embraced many elements of this practise. There was scientific curiosity, though this was tempered with caution and he was prepared to let an idea go when no advantage could be demonstrated. He may have been stubborn and hard-nosed at times, but he was no fool.

Within the limitations imposed by the LNER's Board and the REC on locomotive construction, there was little room to manoeuvre. Nevertheless, Thompson was still able to push through a number of projects in a search for greater efficiency and standardisation. Although their gestation period may have been long, and the number of engines affected generally quite small, as the Q4/ Q1 project proved, it was still an interesting and note-worthy programme. And 1942 saw him begin develop-ment of three more classes before the contentious issue of P2s entered the fray – the Great Central designed J11 0-6-0 goods engines, Gresley's D49 4-4-0 and his own B1 4-6-0.

The J11 (the Great Central Railway Class 9J) was another Robinson design that first appeared shortly after the turn of the century and, by 1910, 174 had been built. Eighteen served on the Western Front in the Great War where they would have been known and observed by Thompson. Despite their age, they were still doing good work in 1941 when he became CME and began formulating his ideas on standardisation. Very early in this process he reasoned that this programme should include an 0-6-0 tender engine and saw the J11 as one model that might fill this slot.

As designed by Robinson, these engines had two inside cylinders, Stephenson's link-motion, slide valves, saturated boilers and Belpaire fireboxes. Over the years, they were modified with the addition of superheaters and piston valves. But this was a slow running, low priority programme that appears to have only reached completion in 1946. So, when Thompson took over as CME, many of the class were in original condition with both marques running in great numbers. From this, it is probably safe to assume that the class were successful and effective in service in both forms.

When contemplating standardisation, Thompson was sufficiently impressed with these light goods

engines to include the concept in his plans, but in a modified form. He duly authorised drawing office staff at Doncaster to flesh out his ideas and in due course a prototype appeared. A superheated engine was selected for modification and entered the workshops at Gorton in early 1942 and was turned out for inspection a few months later in July as a J11/3. To all intents and pur-poses, it looked little different from its sisters; nonethe-less, it did contain a number of changes. There were new cylinders, though their dimensions were identical to the originals. The valve gear was modified with the removal of the rocking shaft and there was an increase in valve travel to 6in. The unbalanced side valves were altered and maximum cut-off in full gear was reduced from 79 per cent to 70 per cent. These alterations meant that the engines' frames had to be modified and the boiler raised by four inches with the chimney reduced in height to keep within the loading gauge.

In the months that followed, the engine when tested seems to have been sufficiently effective to warrant the conversion of another thirty during Thompson's tenure. But that was all. As most of the class remained largely as built, until scrapped in the late 1950s and '60s, it would seem as though any improvements achieved by rebuild-ing were marginal to say the least.

The D49 conversion followed a similar pattern, but in this case took Thompson's ideas on two cylinders, as opposed to three, a step further. The planning for this work sat alongside the J11 project and in August 1942 engine No. 365, *The Morpeth*, appeared at Darlington where originally built in late 1934. This engine was cho-sen as a prototype for the CME's ideas because she was in the works for repair following damage to her cam-shaft. But it wasn't a quick project to come to fruition, suggesting a great deal of thought about requirement and the need for standardisation before conversion work could begin.

The D49 class had been built in three forms, although each carried three cylinders and steam chest in a sin-gle casting, the same boilers, conjugated valve gear and 6ft 8in driving wheels as standard. Twenty-eight D49/1s were built with conventional piston valves between 1927 and '29 and in 1928, six D49/3s appeared with poppet valve gear. This wasn't a success and by 1938 they were fitted with conventional piston valves. The D49/2s were initially designed using the compound expansion principle, but Gresley didn't pursue this idea

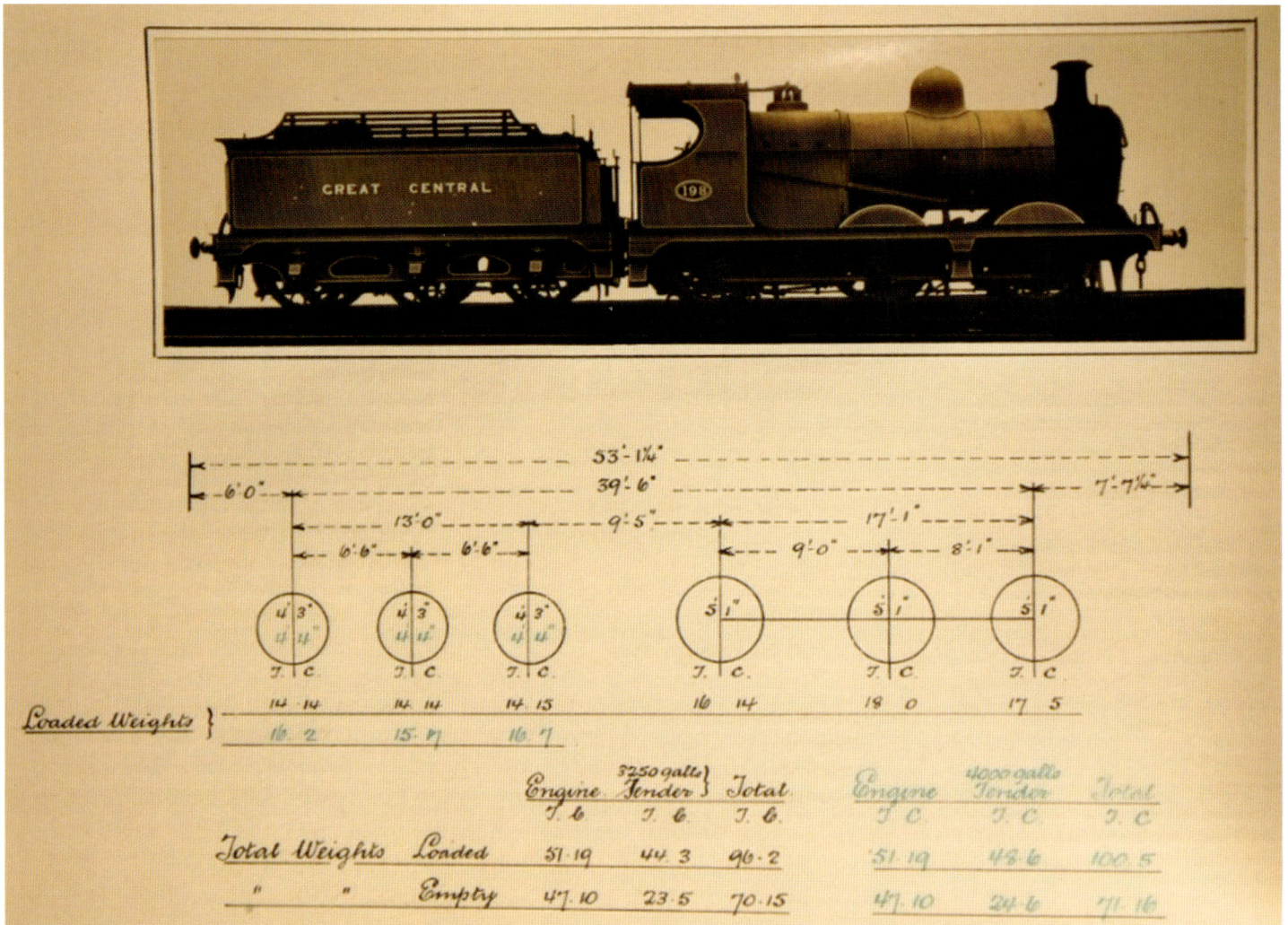

Thom's record of the Class 9J (later the LNER's J11) when serving with the Great Central Railway at Gorton. (*RT/THG*)

Left: How D49 engine No. 365, '*The Morpeth*', appeared after reconstruction in 1942. *Opposite*: how Robert Thom recorded its original construction and the original outline of the D49s. (*RT/THG*)

TYPE D-49 (PART 2)

4-4-0 EXPRESS PASSENGER TENDER ENGINES (3 cyl.)

NEW ENGINES. **BUILT :- DARLINGTON WORKS**

BOILER.
BARREL Outs. Dia.' 5'-6"
Length. 11'-4⅝"
FIREBOX Outs Length.O/S 8'-11⅞"
GRATE AREA 26 sq ft.
WORKING PRESSURE 180 lbs/sq in.

HEATING SURFACE.
FIREBOX 171.5 sq ft
TUBES 871.75 "
FLUES 354.53 "
SUPERHEATER. 271.8 "
TOTAL. 1669.58 sq ft.

CYLINDERS (3) 17'dia.' x 26'stroke.
DRIVING WHEELS 6'-8'dia.'
WEIGHT ON DRIVERS 41 Tons 10 Cwt.
TOTAL WT. OF ENGINE IN WORKING ORDER 64 Tons 10 Cwt.

ENGINE Nº	DATE SENT INTO TRAFFIC.	SUPERHEATER.	Nº OF ELEMENTS	REMARKS.
205	10.7.34	Robinson	24	" The Albrighton "
214	14.7.34	"	"	" The Atherstone "
217	17.7.34	"	"	" The Belvoir "
222	20.7.34	"	"	" The Berkeley "
226	23.7.34	"	"	" The Bilsdale "
230	10.8.34	"	"	" The Brocklesby "
238	17.8.34	"	"	" The Burton "
258	22.8.34	"	"	" The Cattistock "
274	28.8.34	"	"	" The Craven "
279	4.9.34	"	"	" The Cotswold "
353	12.9.34	"	"	" The Derwent "
357	22.9.34	"	"	" The Ferrie "
359	28.9.34	"	"	" The Fitzwilliam "
361	4.10.34	"	"	" The Garth "
362	11.10.34	"	"	" The Goathland "
363	15.11.34	"	"	" The Grafton "
364	19.11.34	"	"	" The Grove "
365	1.12.34	"	"	" The Morpeth "
366	7.12.34	"	"	" The Oakley "
368	12.12.34	"	"	" The Puckeridge "

and decided to fit Lentz valves operated by rotary valve gear instead. In this form, forty-two engines were constructed between 1929 and '35, including *The Morpeth*.

Comparability trials were carried out between the different types of D49s in 1935-36 and these showed the piston valve version to be superior. Following this, it seems there were proposals to convert the D49/2s to this form, but the coming of war and changed priorities curtailed these plans, except in the case of engine No. 365. In 1939, she was fitted with variable rotary cam poppet valve gear controlled by steam pressure rather than by springs. In this form, she ran until 1941, when the camshaft was damaged and the engine placed in store where she became the focus of Thompson's thoughts and plans.

She retained the boiler, but the three-cylinder mechanism was replaced by two inside cylinders, with the Stephenson motion used to operate the piston valves. These valves were of the same diameter as those on the D49/1s but had reduced travel. This overall configuration bore hallmarks of the arrangement used on the successful Robinson-designed two-cylinder D11 4-4-0 'Improved Director' Class that appeared in 1919 on the

Great Central Railway. Construction of this class continued under Gresley and would have been seen, and possibly admired, by Thompson. Such were his feelings on the subject that the modified locomotive, simply designated 'D', quickly featured in his standardisation plans.

However, trials run from Neville Hill Shed in Leeds, and then when based at Haymarket and Starbeck in Harrogate, quickly showed that the 'new' design was inferior in some respects to the originals. This was nowhere more apparent than in No. 365's big end brasses, which tended to run hot when high cut offs were used. Analysis also showed that the problem was exacerbated when the locomotive was operated by unfamiliar footplate crew, who tended to shovel ash over the big end. Due to a perceived fault in the ashpan, this allowed contamination to enter the big end which did little to improve performance or reliability. However, with a regular crew this didn't seem to have been a problem and the engine was known to have turned in fair performances. So, with no obvious advantages to be gained from continuing the experiment, no other locomotive was modified in this way and the programme was eventually dropped. Undoubtedly though, this project

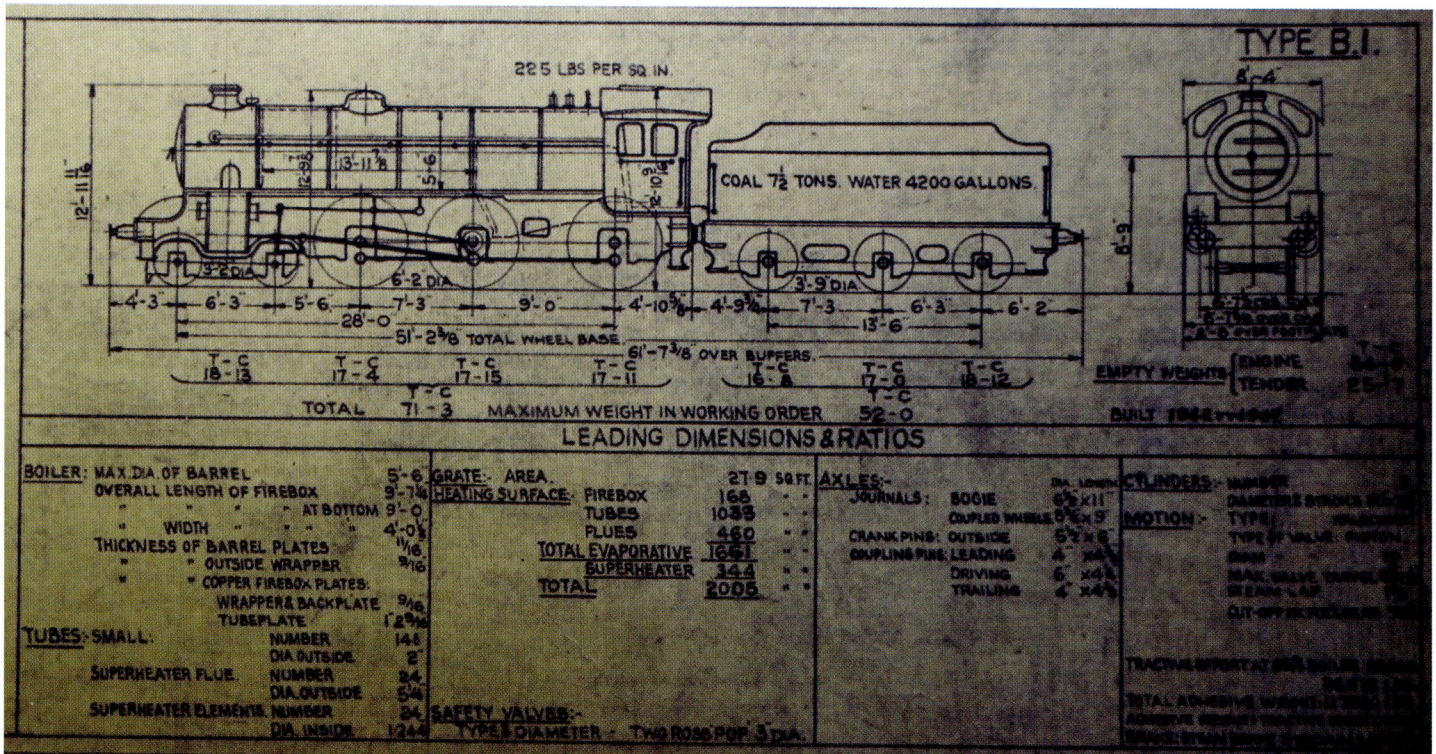

The B1's diagram showing the broad layout and dimensions. In looks it was clearly an LNER engine with its familiar balanced lines.

added to Thompson's developing knowledge of design and so inform his next project – the 4-6-0 B1.

It was at about this time that Richard Hardy came into direct contact with the CME again in a chance and revealing meeting as he took an 'unofficial' footplate ride to widen his experience:

'I had just left Bob Foster, having come with him from Doncaster, and crossed over to the up side to catch a slow train back home. Gaining the darkened platform, I found myself walking towards Edward Thompson! I had been working with enthusiasm for hours and as most boys believe that the blacker one gets, the better, I was not a pretty sight. Thompson, on the other hand, was elegantly dressed and looking down at me from a seemingly great height. There was no escape and evasion was not only impossible but also unthinkable – so it had to come out. "Sir, I've been working on the footplate but I haven't a pass and I know that I should not have been on an engine without one". His reply, with an understanding smile, I shall never forget. "Sonny, I'm delighted to hear that you are interested enough to do this in your spare time. Are you going to Doncaster?"

'At that moment the Doncaster slow ran down and, striding to the nearest third class open coach, he imperiously beckoned to me to follow him. We sat side by side, at his direction, in a pair of bucket seats and he told me of his plans for the future, of the classes of engine that he was going to rebuild, of the mixed traffic engine that was going to be the B1 and so on. He held the engines of John Robinson in high regard and told me that the rebuilt J11 and the O4 were going to become standard in their field.'

For such a remote man, this openness, especially to one so young and so junior in the organisation, is illuminating. On one hand it suggests a man of great warmth and understanding, and on the other it underlines the transparency of his thought processes and the boyish interest he took in this aspect of his work. Either way, his approach captured this young man's imagination and left an impression that clearly affected him deeply.

But what of the B1? When it came to this programme, R.A. Riddles, a leading light under Stanier on the LMS who would later become BR's first CME,

expressed a thought provoking view in a letter he wrote during May 1968:

'There was on the London and North Eastern Railway no general purpose mixed traffic engine, such as Stanier's Class 5, until Edward Thompson, who succeeded Gresley, produced his excellent B1 Class 4-6-0 with two cylinders, which was probably the most useful engine ever built for that line.'

Interestingly he then offered his opinions on Gresley's legacy to Thompson:

'On the LNER, Gresley, great engineer though he was, embarked on a policy which was the very antithesis of the Churchward school. Though he was forced to follow Churchward's ideas to obtain the best results from his locomotives, he never attempted any standardisation. His engines were frequently tailor made to meet local conditions; and he designed a range of engine classes which were mostly fitted with three cylinders and a valve gear which was difficult to maintain. '

Such views are revealing because they are the assessment of an experienced and highly professional outsider and not an LNER man who might be swayed by tribal loyalties or personal likes or dislikes. Basically he had 'no axe to grind' and could appraise developments without a hint of bias. Just as William Stanier, through Ernest Cox, had fairly assessed the problems with Gresley's conjugated valve gear when asked to do so in 1942, so Riddles demonstrated equal impartiality. Both men agreed that Gresley was a talented engineer, but also recognised his limitations. In this even-handed way, they were also content to give credit to Thompson, where due, for his efforts in bringing some order to the muddle and round off what Gresley had started. In some ways, they seem to be inferring that between them the two CMEs had complementary talents that could have better served the LNER if they had been able to work together more effectively. To this end Riddles added:

'We heard rumours of disagreements, which to be frank are quite common in any organisation, often go unresolved and can fester. In this case it was clear to Stanier and myself that their gifts were many-sided and covered all disciplines most effectively. But they often seemed unable to harmonise these skills and get the best out of each other. Strong willed, ambitious men with a clear sense of destiny are often like this. They cannot stand being corrected or being deflected from their goals. However, they survived and forged a partnership of sorts, but together they were capable of much more. Ideally, Thompson should have been sitting in the seat occupied by the ebullient but erratic Bulleid and been deputy CME at the same time. In this way locomotive policy, management of all the workshops and design would have been harmonised and managed much more effectively than they were.'

Nevertheless, Gresley still achieved a great deal and Thompson supported him by bringing order and greater productivity to the workshops. But there remains a conundrum; what might have been achieved if the

relationship had been closer and more technically inclusive? If so, it might have helped Thompson develop his design skills and better equip him for the time when he might become CME himself. As it was, these talents remained unrefined and untested and this placed him at a distinct disadvantage when his turn came to lead. But did this matter, after all engineering design is rarely, if ever, placed in the hands of just one person? There will always be a leader, but generally it is the led who take on detailed planning and construction tasks. And this returns us to the question of who truly designs something as complex as a locomotive?

Gresley certainly acted as instigator when a requirement was identified by the operational side of the LNER. He also provided an outline and contributed ideas, but ultimately it was Spencer and the small HQ team who translated these proposals and then it was the drawing office where the fine detail was considered

The first B1 gradually comes together at Darlington in late 1942. (*ET/DN*)

DESIGN AMBITIONS • 223

and developed into a workable solution for the CME to approve. With Thompson, the same would have applied and anything he produced would have had the 'team' stamp upon it. However, the responsibility for success or failure would have fallen squarely on the shoulders of the CME and not the many contributors. In the same way, Thompson's work on Gresley's P2s and Pacifics, the D49 and J11s and others would ultimately have been a team effort with pressure being applied by a number of people in his own organisation or the running department to reach certain conclusions. With such conflicting demands and operating under the stringencies of war, it is small wonder that anything of value appeared at all, but it did and the B1 can probably be judged the most 'useful' of all those engines that emerged, as Riddles suggested.

When describing the development of the B1, the noted LNER historian W.B. Yeadon, who appears to have been no great fan of Thompson, quoted the words of an unnamed CME:

'When he [Thompson] wasn't different from Gresley, then he built a good engine.'

Yeadon then underlined this view by saying that the B1, which in his words 'acquired a favourable reception', took the cylinders from Gresley's K2 2-6-0 design, coupled wheels from the V2 and had a boiler 'for which Gresley signed the drawings in April 1939'. He then searched for any element of the design for which Thompson might be credited, but drew few favourable conclusions. The boiler pressure had been increased from 220lb. to 225lb. and the steam supply passages in the cylinders had been *smoothed out*. And with that, he dismissed Thompson's work and marked the B1 down as being a Gresley engine. But is this a fair assessment?

There is a view that by the early twentieth century there was very little innovation or anything truly original to add to the design of steam locomotives. So most engineers simply adopted a mix and match arrangement, taking, refining and adapting established concepts when considering a new engine. In fact, Gresley is quoted by Oliver Bulleid as saying 'when you run out of ideas then copy the best', so even he seemed to recognise the shallow pool from which designers could draw inspiration and the limited options available in their science. Thompson, only too aware of the many limitations imposed on him, followed this same route and drew together, in a very practical way, the best of what

was available, just as Gresley had done with his many locomotives.

When considering a standard mixed traffic 4-6-0 engine, Thompson's initial thoughts fell on the B17 Class as a reasonable model to follow, but with two cylinders, not three. To achieve this, he chose to use cylinders based on Gresley's pre-Great War H3/K2 Class, which measured 20in by 26in, matched to Walschaert valve gear. At the same time a standard 5ft 6in diameter boiler, designated No. 2 and based on diagram 100A, was chosen. With this outline in place Edward Windle and his staff produced an initial design for the CME to ponder.

As the months passed, he considered how the layout might be simplified to ensure easier maintenance and more effective running in wartime. With his long history of analysing and modifying industrial processes, this approach had become second nature to him and he applied the same principles to locomotive design. So when Windle submitted new drawings and a diagram in 1942 the design had been tweaked with modifications made to the cab, steam pipes and running plates. The grate area had also been expanded and the boiler's pressure marginally increased to 225lbs. In addition, a redesigned bogie had been introduced. It is reported that the central rubbing plates, which had become a standard fit, were detached and replaced by spherical side bearers, which were attached to the engine's frame, through which the load was conducted to the bogie frames. This idea passed muster but over the years the bogie design would be subject to additional modifications, particularly to the stretcher plates.

This final design was approved in mid-1942 and a submission went to the Locomotive Committee seeking approval to begin construction. In the minutes of the meeting, Thompson is recorded as asking for 'ten engines of two-cylinder type, entirely composed of standard parts which will be roughly equivalent to the K3 engines . . .' Although being given permission to go ahead the need for a prototype was considered necessary and this was duly completed at Darlington and entered traffic on 12 December.

Throughout its construction, Thompson was recorded as visiting the workshops regularly and taking a close personal interest in all elements of the work, riding on the footplate on its first day of operations. In many ways, the project espoused principles which

The first B1 appears in black, numbered 8301 and named *Springbok*. It is said that the name was chosen as a mark of respect for Jan Smuts, the South African Prime Minister and a member of Churchill's War Cabinet, and the large contingent of South Africans who fought in the First and Second World Wars. If so, Thompson, as an old soldier himself, would have approved of this move. The next thirty-nine built followed a similar pattern and were named after different breeds of antelope – Eland, Impala, Gazelle and so on. (*AE*)

had become second nature to him, reflecting the need for economy and efficiency, especially in wartime. So production encompassed such things as welding as opposed to using steel castings and maximum use was made of fabrication techniques. In addition, the use of many readily available components meant that existing jigs, patterns and tools could be employed rather than building new. It was certainly production on the cheap, but was nonetheless effective and the end result didn't bear any physical signs of being driven by austerity – although an austerity engine is what it was.

With so many other pressing demands on the workshops, the construction schedule for the other nine of class proved to be a slow business and it would take until June 1944 for this initial batch to be completed. Another 400 would follow, but the war would be long over before the programme began again and it would only reach fruition in 1952. With such slow progress being made, other ways of boosting the number of standard mixed traffic 4-6-0s available were considered. One alternative that Thompson proposed was the reconstruction of the Robinson designed four-cylinder B3s, six of which had been built for the Great Central Railway between 1917 and 1920. They had not been particularly successful and were noted for their heavy coal consumption.

To try and improve their performance, Gresley decided to strip away the Stephenson valve gear and replace it with poppet valves operated by Caprotti valve gear. Although the first two, Nos. 6168 and 6166, appeared in this guise during 1929, it would take another ten years for the next two to be completed, with war intervening before the last two could be dealt with.

In 1943, engine No. 6166, *Earl Haig*, suffered cracked cylinders and whilst awaiting repair was selected by Thompson and his team to be turned into a B1 of sorts. It was, to all intents and purposes, an experiment in recycling, taking an engine probably nearing the end of its life and giving it a second wind. Some major components, such as the wheels, bogies, tender and sections of the main frames were re-used, but that was about all. Amongst other things, a new round topped boiler of the 100A pattern was fitted, plus two outside cylinders actuated by Walschaerts valve gear. When leaving the works in October 1943, the casual observer could be forgiven for thinking it was a B1; nevertheless the engine retained its original classification, but modified to B3/3.

It seems that 6166 performed fairly well but suffered from cracked frames, which affected her availability. So with this in mind, no more were rebuilt and this experimental programme came to an end. However, as the one engine rebuilt she lasted longer in service than her five sisters, being withdrawn in 1949.

Meanwhile, testing of the B1s had begun and continued into 1944, with the later phase specifically designed to compare the engine with those which this 'standard' design was due to replace. These were overseen and managed by Bert Spencer, who by then had returned to a role more akin to that occupied under Gresley. Over the next two years, until Thompson's retirement, he worked closely with the CME on his standardisation plans and a post-war locomotive development programme. The files that remain identify his

contribution to these tasks and the level of analysis he provided. On 26 May 1944, for example, he met with all the Locomotive Running Superintendents, on behalf of the CME, to agree the test programme and the classes to be included – B3, B6, B12, B17, D11, D40, D49, K2 and many others. During this meeting, he set the test criteria and locations from across the LNER's network. He was then involved in the programme, regularly reporting progress to Thompson and providing analysis for the formal Standardisation Report released in late 1945, much of which he appears to have drafted under the CME's guiding hand.

Engine No. 8301 enters service. Comprehensive testing of the class wouldn't begin until 1943 when No. 8303 underwent analysis on lines in Scotland. These showed that the locomotive was 'free steaming, with good acceleration, despite poor quality coal. On steep and varied gradients, the engine proved to be an excellent starter, but the ride, at times, could be uncomfortable and uneven, due, in part, to the use of cut-offs below 25 per cent. It is concluded that this may be due to high cylinder compressions'. (*ET/DN*)

Engine No. 6166 before and after reconstruction. A weakness in her frames caused occasional fractures to appear. From the few records still available it seems that this may have been a problem that afflicted the originals and wasn't eradicated by re-building. (*ET/DN/RH*)

It seems that he also took a keen interest in the P2 modification programme, which during 1942-43 was moving to fruition, although it was a task handled primarily by Windle and his drawing office. In Chapter Seven, the background of this project and the wider concerns over the conjugated valve gears were discussed. The way ahead, largely supported by Charles Newton and his Divisional General Managers, now seemed clear, allowing the CME to produce something that better met their needs. However, it wouldn't be a quick process, with only one locomotive, No. 2005, finished in January 1943, the others following suit during April and December the following year. It was a programme that ran alongside

A B1 painted green in the immediate post-war period. With the end of hostilities, traditional LNER colour schemes began to be re-established and a new numbering system was adopted. Here engine No.1003, *Gazelle*, stands ready for departure from Liverpool Street Station. This engine received her new colour scheme in late 1945 specifically so that she could undertake Royal Train workings, with one particular duty being on the London to Wolferton station route, for Sandringham. (*AE*)

the creation of four new Pacifics, which Thompson pushed through on the back of the V2 programme.

In the background to all this lay a study commissioned by Newton and undertaken by the LNER Post-War Development Committee to try and establish the railway's future needs. It was chaired by O.H. Corble, who was in charge of Ancillary Services, and had senior managers from all departments, with Edward Windle the CME's representative. In 1943, a successful end to the war still seemed a distant possibility, almost impossible to visualize; nevertheless, Newton wanted a plan that could be developed as the future unfolded. Their first 48-page report appeared in mid-1943 and every aspect of railway working was included with an estimate given of need and cost. It was an ambitious programme with future civil engineering projects, locomotive and rolling stock needs at its core. Steam isn't referred to directly, but electrification is, with the resurrection of the pre-war programme being given high priority. However, the paper does set out targets for future locomotive development:

'Post-war traffic will be characterised by demands for increased speeds, frequency and punctuality of service, freight and passenger . . . to have freight trains capable of maintaining higher speeds and hauling loads of 500 tons (70mph as a maximum and at least 45mph as an average).'

On the cover of his copy of the report, Newton has written 'Standardisation of locomotives and rolling stock is essential if we are to make this work'.

And earlier he sent a memo to Thompson encouraging him to 'press ahead with this work in all haste, but with due regard given to other priorities'. So sanctioned, the CME increased the level of experimentation and at the same time tried to narrow down the number and types of engines to be included in this plan. But wartime need still took priority and he must have realised that such a programme would only come to fruition when the conflict had been fought to a successful conclusion. In tackling this work, Thompson set down a number of guidelines during 1943 in a draft paper for Newton; it was a document that Bert Spencer kept, suggesting he was involved in the drafting process:

'Standardisation is not intended to lay down hard and fast rules from which there can be no departure. It is only necessary to see where the bulk of the traffic can be dealt with by a limited number of locomotive classes, keeping in mind the necessity for continuous study and testing to judge whether improvements or modifications are required from time to time.

'By this means the advantages of standardisation can be secured without involving the stagnation so far as research and development are concerned. If improvements were considered desirable in one of the standard types, one or two locomotives would be selected for experimental purposes. These, after modification to incorporate the new devices and new ideas, would be tested against unaltered engines, and if they proved satisfactory would form the basis for a change in the standard.

'From this point we need to consider a more comprehensive policy, the first step being to divide locomotive types, totalling 166, into three Groups:

'The new standard types which will be constructed when it has been established that a demand cannot be met by one of the existing types.

'The second group includes existing locomotive types which are considered worth maintaining until the end of their useful lives – new boilers will be built for them as required and they will not be broken up until they become obsolete (there are eleven types in this group - the A1 [later called A10s], A3, A4, B17, D49, B16, K3, V2, O4, V1 and V3).

'The third group includes all the remaining locomotive types, all considerably older types which are no longer satisfactory or whose work could, with advantage, be transferred to one of the new types in group one. Nevertheless, this is only a general policy, and not an invariable rule.'

Interestingly, in his paper Thompson makes only a passing reference to streamlining and here the entry simply lists the new standard A1 Pacific as being streamlined. Too much may be read into this, because the Pacifics he eventually produced didn't follow the classic A4 outline. The only nod to this science that was included was in the method of smoke lifting applied – aerodynamic fins around the chimney or more traditional smoke deflectors. Perhaps of greater significance was his expressed wish to leave the A4s as built, and for that matter the A3s. For someone who was subsequently accused of being against anything Gresley and determined to destroy his legacy, this is an interesting outcome. The truth would seem to be that he wasn't but only tackled his predecessor's engines when there was a pressing need to do so – a need driven by the running department.

Having slowly established the pattern of the first of his new standard locomotives a Pacific was the next in line. And the P2 conversion became the first step in this four stage evolution.

When planned in the early 1930s, the P2s were to be built in conventional form, but different degrees of streamlining were then applied by Gresley and his team. The Thompson/Windle redesign saw all air smoothed casing removed and the first two diagrams appearing in 1942 captured the traditional Gresley look. But here the similarities ended. Three cylinders were retained, with their diameter reduced from 21 to 20in., though their stroke remained the same at 26in. As predicted, the conjugated valve gear was removed, with all cylinders being served by independent Walschaerts valve gear. The P2 connecting rods were re-used. To accommodate this, the outside cylinders had to be placed to the rear of the leading truck. This created a clearance problem and meant that the middle cylinder had to be set well forward of the outside cylinders, between the frames, and would drive the front set of wheels. Meanwhile, the outside cylinders drove the centre set of coupled wheels. This configuration gave the engines a stretched, slightly unbalanced look, aesthetically not pleasing to some. However, when speaking to Brian Reed a few years later, Thompson expressed some doubt over this solution. 'I wasn't sure if I had done the right thing and

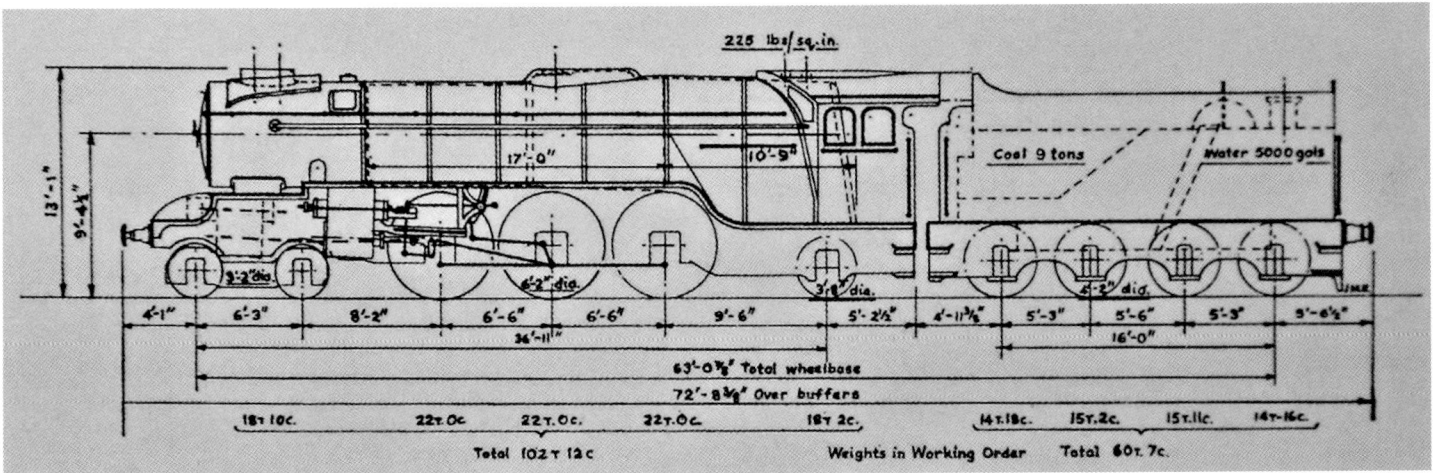

The P2 conversion gradually takes shape during 1942 as debate over the future of engines with Gresley's conjugated valve gear came to an end. These two diagrams (above dated April 1942, below as built) show the interim and final stages of the design.

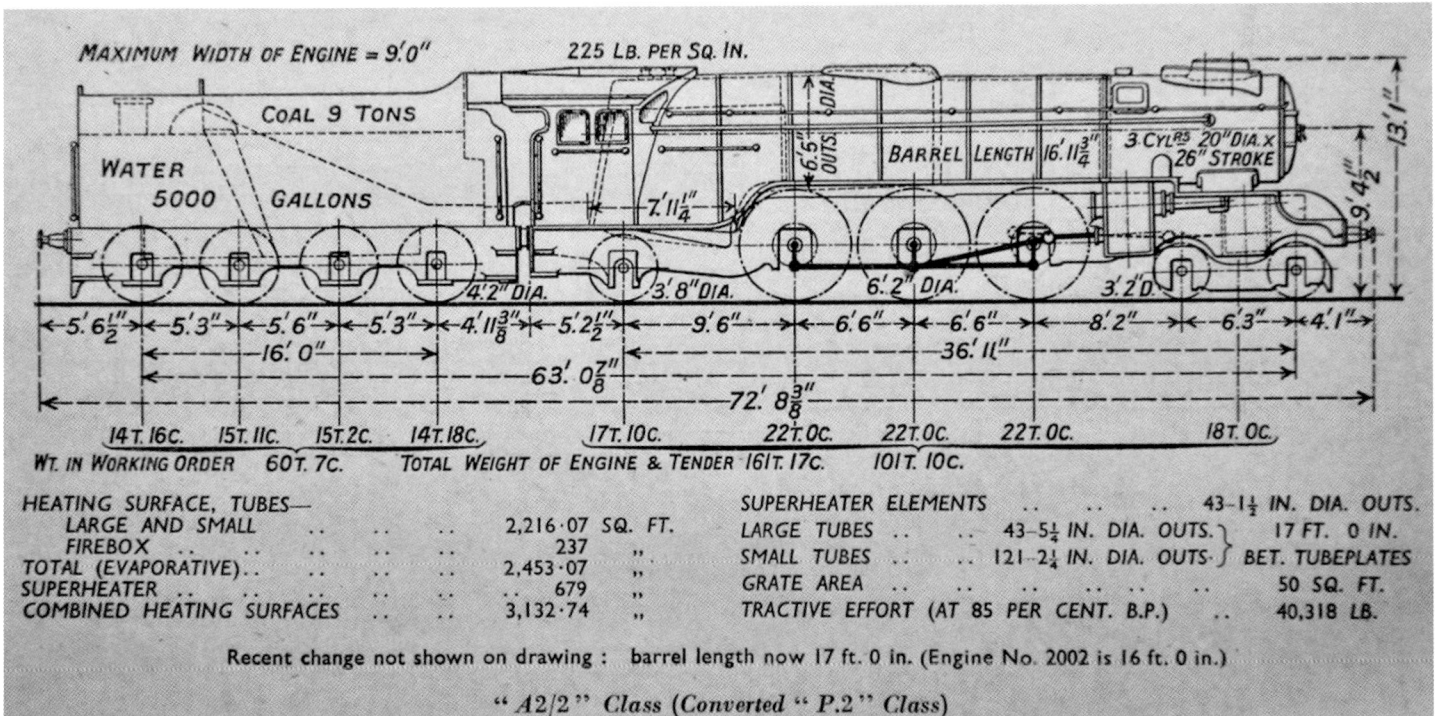

HEATING SURFACE, TUBES—		
LARGE AND SMALL	2,216·07 SQ. FT.	
FIREBOX	237 "	
TOTAL (EVAPORATIVE)	2,453·07 "	
SUPERHEATER	679 "	
COMBINED HEATING SURFACES	3,132·74 "	

SUPERHEATER ELEMENTS	43—1¼ IN. DIA. OUTS.	
LARGE TUBES	43—5¼ IN. DIA. OUTS.	17 FT. 0 IN.
SMALL TUBES	121—2¼ IN. DIA. OUTS.	BET. TUBEPLATES
GRATE AREA	50 SQ. FT.	
TRACTIVE EFFORT (AT 85 PER CENT. B.P.)	40,318 LB.	

Recent change not shown on drawing : barrel length now 17 ft. 0 in. (Engine No. 2002 is 16 ft. 0 in.)

"A2/2" Class (Converted "P.2" Class)

afterwards wished that I had placed all cylinders in line, as with the later Peppercorn Pacifics.'

Trial and error is an essential part of any engineering project and it is interesting to note Thompson's thought processes when faced with technical data based on trials and in service experience. From this it is safe to assume that he wasn't a man who became fixated on one solution to the detriment of any other. After retirement, he carefully followed the progress of the work he had initiated and occasionally visited his old deputy, now CME, up until Peppercorn's own retirement. He seems to have held the younger man in high esteem and it is interesting to note that he saw the benefits of the modifications his successor approved.

The rebuilt engines included many other changes. Driven by the need to stop the chimney fouling the superheater assembly, the boiler was shortened by two feet and a longer smokebox fitted. At the same time, the boiler pressure was also increased from 220 to 225psi, so reflecting the work undertaken on the B1s.

Engine No. 2005, minus nameplates, as she appeared after rebuilding. She would run in this anonymous state from January 1943 until June 1944 when *Thane of Fife* was re-attached. The black colour scheme slowly emerged during the war as did 'NE' letters on the tender. A purely functional choice of colour, but some thought it sat well on the express engines it graced. (*PR/RH*)

All these changes left the firebox with the same heating area, but reduced the flues and tubes from 1,334.2sqft to 1,211.57sqft and 1,122.8sqft to 1,004.5sqft respectively. Likewise, the total evaporative and superheater surfaces were marginally smaller, which gave new totals of 3,490.5sqft for the P2 and 3,132.74sqft for the 'new' engine. With all these changes the tractive effort reduced from 43,452lb. to 40,318lb. but this was more than sufficient for any use to which the engines might be put.

A few months after the engine was turned out of the works at Doncaster, Thompson submitted a press release to the *Locomotive Magazine* describing the project. In this he highlighted some of the other changes made:

'The rigid wheelbase has been reduced from 19ft 6in. to 13ft., which gives the engine so much more freedom on the curves that abound on the LNER Scottish lines. The new bogie which takes the place of the existing pony truck and leading coupled wheels has the horns, stays, central control arrangements all of welded construction. The bogie is of the side support pattern, taking the weight of the main frame through the spherical surfaces on to bronze slippers. The centre line of these slippers is in direct line with the main bogie frame. The side control of the bogie is by means of helical springs, which give an initial control load of two tons, the maximum translation of the bogie being 4 in. either side of the engine centre line.

'The original engine already incorporated a spliced front end portion to the main frame, and the renewal of this front end only was necessary. The

frame immediately behind the original leading coupled wheels backward has been retained unaltered.

'The standard form of built-up crank axle, on which extensions to the webs formed balanced weights, has been retained, and the new eccentric, having a throw of 4½in., is fitted on the crank axle. The exhaust passage from the outside cylinders is taken outside the main frames to the inside cylinder casting, making a single blast pipe base in the smokebox to take a double blast pipe and chimney similar to that fitted to the other 2-8-2 engines in service in Scotland.'

Once conversion and a short running in period were completed, the engine was returned to traffic in Scotland in April, where she could be tested and compared to the five remaining P2s. She was simply designated Class A, reflecting the standardisation plan, but this was changed to A2 a little later and A2/2 shortly after the war ended. There are stories that this engine found no favour with Scottish crews, who preferred the Gresley engines. These may be true or may be apocryphal, but either way they are difficult to verify. However, Thompson seemed satisfied with the engine's early performance and was able to report this success to Matthews, Newton and the LNER's Board. In so doing, he sought permission to proceed with the conversion of the other P2s at an estimated cost of £2,400 per engine. In August approval was given, but for reasons that aren't clear work didn't begin for six months and then took until December 1944 to complete.

Now numbered 994, for a few weeks only, and with *Thane of Fife* plates restored, awaits release at Edinburgh Waverley. *(ET/DN)*

This photo of a converted P2 captures some aspects of remodelling in greater detail, particularly the configuration of the smokebox. (*AE*)

The prototype P2 re-enters service during September 1944 in her new guise. Although some think that the A2/2s lost much in looks during rebuilding the 'converteds' were, to my mind, still attractive and were clearly recognisable as Gresley engines. As always beauty is in the eye of the beholder so no one is either right or wrong when expressing a view. (*ET/DN*)

As 1943 gave way to 1944, Britain's railways faced an even greater burden. The war in Europe was reaching a crescendo as the Allies fought in Italy and prepared for the invasion of France. But of more immediate concern to the LNER was the support of the RAF and the US Army Air Force, which were pressing ahead with their massive bombing campaign against Germany. The vast majority of their airfields were along the East Coast and could only continue operations if regularly re-supplied by the railway. The loads moved were massive, with fuel, spares and weapons dominating traffic until the end of the war. Thompson's workshops were also working beyond normal capacity, surviving only by instituting round the clock working. It was at this point that he began sleeping at the office, taking few breaks and eschewing the comforts of his home in Wilfrids Road. In the 14-18 war he had gladly taken on the mantle of the dedicated soldier and his life in the Second World War reflected the same devotion to duty. For a man of his age it was quite remarkable, but inevitably the strain must have been considerable.

Yet he didn't break, though at times the pressure must have brought him close to collapse as it did many others. To a certain extent, planning for the future and developing his standardisation plan may have provided some light relief from the day to day battle to keep the railway running. It was more than an academic exercise, but only just with so few locomotives being constructed or converted as the war dragged on. The pace did pick up a bit after D Day, with victory seemingly drawing

nearer, but not enough to require great effort on the part of the CME or his Chief Draughtsman. And with this the next phase of the plan got underway.

With the P2 proving a success, in Thompson's eyes at least, and the remaining five due to be rebuilt, he decided to take the development of the Pacific Class a step further. With so many V2s in service, and with less pressure on the fleet of locomotives, the CME sought permission to take the last four V2s in the programme and build them as Pacifics. With lessons learnt from the P2/A2 programme he clearly felt it was time to experiment further in refining a standard class 4-6-2 engine.

When undertaking this work, the CME again fed information to the *Locomotive Magazine* describing the project, which the editor duly published:

'The last four of a batch of 25 V2s have been modified by Mr E. Thompson, CME, in the following way, and designated class A2/1.

'A bogie has been provided at the front end of the engine in place of the original pony truck. The two outside cylinders drive the middle pair of coupled wheels, the inside cylinder drives the leading pair of coupled wheels, and the valve gear for the middle cylinder is actuated by a third independent Walschaerts gear instead of the 2 to 1 lever arrangement as fitted to the original engines. The rods actuating the middle cylinder are identical in length with the rods actuating the two outside cylinders. The cut-off in full gear has been increased to 75 per cent.

'The modified construction of the former V2 class has been undertaken as a result of the rebuilding of the 2-8-2 locomotives of the company to the 4-6-2 wheel arrangement, with separate valve gear and the same cylinder positioning as this engine. The boiler of the engine is the standard V2 type with a grate area of 41.25sqft and a total heating surface of 3,110.74sqft. A modification has been made in that these four engines have been fitted with a complete rocking grate and hopper ashpan so that the ashes can be released without necessity for a man to go underneath the engine.

Above and overleaf: The bombing campaign by the RAF and USAAF in 1944 and '45 absorbed huge resources in men and material, the vast majority of which was pulled at some stage by the LNER. Thompson, as did the company's other senior managers, took a keen personal interest in this important work and was known to visit Command HQs and some of the bases to see for himself what was happening and assess what more could be done. The task of supporting both bomber fleets was immense and it is probably true to say that the huge number of new airfields that were needed couldn't have been built without the rail network. Once they were in existence trains were crucial to their continued operational role. For example, it can be shown that the LNER moved more than 30,000 tons of bombs to 15 USAAF airfields in three months between June and September 1944. And this was only a small part of their support task with every squadron involved consuming huge quantities of bombs, ammunition, stores and fuel in a relentless cycle of re-supply. These two photos, which the CME collected, just hint at the size of this daunting task as supplies are moved to support one operation by one squadron on one day in 1944. (*LJ/RH*)

'The cylinders are 19in. in diameter, compared to 18½in. for the V2, which increases the tractive effort from 33,730lb. to 36,387lb. in the engine thus constructed. The bogie is identical with that fitted to the B1 4-6-0 locomotive and the whole bogie stays and spring bracket are constructed by welding. The front end boiler supporting stay, quadrant link brackets and footplate brackets are also welded structures.'

Once completed, and after a short running in period, the four engines were allocated to Darlington shed, but then 3696, *Highland Chieftain* and 3697, *Duke of Rothesay* were moved to King's Cross. At the same time 3968, *Waverley* and 3699, *Robert the Bruce* found themselves at Haymarket.

From these two locations they found regular employment along the East Coast main line where they proved to be 'reliable but unspectacular performers'. They would undergo some minor modifications over the years, the most notable being the removal of the wing type smoke deflectors and their replacement with a larger, more traditional type.

Thompson probably learnt little from these engines that he hadn't already picked up from the P2 programme. But it was a stepping stone nonetheless, helping him and the Chief Draughtsman understand how the standard class Pacific might eventually appear. However, before the next phase of this programme could begin, there were other ideas to explore as the overall development plan came together.

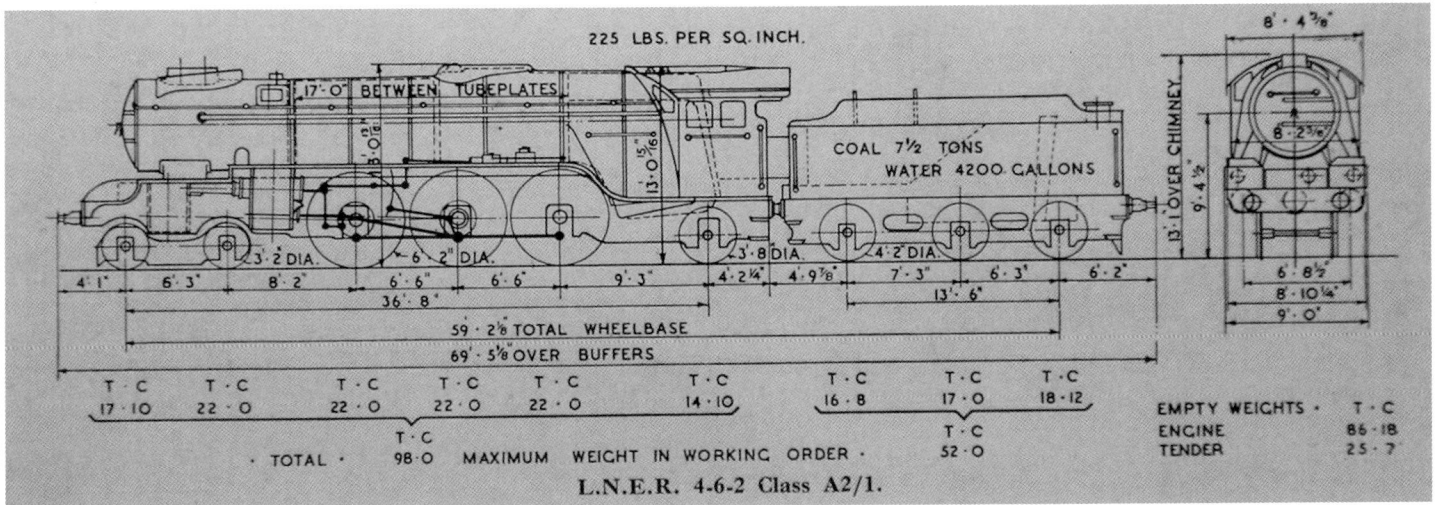

225 LBS. PER SQ. INCH.

L.N.E.R. 4-6-2 Class A2/1.

The A2/1's diagram and specification as published in July 1944. They retained the six wheeled tenders that accompanied the V2s but these were found to be lacking in capacity and so eight wheeled tenders were eventually attached, one of them from A4 No. 4469 which had been written off following bomb damage at York in April 1942.

L.N.E.R. 4-6-2 Class A2/1 No. 3696.

BOILER :
Maximum diameter of barrel ... 6ft. 5in.
Overall length of firebox .... 9ft. 5⅝in.
Overall l'gth of firebox at bottom 6ft. 8in.
Overall width of firebox at bottom 7ft. 9in.
Thickness of—
Barrel plates ...... 23/32in. and 25/32in.
Outside wrapper .... 9/16in.
Copper firebox plates—
Wrapper and backplate .... 9/16in.
Tubeplate .... 9/16in. and 1⅛in.
TUBES :
Small—
Number 121
Diameter outside .... 2¼in.
Superheater flue—
Number 43
Diameter outside .... 5⅛in.
Superheater elements—
Number 43
Diameter inside .... 1.244in.

GRATE : Area .... 41.25 sq. ft.
HEATING SURFACE :
Firebox 215   „   „
Tubes .... 1,211.57   „   „
Flues .... 1,004.5   „   „

Total evaporative .... 2,431.07   „   „
Superheater .... 679.67   „   „

Total .... 3,110.74   „   „

AXLES :
Journals—   Dia. Length
Bogie .... 6½in. by 9in.
Coupled wheels .... 9½in. by 11in.
Trailing wheels .... 6in. by 11in.
Crankpins—
Outside .... 5½in. by 6in.
Inside .... 8¼in. by 6in.

Coupling pins—
Leading .... 4⅛in. by 3⅛in.
Intermediate .... 6in. by 4⅛in.
Trailing .... 4in. by 4⅛in.
CYLINDERS :
Number 3
Diameter and stroke .... 19in. by 26in.
MOTION :
Type (inside and outside) ... Walschaerts
Type of valve .... Piston
Diameter of valve .... 10in.
Maximum valve travel .... 6⅜in.
Steam lap (inside and outside cyls.) 1⅝in.
Cut-off in full gear .... 75 per cent.
TRACTIVE EFFORT at 85 per cent.
boiler pressure .... 36,387lb.
TOTAL ADHESIVE WEIGHT ... 147,840lb.
ADHESIVE WEIGHT divided by
TRACTIVE EFFORT 4.06
BRAKE ... Steam brake and vacuum ejector

Above and overleaf: Engines 3696 and 3698 as they appeared when leaving the works at Darlington in May and November 1944 respectively. (*ET/DN*)

Two pictures showing the cab layout of an A2/1, highlighting newly installed, and experimental electrical equipment. Under Thompson's leadership there were a number of modifications such as this to improve the working conditions of the footplate crew. All these developments were duly written up in the *Locomotive Magazine* beginning with the words 'To overcome the disadvantages of oil burning headlights and to provide engine crews with illuminated gauges and control points in cabs, the LNER has evolved a system of electric lighting in conjunction with Metro Vickers Electrical Co Ltd. Four Class A2/1 Pacific locomotives are to be provided with this equipment as an experiment'. (*ET/DN*)

A2/1 now numbered 508 (*Duke of Rothesay*) and fitted with more conventional smoke deflectors is captured at Potters Bar with an 'up express' shortly after the war. (*PR/RH*)

And these weren't all related to the locomotive fleet, because most of Thompson's efforts were still directed towards the workshops and the role they played in keeping the railway going at a critical time. As a production engineer, he was constantly searching for ways of improving flow rates and identifying pinch points. One issue that taxed him was the inability of the running sheds to undertake some repairs. It was an issue that E.S. Beavor highlighted when describing problems shed fitters had when maintaining engines fitted with the conjugated valve gear. Thompson sought improvements, but the problem wasn't satisfactorily resolved in his time, perhaps due to staff shortages and other priorities, so remained a cause of unnecessary downtime. But there were some successes and two reports have surfaced suggesting that improved support at the sheds did enhance availability of the A4s in particular.

Wartime working conditions, particularly during the hours of darkness, always created difficulties when servicing engines. To try and alleviate this problem Thompson and his team used their powers of invention and improvisation. One interesting example of this was the 'Light Tunnel' introduced in late 1943 to speed up the servicing of locomotives overnight. In the blackout this had become increasingly difficult and pre-fabricated pod shaped buildings, with openings at both ends, were introduced. In these structures, a loco could be placed, in steam over a pit in well-lit conditions for examination. They proved successful and remained in service until the end of the war.

Perhaps of greater significance to the maintenance programme was a system developed under Thompson's guiding hand and given the title of 'Rapid Repair of Locomotives'. For a long time, he had tried to cut down the time taken for an engine to be stripped, repaired and returned to traffic. By 1943, these efforts had resulted in a streamlined process, described in some detail in the *Locomotive Magazine*, which reduced the turn round time to a mere sixteen days, when before it had been more than thirty. It was an achievement that drew a positive response from the REC and the Mount Committee, both of which had been highly critical of each company's performance.

Another development of note concerned boiler repairs. It was a newly introduced scheme which:

'Embodied the use of gantry structures for containing the boilers during the operation of stay drilling, tapping and stay running-in, which operations are carried out by the use of portable electric machines of high frequency. The various repair stages are arranged in line to form a progressive process and boilers of all sizes are inverted during the process in order to give maximum accessibility to all parts during repair.

'By this process much time and transport is saved, compared with previous practice, which necessitated moving the boilers from one shop to another for repairs after stripping and prior to replacement in the engine frames. The whole process is now carried out in one shop, with further time saved by having all tools fixed in position available for immediate use.'

When assessing a person's reputation or their achievements, it is often the case that the mundane or ordinary is overlooked. Yet it is often on the successful accomplishment of such things that a company's profit and future rests. Without a sound, well run organisation, a skilled properly directed workforce or the application of effective production and maintenance practices a business will fail; this despite its effectiveness in designing such things as locomotives. Thompson, I believe, represented this less glamorous side of business. Yet all the work he did in making the LNER's workshops run effectively, and in seeking standardisation, proved as important to the company's success as that of any of his contemporaries. Thompson may not have been a locomotive designer of great note, but his eye for detail, matched to keen analytical skills, a common sense approach and sharp management abilities paid dividends in areas of work essential to success in peace and war. Latterly, he is judged by his locomotive projects, but to truly gauge his abilities and achievement you must look more broadly at all his accomplishments.

Although the war was drawing to a close, the pace of work within the LNER didn't slacken, if anything it increased as the fighting reached a crescendo. But with a return to peace growing daily more likely, plans for the future were drawn more clearly into focus. With this in mind, Thompson continued developing his standardisation plans in the hope that implementation would soon become a reality. And here his thoughts on a heavy goods engine are of interest especially as they focussed on a Class which had featured in his life since the 14-18 war – the 1911 Robinson designed two-cylinder 2-8-0 O4s. By 1944, the LNER still had a substantial number of

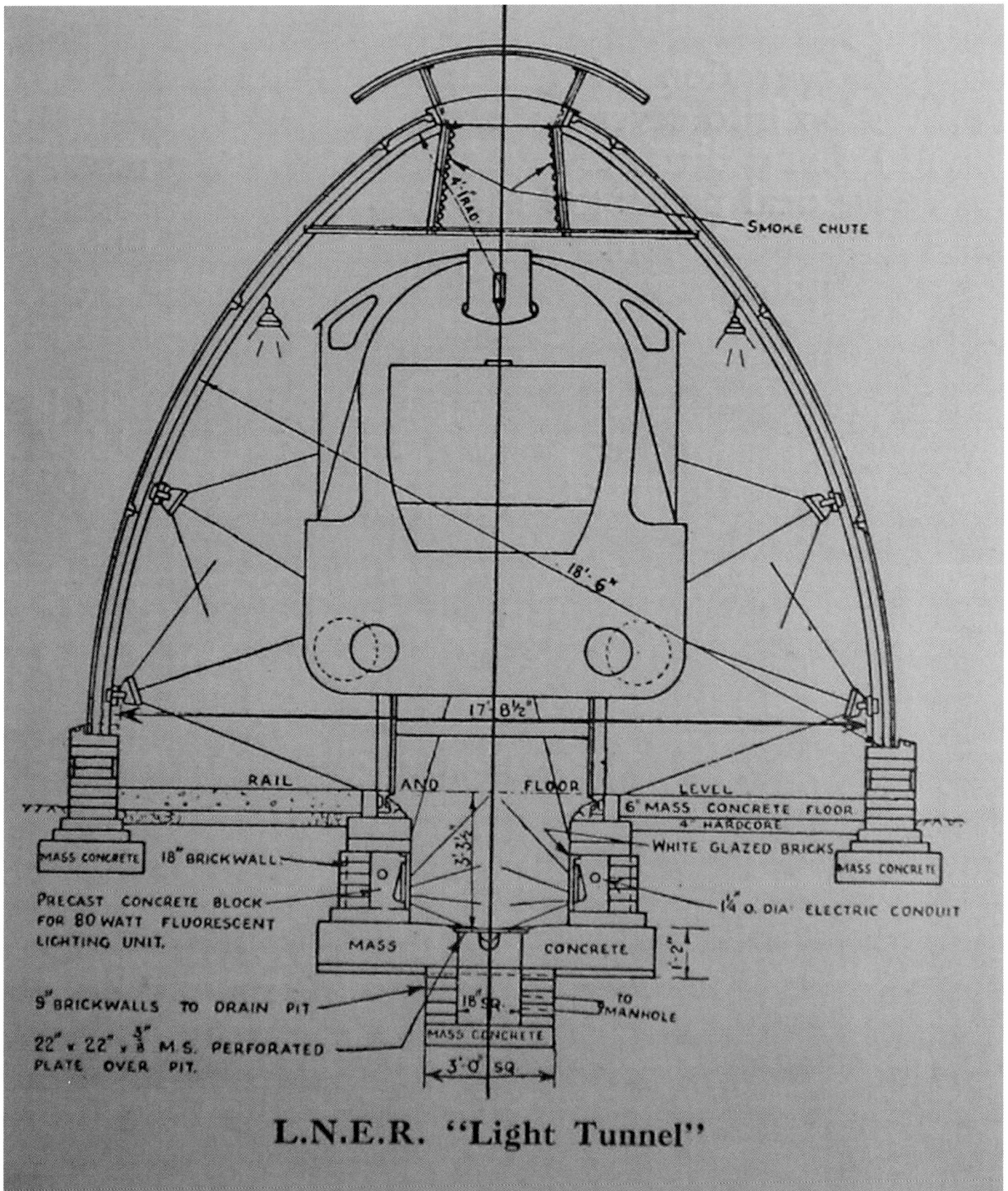

SMOKE CHUTE

18'-6"

17' 8½"

RAIL AND FLOOR LEVEL

6" MASS CONCRETE FLOOR
4" HARDCORE

MASS CONCRETE 18" BRICKWALL

WHITE GLAZED BRICKS

MASS CONCRETE

PRECAST CONCRETE BLOCK
FOR 80 WATT FLUORESCENT
LIGHTING UNIT.

1¼" O. DIA· ELECTRIC CONDUIT

MASS   CONCRETE

9" BRICKWALLS TO DRAIN PIT

TO MANHOLE

22" × 22" × ⅜" M.S. PERFORATED
PLATE OVER PIT.

18" SQ
MASS CONCRETE

3'·0" SQ

L.N.E.R. "Light Tunnel"

The 'Light Tunnel', a simple cost effective solution to a pressing problem designed and introduced by Thompson and his team.

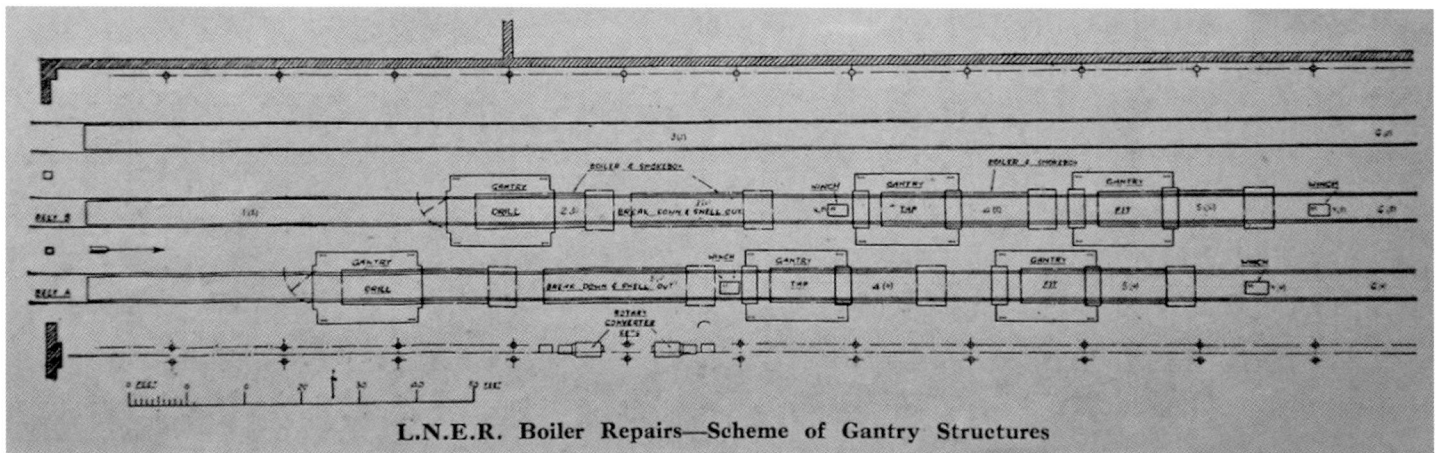

L.N.E.R. Boiler Repairs—Scheme of Gantry Structures

Another Thompson-run workshop programme inspired by Henry Ford's production line techniques. Here boilers are stripped and repaired in a compact, well designed facility. (*ET/DN*)

these locomotives in service, some having already been modified under Gresley's guiding hands, but whether they were an ideal class on which to base a future development programme was quite another thing. So Windle set to work applying Thompson's ideas and the first of the conversions appeared in

early 1944 as the Class 01. Over the next five years another fifty-seven would be built.

The frames and wheels were retained but the boiler and cylinders were changed to mirror those applied to the B1s, with Walschaert valve gear added. A new cab and a raised running plate were also included in the design.

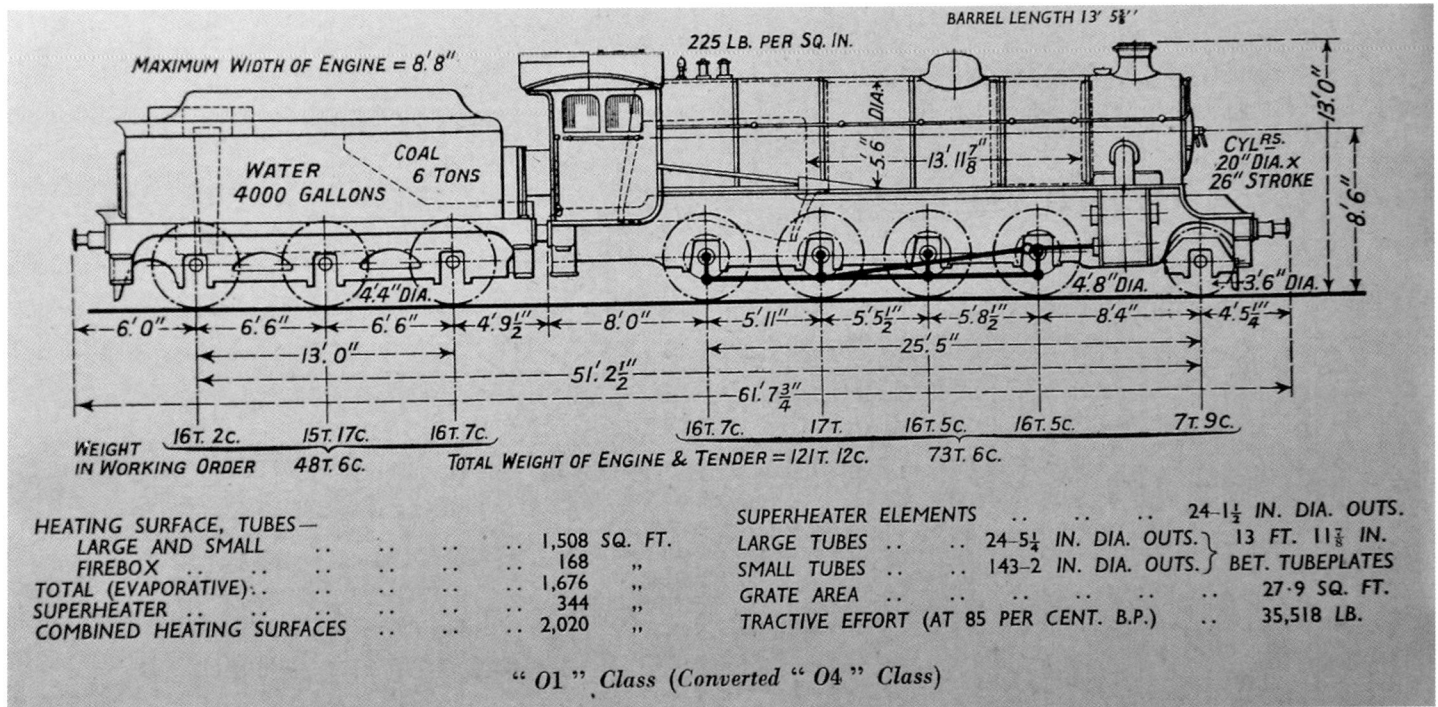

MAXIMUM WIDTH OF ENGINE = 8' 8"
225 LB. PER SQ. IN.
BARREL LENGTH 13' 5⅛"

WATER 4000 GALLONS | COAL 6 TONS
CYLRS. 20" DIA. X 26" STROKE

HEATING SURFACE, TUBES—					
LARGE AND SMALL				1,508 SQ. FT.
FIREBOX				168 "
TOTAL (EVAPORATIVE)				1,676 "
SUPERHEATER				344 "
COMBINED HEATING SURFACES				2,020 "

SUPERHEATER ELEMENTS .. .. .. 24-1½ IN. DIA. OUTS.
LARGE TUBES .. .. 24-5¼ IN. DIA. OUTS. ⎫ 13 FT. 11⅞ IN.
SMALL TUBES .. .. 143-2 IN. DIA. OUTS. ⎬ BET. TUBEPLATES
GRATE AREA .. .. 27·9 SQ. FT.
TRACTIVE EFFORT (AT 85 PER CENT. B.P.) .. 35,518 LB.

"01" Class (Converted "04" Class)

The Class O1 from diagram to reality – in this case engine No. 6216 which emerged from Gorton works in January 1946. She would remain in service until November 1962. Some would last longer and still be going in 1964-65, suggesting that the design was a success. (ET/DN)

Whilst this was happening, another proposal was pursued that saw other O4s upgraded, but staying largely as inherited by Thompson. A group of these engines would receive the new cabs and B1 type boiler only. In this guise, ninety-nine would be rebuilt between 1944 and 1957, becoming O4/8s in the process.

Throughout Thompson's time as CME the A4s continued to ply their trade successfully without significant modification being attempted. Throughout this period, the CME continued to take a benign interest in them, which must have surprised those ready to accuse him of challenging and damaging Gresley's legacy. But he was the first to recognise good design and if it worked effectively to leave well alone until forced to intervene in some way. So, during 1942, in response to growing concerns about the A4s' ability to start with very heavy wartime loads, he took action and issued a memo authorising an 'increase in the valve travel from 5¾in. to 6¾in., in full forward gear. Once completed this should allow the cut-off position to be advanced from 65 per cent to 75 per cent and, in theory, improve these engines' performance'. The first engine, No. 4499, was modified in March 1943, with five more completed by July 1944 after tests confirmed some improvements in performance. This work resumed in early 1946, but it took until 1957 for all the class to be converted, suggesting that peacetime loads were smaller and within the capabilities of the class.

If the A4s survived Thompson's attention, another of Gresley's Pacifics fared less well. By 1944, his pioneering A1s (now designated A10s) were all approaching twenty years of age or more. Like most locomotives of the time, they had become the worse for wear due to the heavy demands of war and minimal maintenance. It is inevitable that high performance engines such as the Pacifics

Engine No. 3755 as she appeared in 1946. Up to that time she had carried the number 6578. This locomotive spent her life as a Class O1 in the North-East until condemned in November 1962. (*PR/RH*)

should suffer more than other types because they tended to be worked to their maximum capacity over prolonged periods. Some of them had been modified to reflect the changes introduced when the A3s appeared in late 1928. This work actually began in July 1927, but only proceeded at a snail's pace with the bulk of the engines only being modified under Thompson's guiding hand. For some reason, No. 4470 *Great Northern* wasn't included and by 1944 was reported by Richard Hardy as being 'an average old tub with nothing much to write home about at that time – a low pressure A1 rarely used on the heaviest jobs.'

So despite being the first of Gresley's Pacifics, she had become no more than just another engine that had slipped down the pecking order. In this guise, she became a candidate for rebuilding and a controversy was born, fuelled by the knowledge that *Great Northern*'s competitor in 1922, Raven's Pacifics, had ended their days ignominiously in Gresley's hands only a few years earlier. It was an injustice that was supposed to have festered in Thompson's mind, who, when an opportunity arose took his revenge by destroying Gresley's masterpiece. As a work of fiction it has many merits – clichés, a hero and a villain determined to do his worst. But the reality of life in a hardnosed, unsentimental business trying to survive in turbulent times is very different from the neat world of fiction. If there was any truth to these stories, then Thompson could have chosen far more important targets to reconstruct than one tired old engine – the A4s or A3s for example. But his continued support of both types and his lack of meddling in either design suggests a clearer, more honourable motivation.

Engine No. 4464, *Bittern*, painted black for wartime use and safe in Thompson's hands. In 1947 she was painted garter blue at the end of a period of General Repair and renumbered '19'. Following nationalisation, she became No. 60019 and she would survive in service until September 1966, when sold for preservation. (*ET/RH*)

Above and below: Engine No. 1470, the first of a class as she appeared when built to Gresley's design for the GNR in 1922. (*PR/RH/DN*)

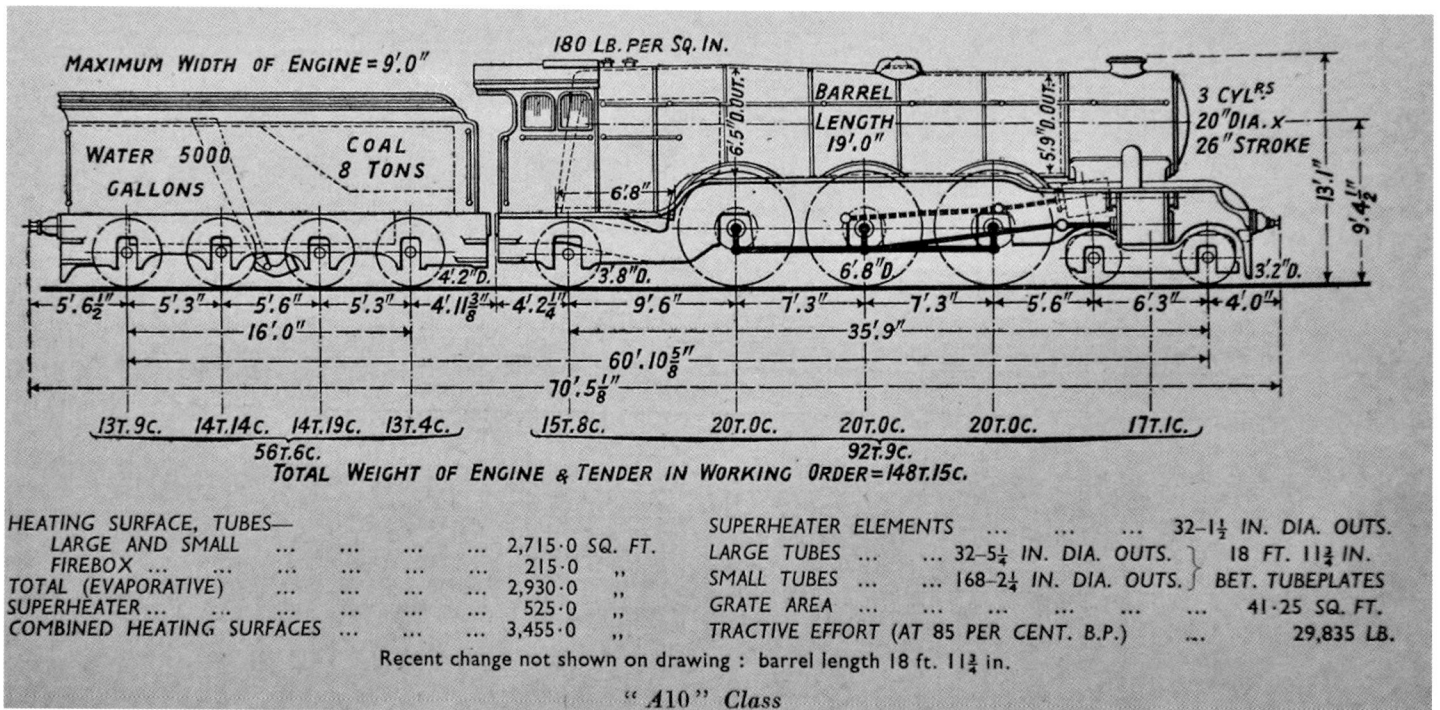

HEATING SURFACE, TUBES—
LARGE AND SMALL ... ... 2,715·0 SQ. FT.
FIREBOX ... ... 215·0 ,,
TOTAL (EVAPORATIVE) ... ... 2,930·0 ,,
SUPERHEATER ... ... 525·0 ,,
COMBINED HEATING SURFACES ... ... 3,455·0 ,,

SUPERHEATER ELEMENTS ... ... 32–1½ IN. DIA. OUTS.
LARGE TUBES ... ... 32–5¼ IN. DIA. OUTS. ⎱ 18 FT. 11¾ IN.
SMALL TUBES ... ... 168–2¼ IN. DIA. OUTS. ⎰ BET. TUBEPLATES
GRATE AREA ... ... 41·25 SQ. FT.
TRACTIVE EFFORT (AT 85 PER CENT. B.P.) ... 29,835 LB.

Recent change not shown on drawing : barrel length 18 ft. 11¾ in.

" *A10* " *Class*

The only real issue seems to have been whether to upgrade this engine to A3 standard or let her become an experiment in producing a standard class Pacific at minimal cost, mirroring Thompson's other work. On face value, neither of these options seem to be contentious issues. But it is the choice of 4470 which appears to have raised eyebrows when another, less historically important, engine might have been chosen instead. There are some hazy, unconfirmed reports that Thompson selected 4470 deliberately against advice with Edward Windle possibly pleading the case for an alternative. Unfortunately,

Windle doesn't appear to have recorded his memories or thoughts so only conjecture remains. The only reliable source of information that can be quoted with any certainty remains Richard Hardy, who by 1944 had progressed to the drawing office at Doncaster when the 4470 project was in hand. He later recalled in a letter that:

'The drawing office team were a hard bitten group of engineers and never a word did I hear regarding the selection of No. 4470 for rebuilding. Most of them, including Windle, were steeped in the

Gresley tradition but the choice of this engine meant nothing to them at the time. As for me I was a 21-year-old and full of romantic ideas about engines, foot-platemen and running sheds – the practical life. I was acquainted with 100s of engines on a personal basis from Pacifics to C12s, GN Atlantics and all the lusty Great Central designs. So if anybody should have got uptight, it should have been me – and I never gave it a second thought….she wasn't one of the best anyway.

'Maybe Edward Thompson did refuse to change the number that had been submitted to him, based on which engines were due for a heavy general repair.

When a locomotive was required for a special event or for rebuilding, the Running Superintendent, in this case George Musgrave, would be asked to nominate an engine. It is quite likely that a tidy minded clerk at Gerrard's Cross put together the number of the first of the bunch and why not? A letter would be written, the selection approved and by the time the news reached Thompson, the die had been cast. It is possible that Windle did remonstrate with ET over the choice and it is equally possible that his chief told him that 4470 was Musgrave's choice and that would have been an end to it. We have no means of knowing otherwise today but

One of *Great Northern*'s surviving Repair Cards which came up for sale with Sheffield Railwayana Auctions. Others may exist but a complete file of her maintenance records has yet to come to light and may have been destroyed when main line steam locomotion came to an end. (*THG*)

TYPE A-1.

250 LBS PER SQ IN.

COAL 9 TONS.

WATER 5000 GALLS

LEADING DIMENSIONS & RATIOS

BOILER:		CYLINDERS:
MAX DIA OF BARREL — 6'-5	GRATE AREA — 41.25 SQ FT	NUMBER — 3
OVERALL LENGTH OF FIREBOX — 10'-5½	HEATING SURFACE: FIREBOX — 231.2	DIAMETER & STROKE 19 × 26
" " " AT BOTTOM — 6'-8	TUBES — 1281.4	MOTION: TYPE. OUTSIDE WALSCHAERT
" WIDTH — 7'-9	FLUES — 1063.7	INSIDE
THICKNESS OF BARREL PLATES ⅞ & 9/16	TOTAL EVAPORATIVE — 2576.3	TYPE OF VALVE. PISTON
" OUTSIDE WRAPPER 9/16	SUPERHEATER — 748.9	DIA. " — 10
" COPPER FIREBOX PLATES	— 3325.2	MAX VALVE TRAVEL 6¾
WRAPPER & BACKPLATE 7/16		STEAM LAP INSIDE CYL 1⅝
TUBEPLATE 9/16 & 1¼		" OUTSIDE ⅝
TUBES: SMALL. NUMBER 121		CUT-OFF IN FULL GEAR 75%
DIA. OUTSIDE 2¼		TRACTIVE EFFORT AT 85% BOILER PRESS
SUPERHEATER FLUE NUMBER 43		37,400 LB
DIA. OUTSIDE 5¼		TOTAL ADHESIVE WEIGHT 147,840 LB
SUPERHEATER ELEMENTS NUMBER 43	SAFETY VALVES	ADHESIVE WEIGHT: TRACTIVE EFFORT 3.9
DIA. INSIDE 1.244	TYPE & DIAMETER TWO ROSS POP 3½ DIA	BRAKE: STEAM BRAKE

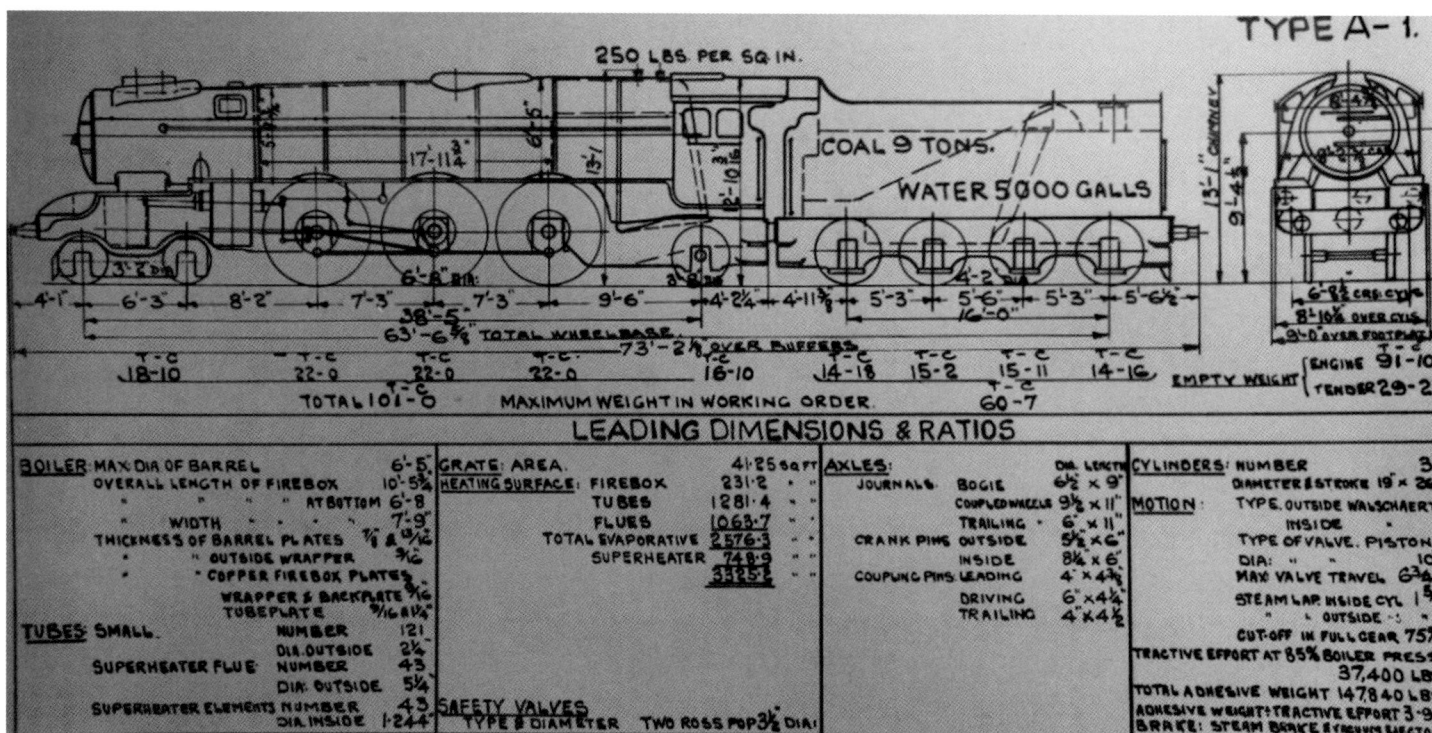

The plan for engine No. 4470 comes to fruition. To some it was sacrilege but to me the engine, though different, was nonetheless striking in appearance and still demonstrably a Gresley styled engine.

this is how a choice would normally have been made and how railwaymen behaved in the real world. Apart from anything the war was still at its height and the pressure was so intense on ET that I doubt if he had enough time to eat or rest let alone plot such an act.'

Wherever the truth lies, No. 4470 was selected, potentially the first of a number of A10s that might eventually be rebuilt. Planning took some months and in due course, drawings and a diagram appeared incorporating many of the ideas that Thompson and Windle had been developing over the previous two years. But in this process there was also time to consider the question of aerodynamics, which brought into play Bert Spencer. The outline standardisation plan had forecast a potential need for such engines and now some plans were laid down including proposals for streamlining.

No. 4470 entered the workshops at Doncaster on 1 May 1945 and emerged in her new guise on 25 September. It is reported that very little of the engine was re-used, but this may be a slight exaggeration. There were new frames and an A4 boiler (No.9487) producing 250psi amongst other things, but a lot else was retained including the high sided,

eight wheeled tender (No. 5582), which had been attached to this engine in 1937. To improve the engine's performance, the number of superheater elements was increased from 32 to 43, the tractive effort went from 29,835 to 37,397lb. and the coal capacity was marginally increased from 8 tons to 9 tons in an effort to increase her range. The wing type smoke deflectors that had become a familiar sight on the A2/1s and A2/2s gave way to a larger type of 'plate for preventing down draught'. In practice, the small wings had been criticised by footplate crew for not lifting the exhaust away from the engine causing a visibility problem. In due course, the A2/1s would have the larger deflectors added, though of a slightly different pattern, whilst the A2/2s would stay as rebuilt until scrapped in the 1960s.

In October, the intention was that some of the remaining A10s would follow 4470. But with the war ending, the restrictions on funding were lifted, to a certain extent, and new locomotives could once again be built. So rather than rebuild more A10s, Thompson sought approval from the Locomotive Committee to construct sixteen new A1s instead. They agreed with this proposal and also to continue upgrading A10s to A3 standard.

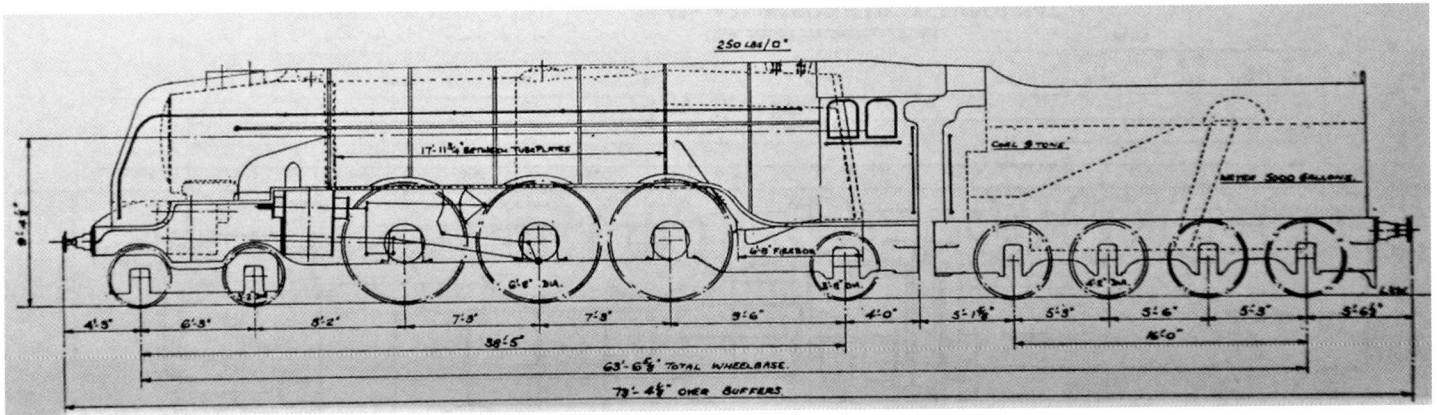

An initial attempt at streamlining an A1 that appeared in 1945. The position of the outside cylinders suggests that this design followed the ideas used when the P2s were converted and the A2/1s were built. It is unclear whether there was any serious intention of building 4470 in this form, but design work continued in the belief that other A10 rebuilds might materialise as air-smoothed engines.

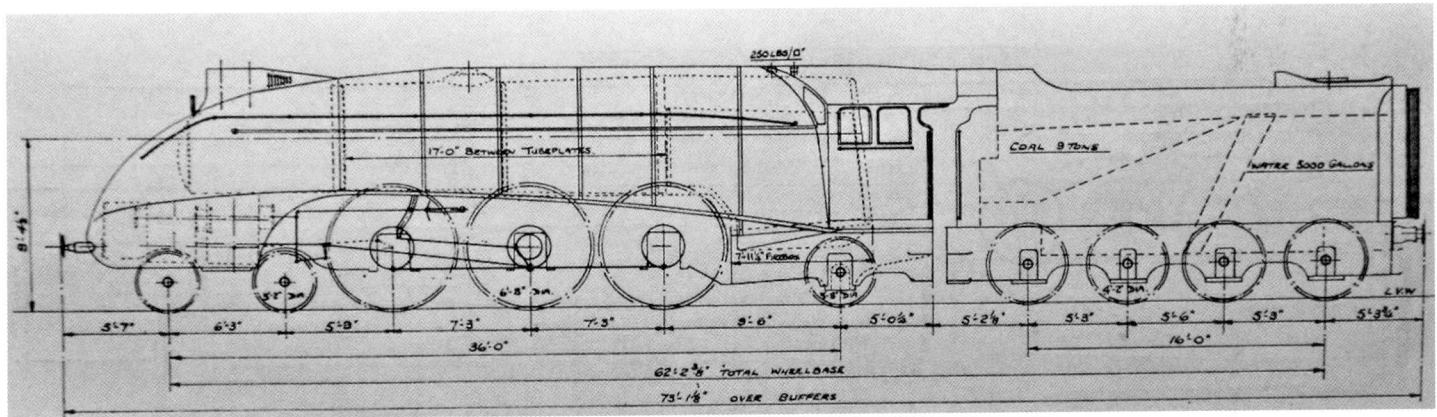

A little later the drawing office produced an A1 streamlined proposal close to the A4 model with cylinders further forward over the front truck. Bert Spencer would later write 'the CME was fully involved in this work and seemed content to press ahead with the stream-lining proposals for the 4-6-2 and even Gresley's 4-8-4 pre-war design, though there was no serious intention to build the latter'. Yet Thompson was 'reliably' quoted as saying no more streamlined engines!

Right and overleaf above: Although dated 1947 these models are recorded as having been built in late 1945 to test some of the stream-lining proposals then being considered. The work was quietly dropped after Thompson's retirement and was never resurrected, new Pacifics being built by Peppercorn proceeded along more traditional lines. It is rumoured, but unconfirmed, that several of these models sat in Thompson's office. (*ET/DN*)

No. 4470's reconstruction proceeds apace at Doncaster. (*ET/DN*)

According to a summary contained in the RCTS's influential 1973 publication that focused on the LNER's Pacifics, *Great Northern* was thought to be a better engine rebuilt than she was as an A10. But then they went further and judged that its performance was superior to the average A3 or A4 of the day, before all were fitted with the Kylchap exhaust system. So, on this basis, reconstruction seems to have been justified. But more proof of this had to wait until a full testing programme could be initiated and it took until

1947 for this to happen. By then Thompson had retired and played no part in these process, so it was left to his successor to oversee the validation of this reconstruction work.

In terms of serviceability, the engine's first twelve months of operations showed a moderate amount of time in the workshops – six brief visits for minor maintenance, not unusual for a new engine. But of more concern was an apparent weakness in the front end of the frames caused, it seems, by vibration and the positioning of the cylinders.

(Above and right) 4470 emerges from the workshops and is fired up to begin a period of test before being allocated to King's Cross in October 1945. Shortly afterwards she would receive her new deflectors. (*ET/DN/RH*)

Strangely enough this reflected a problem found with Stanier's Princess Royal Pacifics, which had a similar stretched look and outside cylinders positioned aft of the leading truck. To correct this defect, the front frames were cut back and new sections fitted, but this didn't eradicate the problem entirely and the high stresses imposed still caused problems. It was a problem that was only truly resolved when Tom Coleman took the design and developed it into the Princess Coronation Class. Peppercorn would, as CME, find a similar solution when later building more Pacifics for the LNER.

As an experiment, the *Great Northern* project proved of some value and was part of a process which would evolve into Thompson's A2/3s and Peppercorn's A1s and A2s in time. But was the programme cultural vandalism as some have suggested, conducted out of spite on Thompson's part or simply a valid engineering project? The evidence in either case is slight, with many stories seeming to be apocryphal or simply unsubstantiated conjecture. Finding a way through this mass of often conflicting material so long after the event is difficult, but Richard Hardy's assessment has a ring of truth. To me, Thompson's programme wasn't engendered by malice; if so, he would surely have seen the A3s or A4s as better targets. The fact that he left them alone and continued to support the A10s' upgrade to A3 standard speaks volumes. But there is another point to consider in all this. Thompson, as he recorded later, admired Gresley greatly. What he respected less was his predecessor's often rigid, inflexible approach to the question of cylinder numbers and the 2-to-1 solution which seemed to dominate his designs. If anything, Thompson was prepared to look more widely, select the best from Gresley's work and experiment with other ideas in an effort to improve the breed. He wasn't always successful and lacked the design skills of his predecessor but at least he tried hard in very difficult circumstances.

May 1948 and *Great Northern*, now under BR ownership but carrying number 113 which she received in October 1946. She will be renumbered 60113 five months after this picture was taken. Here she makes ready to depart from King's Cross pulling the prestigious Yorkshire Pullman. It seems that this was to become one of her regular turns. *(PR/RH)*

Now numbered 60113 and in BR service. In this guise she lasted until November 1962 before being condemned and scrapped. (*THG*)

During the war years everybody with a garden or an allotment was encouraged to grow their own vegetables or keep poultry in a bid to eke out their rations. The LNER actively supported this as this photo bears witness – Thompson and Thomas Cameron, Regional Divisional Manager Scotland, lean on the fence whilst Charles Newton superintendents the 'workers' on an allotment created 'somewhere in Southern England' though in reality at the LNER's wartime HQ at Hoo. (*THG*)

Before moving on to describe Thompson's final years as CME I think it worth recording Hardy's last words on this subject, in which he contemplated this issue and the question of double standards:

'Had a drastic rebuild of an Ivatt Atlantic been contemplated in Gresley's day, nobody would have lost any sleep if No. 3251, the original 1902 engine, had been chosen. Did anyone bat an eyelid when No. 8900 *Claud Hamilton*, the first and famous GE 'Claud', was selected in 1933 for the first comprehensive rebuild to Class D16/3 and stripped of all its glorious brasswork. Of course not!'

Although the needs of war and locomotive development and maintenance programmes tended to dominate Thompson's schedule, there were other projects in which he was involved. Two of these are of particular note. One because it related to the war, the other to peace. Rolling stock was as important to the war effort as the locomotives. Having the correct quantities and varieties was enormously important if the military were to be adequately supported on many fronts. The LNER even produced hospital trains to support the American Army and assigned B12 engines to pull them, no matter in which region they might be needed. Following D Day, with casualties steadily mounting, these trains proved crucial in moving large numbers of wounded soldiers to hospitals across the country; all duly reported in the LNER's *Journal*. In 1945, Thompson took on another important task, because of the company's proven ability to support the USAAF as well as the US Army over the previous two years.

With the Allies pushing the German Army back across Western Europe, General Eisenhower and his staff needed a mobile command centre to help control events. To achieve this, it was deemed essential for a carriage to be provided and to the LNER fell the honour of producing a suitable vehicle for use at the Front. In many ways, this was reminiscent of carriages and trains produced for service in France and Belgium during the Great War, one of which was used regularly by Thompson's old friend Cecil Paget. But in this case, the level of fittings and protection were much greater. To this end, the carriage was heavily armour-plated, with bullet-proof glass and strengthened shutters and ventilators provided. It was also fitted with sufficient communications equipment to allow Eisenhower to stay in contact with his generals

and it also retained six pre-war sleeping berths, with shower and toilet facilities added. When last heard of it was reported as being 'somewhere in Europe' and seems to have found a role in post-war Germany as the allies sought to bring order to a defeated country.

As this wartime project came to an end, the thoughts of the LNER turned towards peace and the need for new carriages to meet future demand. Here Thompson's work would prove important, especially as it harked back to his correspondence and discussions with Gresley before the Great War. In the debates that followed, the need to strengthen carriages by using steel was a central theme. But change was slow in coming, despite the pressing safety issues, but in 1944-45, some of Thompson's thoughts and beliefs finally found a voice. However, the publicity produced by the LNER to mark the introduction of new carriages tended to focus on improved access, quality of fittings, better views of the passing countryside and ease of access. For some reason, they felt no need to add an assessment of their improved strength and ability to better survive an accident. Nevertheless, these were key issues that had played on Thompson's mind for many years. But it was a developing science that would only gain added strength in the post-war years as one serious accident followed another. The legacy of Harrow, Lewisham, Lichfield and many other incidents would continue to highlight an issue of which Thompson had been aware of most of his adult life and sought to improve.

As the war ended, the CME prepared for a final flourish of activity before retiring. With twelve months or so to go, he clearly wished to pull together all the strands of his standardisation plan and set out a clear policy for the future. But an even bigger change was taking place in 1945 that might negate all these efforts. A landslide General Election victory for the Labour party on 26 July announced an age of nationalisation for key industries and it soon became apparent that the railways would be absorbed in this massive programme.

With no clear statement of policy immediately emanating from their political masters and with uncertainty over which direction might be taken, there was no alternative but to press on as before. So Thompson continued with his experiments on existing classes – the K3, K4, B16 and B17 in particular. In addition, he set in motion the next stage of his Pacific programme and put in place his final selection of types for inclusion in his standardisation plan, including one new class, the L1.

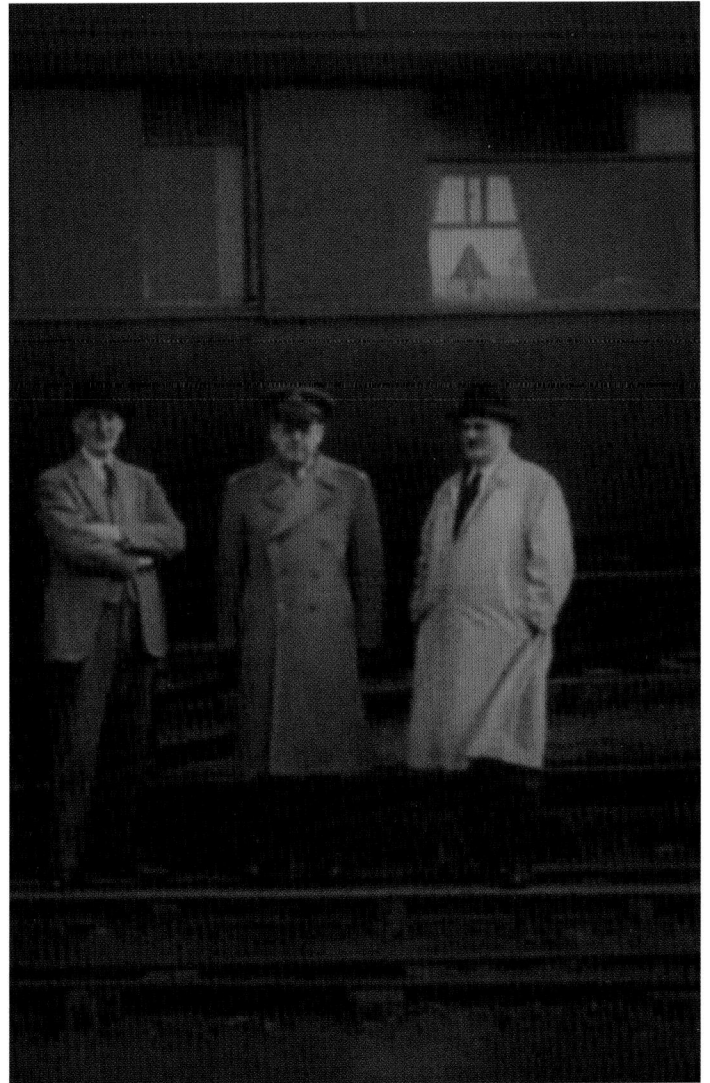

Supreme Headquarters
ALLIED EXPEDITIONARY FORCE
Office of the Supreme Commander

15 April, 1945.

Dear Sir Ronald.

I must write to thank you personally, as
Chairman of The London and North Eastern
Railway, and all those members of your staff
who have done such fine work on the new
"Bayonet". I am indeed grateful to you.

Would you please extend my special thanks to
Mr. E. Thompson and Mr. A. H. Peppercorn, the
Chief and Assistant Chief Mechanical Engineers
at Doncaster, who rendered such invaluable assistance to Colonel Bingham.

The wholehearted cooperation of the British
Railways at all times during this war will
always stand out as one of the finest examples
of Anglo-Americanism.

With renewed thanks.

Sincerely
Dwight Eisenhower

Sir Ronald W. Matthews
Lime Tree Cottage
Letwell
Nr. Worksop
Notts., England

A rather different task for Thompson and his team to handle – production of a command and control vehicle to accommodate the Allied Supreme Commander, Dwight D. Eisenhower, whilst in Europe. Copies of the letter from Eisenhower were circulated widely across the LNER as were the photographs of the carriage's compartments and of Thompson and Peppercorn posing with Colonel Bingham, who acted as liaison officer during construction. (ET/DN)

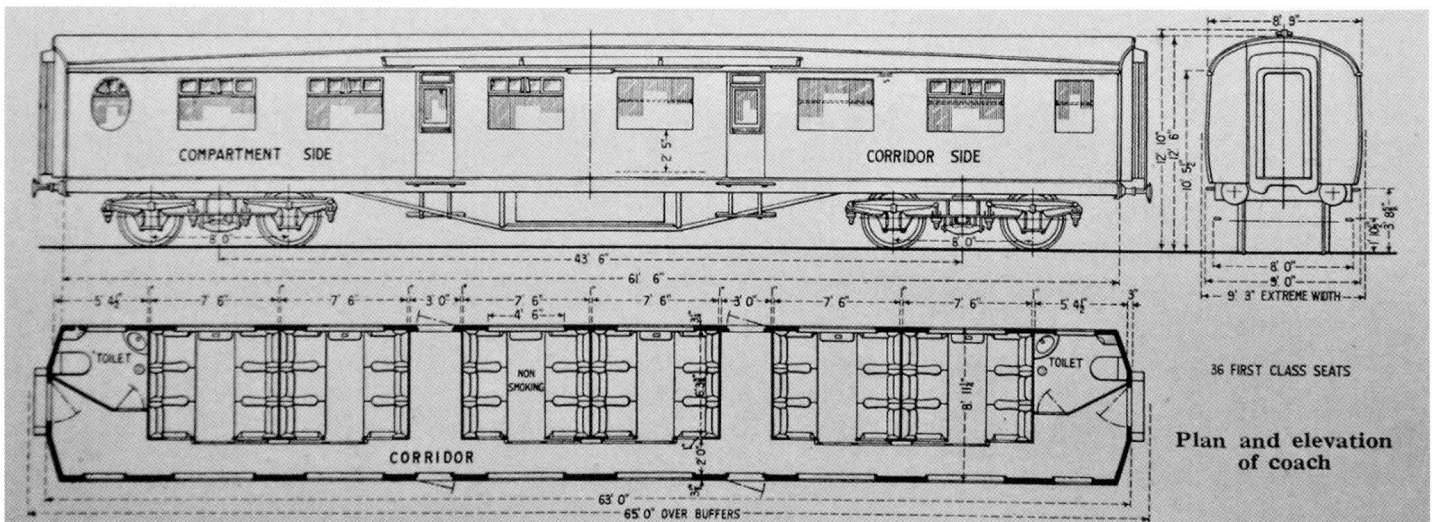

The first of a new breed of carriage on the LNER – a first class corridor coach of steel and timber composite construction. This unit ran for the first time on 11 January 1945. (*PR/RH/DN*)

These new engines were developed by Thompson and Windle in response to a demand from the running department for a modern version of the old Metropolitan Railway K Class. Six of these engines, designed by George Hally and built by Armstrong Whitworth in 1925, were acquired by the LNER in 1937 to supplement its fleet in the London area. In the years that followed, they proved useful in both goods and passenger roles. But by 1943, they were reaching the end of their lives and a replacement was sought. At this stage, eighty Gresley V1s and ten V3 three-cylinder 2-6-2Ts were available, but were deemed insufficient for this task, or so it seems. So, the L1 was the CME's response to this demand, with standardisation of parts a key part of the plan. Shortly after the design was approved, construction of thirty was authorised. Clearly from the number ordered it wasn't simply a replacement for the L2 but was intended to have

wider application across the system as a standard class engine.

The boiler was based on the V3, uprated to a working pressure of 225psi, but fitted with a larger firebox and longer water tanks. Two B1 type cylinders were used, coupled to Walschaerts valve gear and 5ft 2in diameter coupled wheels. In this form, the first engine appeared in April 1945 painted in LNER green livery to reflect the end of the war. Little time was lost in subjecting the locomotive, numbered 9000, to a full dynamometer testing programme. Between September and November an extensive set of trials across the network were held under the control of George Musgrave, the Locomotive Running Superintendent, who had strongly advocated the L1s' construction. To aid analysis, this engine was compared to four other classes – the A5, N1, C1 and C4 – which Musgrave confirmed 'the L1 may replace in service'.

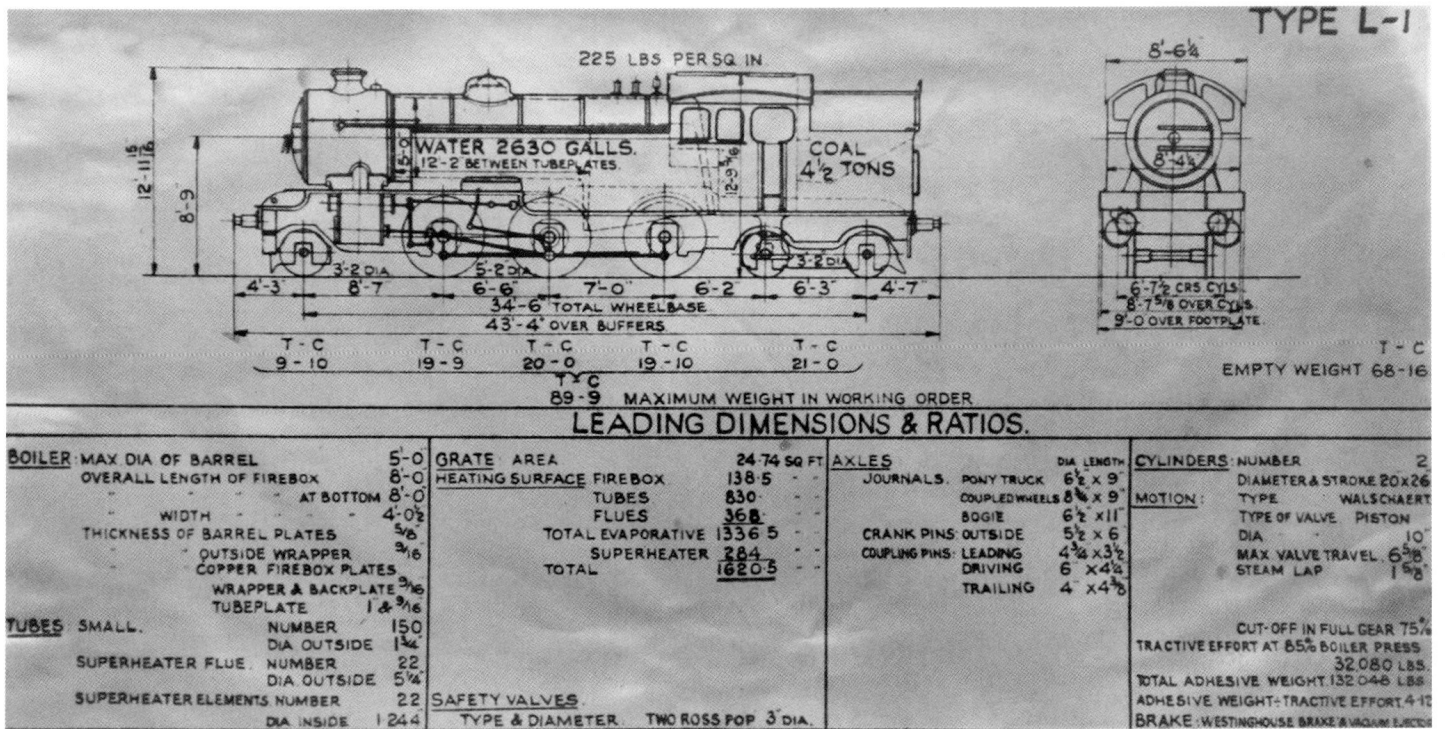

TYPE L-1

225 LBS PER SQ IN

WATER 2630 GALLS. 12-2 BETWEEN TUBEPLATES.

COAL 4½ TONS

3-2 DIA 5-2 DIA 3-2 DIA

4'-3" 8'-7" 6'-6" 7'-0" 6'-2" 6'-3" 4'-7"

34'-6" TOTAL WHEELBASE
43'-4" OVER BUFFERS

8'-6¼" 8'-4¾" 6'-7½" CRS CYLS 8'-7⅝" OVER CYLS 9'-0" OVER FOOTPLATE

T-C 9-10   T-C 19-9   T-C 20-0   T-C 19-10   T-C 21-0   T-C EMPTY WEIGHT 68-16

T-C 89-9 MAXIMUM WEIGHT IN WORKING ORDER

LEADING DIMENSIONS & RATIOS.

BOILER		GRATE AREA	24.74 SQ FT	AXLES	JOURNALS	DIA	LENGTH	CYLINDERS	NUMBER	2
MAX DIA OF BARREL	5-0	HEATING SURFACE FIREBOX	138.5		PONY TRUCK	6½ x 9			DIAMETER & STROKE	20x26
OVERALL LENGTH OF FIREBOX	8-0	TUBES	830		COUPLED WHEELS	8¾ x 9		MOTION	TYPE	WALSCHAERT
" " " AT BOTTOM	8-0	FLUES	368		BOGIE	6½ x 11			TYPE OF VALVE	PISTON
WIDTH	4-0½	TOTAL EVAPORATIVE	1336.5	CRANK PINS OUTSIDE	5½ x 6				DIA	10
THICKNESS OF BARREL PLATES	⅝	SUPERHEATER	284	COUPLING PINS LEADING	4¾ x 3½				MAX VALVE TRAVEL	6⅝
" OUTSIDE WRAPPER	9⁄16	TOTAL	1620.5		DRIVING	6 x 4½			STEAM LAP	1⅝
COPPER FIREBOX PLATES					TRAILING	4 x 4⅜				
WRAPPER & BACKPLATE	9⁄16									
TUBEPLATE	1 & 9⁄16								CUT-OFF IN FULL GEAR 75%	
TUBES SMALL NUMBER	150							TRACTIVE EFFORT AT 85% BOILER PRESS 32,080 LBS		
DIA OUTSIDE	1¾							TOTAL ADHESIVE WEIGHT 132,048 LBS		
SUPERHEATER FLUE NUMBER	22							ADHESIVE WEIGHT ÷ TRACTIVE EFFORT 4.12		
DIA OUTSIDE	5¼							BRAKE: WESTINGHOUSE BRAKE & VACUUM EJECTOR		
SUPERHEATER ELEMENTS NUMBER	22	SAFETY VALVES								
DIA INSIDE	1.244	TYPE & DIAMETER TWO ROSS POP 3" DIA								

An early diagram of the new L1 Class.

The results clearly pleased him and his report is peppered with such comments as 'the engine steamed and ran freely', 'the engine worked all trains with ease and a good reserve of power' and 'the quick acceleration on rising gradients enabled timing at stations to be met with a certain amount of ease'. In the summary he was quite effusive in his praise, with one reservation, the wheel size – he deemed that 5ft 2in was sufficient for freight work, but 5ft 8in would be better when pulling passenger trains. As a result, he recommended that two types of L1 be constructed, but realised that this might prove impractical.

By the time Thompson retired, the prototype L1 had been hailed a success, but it would be another three years before the remaining twenty-nine would emerge from Darlington. These would be followed by another seventy built by North British and Robert Stephenson & Hawthorn between 1948 and 1950. After a hopeful start, the class came in for some criticism during BR years.

Whilst trying to chart a course through the standardisation programme, Thompson had put together, and periodically modified, a simple booklet outlining types of engines that might fill the eleven selected classes. By early 1946, this had begun to take more definite form with the L1's arrival. Luckily, a copy of these proposals has survived, as has the CME's draft paper outlining the programme. Charles Newton took these proposals and issued them without significant amendment on 26 March to the Locomotive Committee for consideration. In conclusion he urged them to accept the plan in a covering minute and 'recommended that this booklet be approved as the official record of the LNER's plans for standardisation, from which departures will be made only on special authority'.

It is difficult to be sure, so long after the event, if agreement on the types to be included was universal. And here three key figures involved in the plan, Peppercorn, Windle and Spencer, remained silent. However, broad approval might be assumed, particularly as Peppercorn continued to issue slightly modified copies until 1949. The only change he injected seeming to be a modified A2 that appeared during his time as CME.

It is a shame that Peppercorn didn't record his memories of this period. In the absence of any word from him, a void was created that has been filled by others using the unreliable art of conjecture. One thing is certain though, Peppercorn was greatly admired by Thompson and it was he who recommended, in mid-1945, that the younger man 'should relinquish the ME Doncaster post and devote his full time to that of the Assistant CME post.

Engine No. 9000 makes her appearance at Doncaster in April 1945. (*ET/DN*)

Engine No. 67714 on duty at Marylebone in 1948 showing her new ownership and the Westinghouse brakes fitted to meet the requirements of the LNER's Eastern Section. (*BR/RH*)

Mr L. Reeves, ME Scotland, should be appointed in his place at Doncaster'. It was a move prompted by two things – Thompson's desire to have his successor in place and concerns over his own health. The burden he had shouldered during the war was immense and he was badly in need of a rest. So now was the time to plan for the future and give Peppercorn breathing space to prepare himself for promotion. It was a proposal with which both Matthews and Newton agreed, recording their thoughts on the matter in several memoranda. Once he was in post Thompson was able to take a break and, in his own words 're-charge my batteries over several weeks'.

At this time the question of awards for exemplary wartime service was being considered and it is notable that Thompson, amongst all the submissions he made, included Peppercorn. The words he used were honest, to the point, most flattering and were quickly endorsed by the Chairman. In due course, an MBE was conferred on the Assistant CME, along with four MBEs and twelve British Empire Medals to other members of Thompson's staff. It is rumoured, but not confirmed,

that Newton wished the CME to be similarly decorated, but Thompson declined to be included, preferring recognition to go to those who worked for him. An apocryphal tale, perhaps, but not out of character if the many accounts of his generosity are anything to go by.

As his time ran down to retirement, two final locomotive projects drew Thompson's interest. The first contributed to the Pacific evolution, whilst the second focussed on the development of a diesel shunter, a programme initiated in 1941 just before Gresley died which then fell to Thompson to complete.

He didn't record his thoughts on the coming of diesels, but as a practical, business orientated man, who didn't appear to be wedded to any particular form of propulsion, he may have been attracted by the promise of greater efficiency and economy. Either way, the development of diesels by the LNER was a muted affair, even by the standards of the age. If anything, company ambitions leant towards electrification and in the two years after the war partially completed projects were revived by Henry Richards with the chairman's backing.

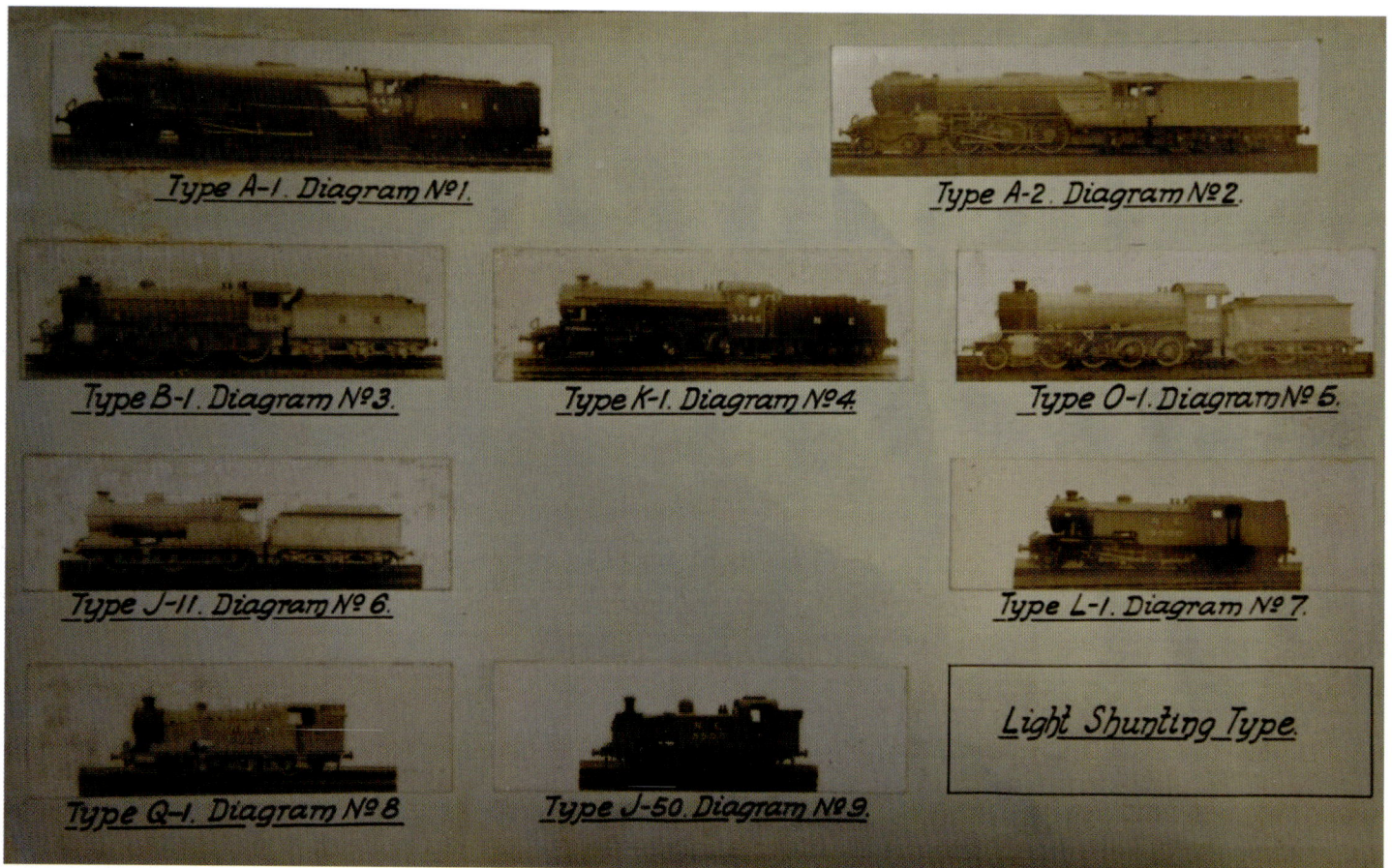

The summary sheet prepared by the CME's team which formed part of the Standardisation Plan that was approved and issued in early 1946, shortly before Thompson's retirement. Although not included in picture form in the booklet it was clear that the A3s, A4s and other Gresley designs, would play a key part in meeting the LNER's future needs. (ET/DN)

On 23 January 1946 one of the CME's longest serving managers, H.A. Butler (left), Traffic Stores Superintendent at Doncaster, retired. Thompson attended the ceremony and gave a brief speech. In it he referred very warmly to Butler and added that 'he had assisted the Company in a way few men had done'. The CME was one to give praise where it was due. With his own retirement only a few months away, the mournful looking CME must have had the future on his mind. Peter Grafton records a conversation between him and his long serving secretary, Ivy Shingler. Seeing a grey wet day through his office window he wondered aloud what one did in retirement on such a day? Without wife or family and without the pressure of work the future may have held few delights for him. (LJ/RH)

The second of the LNER's four Class J45 diesel shunters; later re-designated DES1. All were built at Doncaster in the last two years of the war. (*ET/DN*)

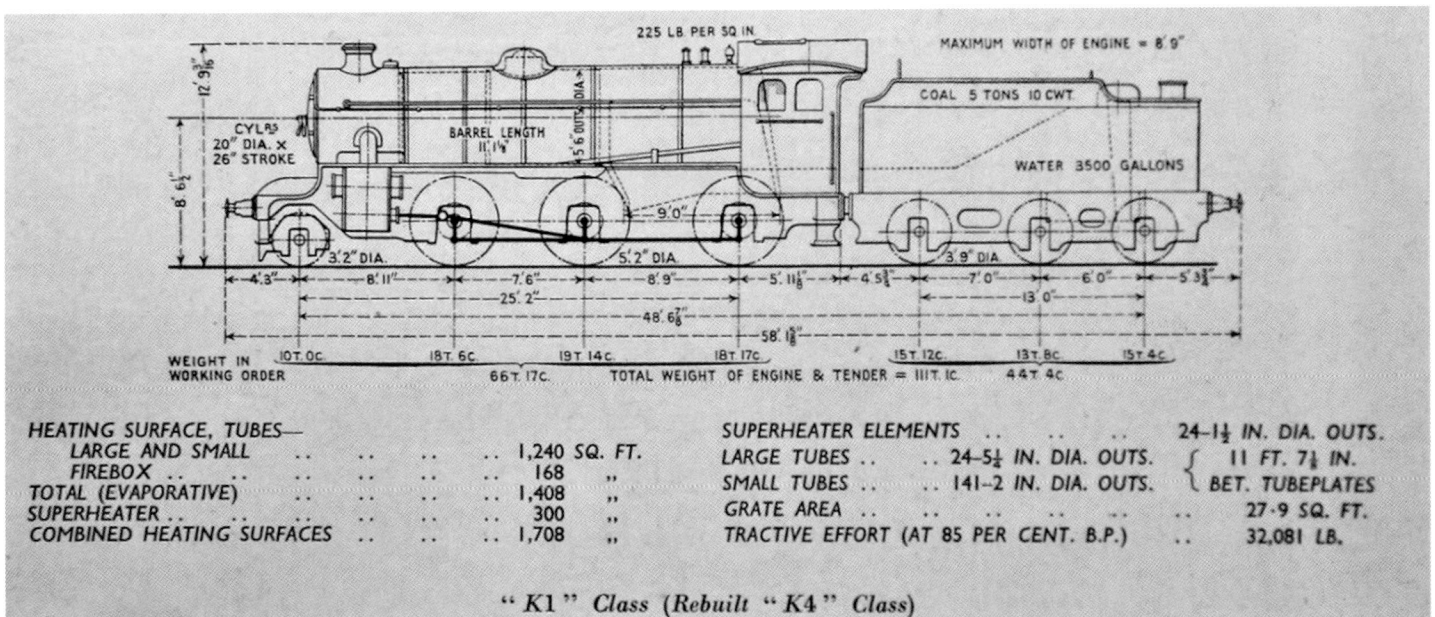

HEATING SURFACE, TUBES—								SUPERHEATER ELEMENTS	..	..	..	24–1½ IN. DIA. OUTS.
LARGE AND SMALL	..	..	..	..	1,240 SQ. FT.			LARGE TUBES ..	.. 24–5½ IN. DIA. OUTS.		{ 11 FT. 7¼ IN.
FIREBOX ..	..	..	..	..	168 ,,			SMALL TUBES ..	.. 141–2 IN. DIA. OUTS.		{ BET. TUBEPLATES
TOTAL (EVAPORATIVE)	..	..	..	..	1,408 ,,			GRATE AREA ..	.. ..		27·9 SQ. FT.
SUPERHEATER ..	..	..	..	..	300 ,,			TRACTIVE EFFORT (AT 85 PER CENT. B.P.)			.. 32,081 LB.
COMBINED HEATING SURFACES	..	..	..	1,708 ,,							

" K1 " Class (Rebuilt " K4 " Class)

Above and overleaf: Experiments on existing classes of engines continued up to Thompson's retirement and afterwards under Peppercorn's guiding hand. Basically they pursued the concept of two-cylinders and standardisation of parts. Perhaps the most significant classes of engines involved are illustrated here. In August 1945 a Gresley K4, engine No. 3445, underwent conversion and re-appeared in its new form as a K1. This was followed a month later by K3, No.206, which when work was completed was re-designated K5. Then, concurrently, there was the re-working of the B17 and their translation into the B2. This rush of work and Thompson's departure allowed him little time to evaluate each development, although the early reports from Musgrave were again fairly positive. It would be left to Peppercorn to consider the benefits and decide whether each rebuilding programme should be continued in the years to come. But here he was soon in the hands of the new BR organisation. All that can be said with any certainty is that when Thompson retired all the projects in which he was involved as CME appeared, for the most part, to be valid and justified.

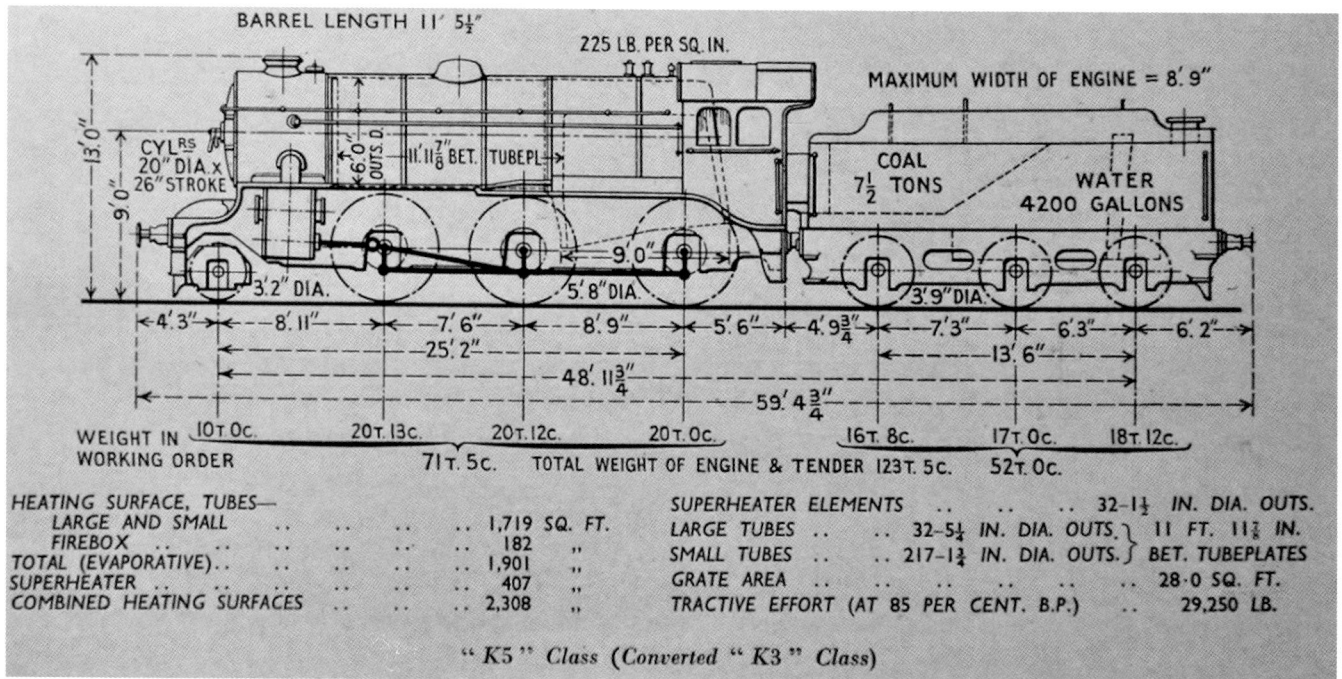

BARREL LENGTH 11' 5½"
225 LB. PER SQ. IN.
MAXIMUM WIDTH OF ENGINE = 8'. 9"

CYLRS 20" DIA. x 26" STROKE
11'. 11⅞" BET. TUBEPL.
COAL 7½ TONS   WATER 4200 GALLONS

3'.2" DIA.   5'. 8"DIA.   3'.9"DIA.

WEIGHT IN WORKING ORDER	10T. 0c.	20T. 13c.	20T. 12c.	20T. 0c.	16T. 8c.	17T. 0c.	18T. 12c.
		71T. 5c.		TOTAL WEIGHT OF ENGINE & TENDER 123T. 5c.		52T. 0c.	

HEATING SURFACE, TUBES—
LARGE AND SMALL .. .. 1,719 SQ. FT.
FIREBOX .. .. 182 "
TOTAL (EVAPORATIVE).. .. .. .. 1,901 "
SUPERHEATER .. .. 407 "
COMBINED HEATING SURFACES .. .. 2,308 "

SUPERHEATER ELEMENTS .. .. .. 32-1¼ IN. DIA. OUTS.
LARGE TUBES .. 32-5¼ IN. DIA. OUTS. ⎫ 11 FT. 11¾ IN.
SMALL TUBES .. 217-1¾ IN. DIA. OUTS. ⎭ BET. TUBEPLATES
GRATE AREA .. .. 28·0 SQ. FT.
TRACTIVE EFFORT (AT 85 PER CENT. B.P.) .. 29,250 LB.

"K5" Class (Converted "K3" Class)

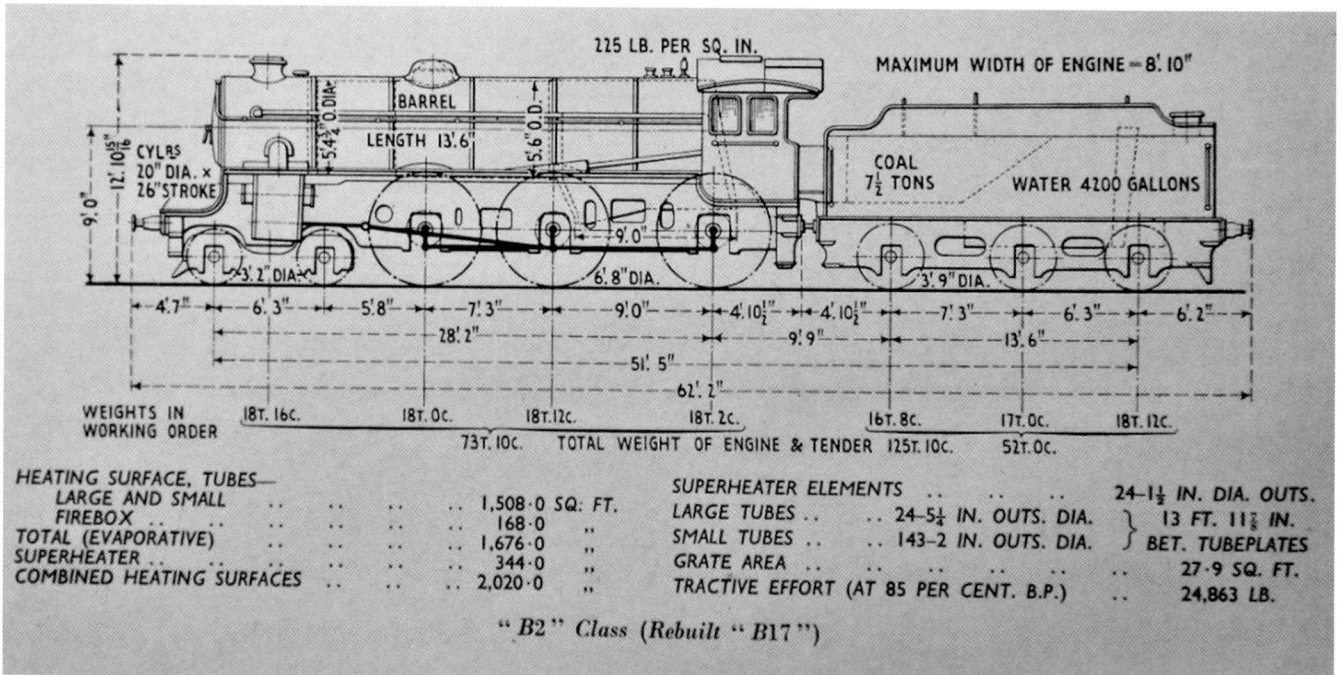

225 LB. PER SQ. IN.
MAXIMUM WIDTH OF ENGINE = 8'. 10"

CYLRS 20" DIA. x 26" STROKE
BARREL LENGTH 13'. 6"
COAL 7½ TONS   WATER 4200 GALLONS

3'. 2" DIA.   6'. 8" DIA.   3'. 9" DIA.

WEIGHTS IN WORKING ORDER	18T. 16c.	18T. 0c.	18T. 12c.	18T. 2c.	16T. 8c.	17T. 0c.	18T. 12c.
		73T. 10c.		TOTAL WEIGHT OF ENGINE & TENDER 125T. 10c.		52T. 0c.	

HEATING SURFACE, TUBES—
LARGE AND SMALL .. .. 1,508·0 SQ. FT.
FIREBOX .. .. 168·0 "
TOTAL (EVAPORATIVE) .. .. 1,676·0 "
SUPERHEATER .. .. 344·0 "
COMBINED HEATING SURFACES .. .. 2,020·0 "

SUPERHEATER ELEMENTS .. .. .. 24-1¼ IN. DIA. OUTS.
LARGE TUBES .. .. 24-5¼ IN. OUTS. DIA. ⎫ 13 FT. 11¾ IN.
SMALL TUBES .. .. 143-2 IN. OUTS. DIA. ⎭ BET. TUBEPLATES
GRATE AREA .. .. 27·9 SQ. FT.
TRACTIVE EFFORT (AT 85 PER CENT. B.P.) .. 24,863 LB.

"B2" Class (Rebuilt "B17")

The development of these diesel locomotives proceeded at a leisurely pace, undoubtedly due to other wartime commitments. It was also a collaborative project between the LNER and English Electric, with the contractors providing the diesel/electric system. Finally, in 1944, the first of four engines appeared at Doncaster with three more added by 1945. They were similar in many ways to engines produced by the LMS, but had a 3in longer wheelbase. Two electric motors were installed, each driving a single axle, which could be disengaged for towing. In addition it had a dual braking system – Westinghouse direct-acting brakes for the locomotive, vacuum for train. Testing proved them to be sound and they were soon allocated to Whitemoor Yard in Cambridgeshire,

FORWARD
THE L·N·E·R DEVELOPMENT PROGRAMME
4ᵈ

ENTERPRISE

As 1946 dawned, the LNER published its 5-year plan to restore the railway after six years of the heaviest wartime use. Perhaps it was simply a 'wish list', but nationalisation 'though on the cards' was far from certain as was the form it might take. There were some who thought that the big four might retain a degree of independence and autonomy. In the meantime, it seemed sensible to pursue their own plans. In this case Thompson's ideas are included verbatim as revealed in these two sample pages. (*THG*)

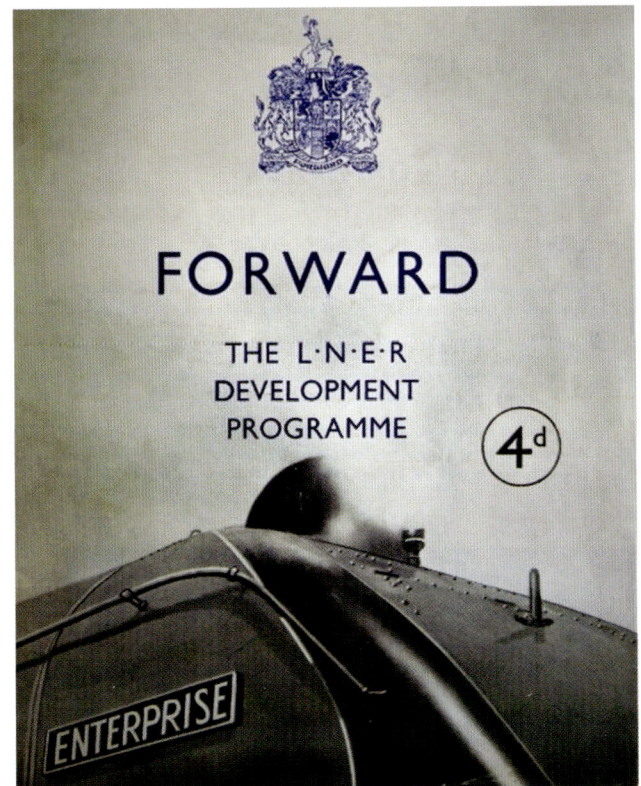

ROLLING STOCK

Here in summary form is our programme :—
THE L·N·E·R FIVE-YEAR PLAN FOR ROLLING STOCK

	To be built by L.N.E.R.	To be built by Contractors.	Total
Locomotives	500	500	1,000
Carriages	2,100	3,400	5,500
Wagons	50,000	20,000	70,000

L.N.E.R. "A.1" 4-6-2 PACIFIC "GREAT NORTHERN" No. 113

LOCOMOTIVES
Immense war-time traffics meant that the scrapping of locomotives had to be postponed, since very few new ones could be built. The fleet of 6,400 engines is to be overhauled and 1,000 old locomotives will be replaced by new machines during the next five years.

STANDARDISATION POLICY
Types are to be simplified ; whilst the engines to be scrapped are of 49 different classes, those to be built will comprise only ten different designs.

L.N.E.R. "A.2" 4-6-2 "PACIFIC" No. 500 "EDWARD THOMPSON"
BUILT 1946 AT DONCASTER WORKS, THE 2,000th ENGINE CONSTRUCTED THERE

The term "standardised" does not mean that design is going to be fettered, or that hard-and-fast rules will be laid down from which there may be no departure. The aim is that a limited number of engine classes shall be able to handle the great bulk of the traffic, and that important components shall be interchangeable within the classes. On the other hand, continuous study and testing will be undertaken to see whether improvements or modifications are required from time to time. Thereby we shall realise the advantages of standardisation without stagnation.

The new standard types include, first of all, two classes of "Pacifics." One will be streamlined for use on the fastest expresses, and will be a modification of the class that already holds the world's speed record for steam traction—126 miles an hour ; the second, such as "Edward Thompson" illustrated on the opposite page, will have rather smaller driving wheels, and will be used for fast passenger work and also fast and heavy freight trains.

HOLDER OF WORLD SPEED RECORD FOR STEAM TRACTION—126 M.P.H.
L.N.E.R. "A.4" 4-6-2 PACIFIC No. 22 "MALLARD"

The next type is a general purpose 4-6-0 locomotive, known as the "Antelope" class, suitable for either passenger or fast freight trains ; no fewer than 400 are included in the programme.

L.N.E.R. "B.1" 4-6-0 No. 1003 "ANTELOPE" CLASS

The first entirely post-war design to appear was the L.1. class mixed-traffic locomotive. One of the class is illustrated on the next page. This engine will undertake passenger and goods services at present handled by a large number of different types of locomotives.

where they would spend most of their lives. In the scheme of things, it was a minor project, but it was one in which the CME is recorded as having taken a close interest. Perhaps he envisaged these types being included as the light shunting engine category of his standardisation plan. His 1946 booklet left a significant gap in this category.

Finally, there was his final exploration of the Pacific concept and his swansong – the Class A2/3 – which had its roots in a proposal to build thirty new stand-ard engines, which was accepted by the Locomotive Committee during 1944. No completion date was set, but as the war drew to a close, the programme came to life and work began in earnest. At the same time, and in accordance with the company's development plan, another thirteen were added to the project with produc-tion set to start in early 1946. With Thompson due to retire in June, it was hoped that the first engine would be ready by then so he could enjoy the fruits of his labours. As things turned out, it entered traffic at Doncaster on 24 May to become the 2,000th engine built at the works.

The specification had a familiar look to it, reflecting the gradual evolution of the class. But despite the changes made, they still bore the distinctive look of Gresley's non-streamlined Pacifics, albeit in a stretched form. There was the boiler producing 250psi and three 19in x 26in cylinders, with the middle unit staggered as before, plus three independent sets of Walschaerts valve gear and 6ft 2in coupled wheels. The new locomotive was also fitted with larger style smoke deflectors, a hopper ashpan, a self-cleaning smokebox, electric lighting and steam brakes. However, the cab was different; the V shape design being dropped in favour of one with a rectangular shaped roof. On first viewing, it seems to have had a more balanced look, though the outside cylinders set back behind the front truck still seem poorly placed to some.

In these last few days of his service, what may have passed through Thompson's mind? Sadly, he doesn't seem to have recorded his thoughts, but they are, perhaps, not hard to divine. Retirement can be a difficult step where pleasure in past achievements can soon be replaced by bleaker thoughts. The step from being lord of all you survey to being a pensioner can be a sobering experience. But in Thompson's case, there may have been some satisfaction in seeing this new locomotive beginning its life; a sense of achieve-ment increased when the first of the class was named *Edward Thompson* in his honour. And with this he quietly departed the scene.

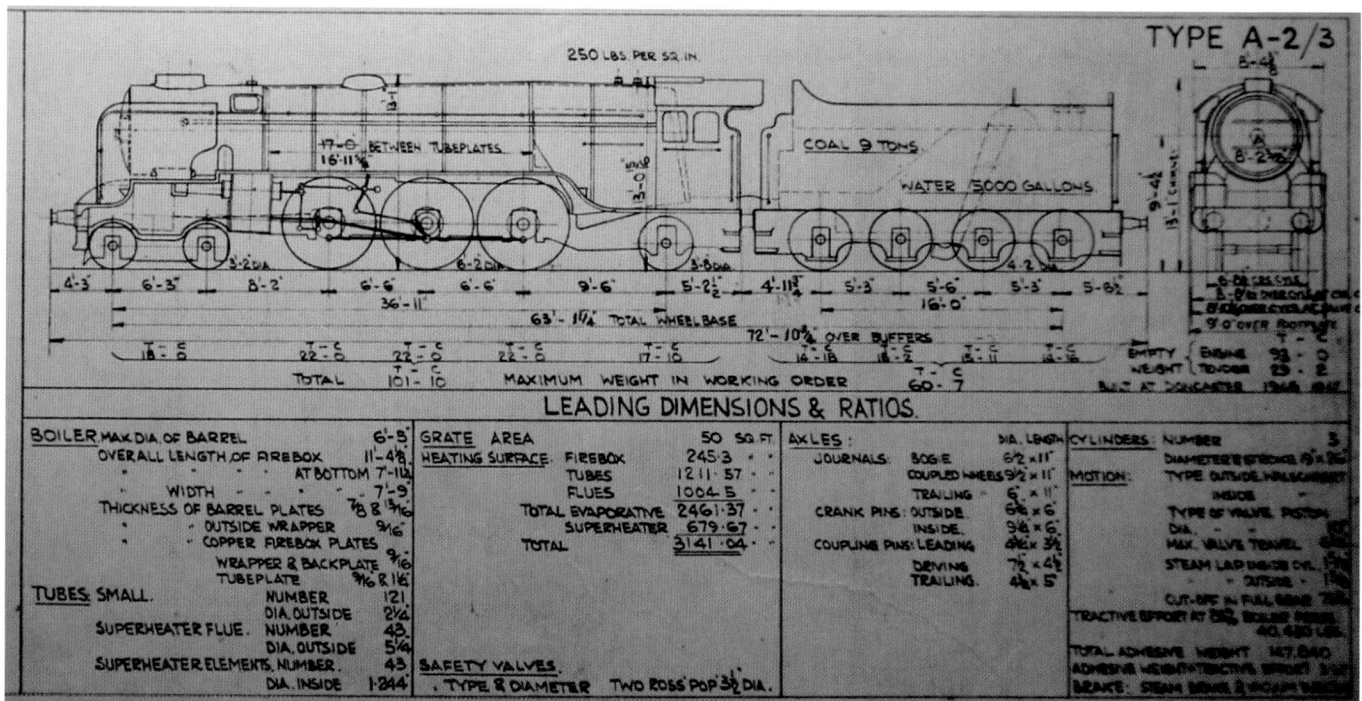

Above: The A2/3's diagram and its dimensions. Opposite above: The second member of the A2/3 Class, later to be named Airborne, has her boiler lifted into the frames at Doncaster in May or June 1946. (ET/DN)

Engine No. 500 works up and down the yard on 24 May 1945. It is reported that Thompson took the controls briefly, though no photograph survives to confirm this. (*ET/DN*)

The engine prepares to back down into Marylebone Station prior to being named on 30 June. (*ET/DN*)

The naming ceremony was led by Sir Ronald Matthews who paid tribute to the retiring CME. Many of the LNER's Board attended as did representatives from his own organisation and the running department. Towards the end of his eulogy Matthews offered a few words to sum up the CME's work. 'That the LNER were able to play their part to the full in the war effort, was due, in large measure to the work of the CME and his staff. In addition to coping with these unprecedented conditions, Mr Thompson found time to design several new types of engine, and to convert certain existing locomotives on improved lines, at the same time establishing a basis for the future standardisation of the locomotive stock of the LNER with a limited number of types. Short as his term of office has been, Mr Thompson has left his mark on the locomotive history of the Company, and it is with this assurance that he is now able to seek his well-earned retirement.' (*LJ/RH*)

Thompson's retirement photograph. It was taken in his office with a picture of his much respected father-in-law prominently displayed in the background. (*PR/RH*)

A career of substance reduced to the barest minimum in the LNER's employment records.

CHAPTER 9

QUIETLY SLIPPING AWAY

In many cases the photos Thompson chose to keep in his archive were not accompanied by a commentary to explain his interest. However, it isn't difficult to understand why he included a particular picture. On the final page of the final album he has carefully added these two photographs. Perhaps he selected them deliberately as a summary of his career or as a reflection of locomotives that interested him. The top picture captures A4 No. 4486, *Merlin*, now numbered 27 in accordance with a system introduced during 1946, at Doncaster. The lower picture portrays one of his A2/3s, in this case No. 517, *Ocean Swell*, which appeared in November 1946, a few months after his retirement. (*ET/DN*)

The end of a working life can mean the end of life itself for some. Never again to feel the pull of responsibility or the challenge of great events can be diminishing, leaving a person barren and rudderless. If it is hard for the common man to adjust and find a new purpose it may be even worse for the uncommon man, for this is what Edward Thompson was. Even if he had had a family to surround him or another absorbing task, it would have been bad enough, but he had neither to distract him. Work, for good or ill, had been the focus of his life and the void retirement left was difficult to fill.

As the war came to an end, he had bought a house in Bexhill-on-Sea, Kent, and made this a base from which to potter. He maintained his membership of IMechE, the MCC and the Oxford and Cambridge University Club in Pall Mall, and is recorded as being a regular attendee at each of them. He seems to have been present at a number of lectures by members of IMechE, but appears to have made no comments on their findings or felt the need to research or present papers himself. But this had been his habit for many years. It is possible, of course, that it was the Institution's extensive library that was the true draw, coupled to the company of old colleagues and friends, of which William Stanier was one. A friendship had grown over the years between them in which, amongst other things, they had congratulated each other on new locomotives – most notably Stanier's Black 5s and Thompson's B1 – and other achievements. They would, in fact, meet very publicly on one important occasion in the years after the war.

CMEs old and new (Peppercorn, Bulleid, Thompson and Stanier) line up for the camera on the day the Rugby Test Centre was formally opened. A4 *Sir Nigel Gresley* was run on the rolling road, whilst Princess Coronation *Sir William A. Stanier F.R.S.* was also in attendance. (*ET/DN*)

Gresley had been chief advocate, since 1927, of the need for a locomotive testing station. In this he was keenly supported by Stanier. Construction work was well underway when war was declared, but was then held in abeyance only reaching a successful conclusion in 1948. Its formal opening on 19 October that year was attended by Stanier, Thompson, Bulleid and Peppercorn amongst others and together they witnessed A4 pacific, *Sir Nigel Gresley*, undergo a test run on the facility's rolling road.

Apart from this it seems that Thompson didn't involve himself too closely in railway business, though he did visit his old stamping ground at Doncaster occasionally and attended Peppercorn's retirement celebrations there at the end of 1949. A year later he viewed one of his B1s, No.61353, on test at Rugby, his only engine to pass through the facility. He later received a personal copy of the report from the test centre's Superintending Engineer, Dennis Carling, an ex-Cambridge and LNER man, who for the duration of the war had served with the Admiralty. In 1945, he had been gathered in by Thompson, as had many hundreds of other people when their wartime duties came to an end, and remained with the company until succeeding D.W. Sanford at Rugby in 1948.

Apart from the B1 and the A4, the only other LNER engine to be tested was a Gresley poppet valved D49, but by then there was probably very little that such testing would reveal about such well-established locomotives.

It is reported that he also took a passing interest in BR's developing locomotive programme as implemented by Robert Riddles, the new organisation's CME. If so he would have found the plans for a new fleet of standard engines, and a preponderance of two-cylinder types, of great interest. In many ways, this mirrored his own ideas and the

60007 is positioned on the rolling road before a trial run. Meanwhile the 'works' are being carefully inspected by a group of engineers. Thompson, it appears, sat on the fireman's seat in the cab observing all that went on. Afterwards Stanier and he travelled together from Rugby to Euston, according to a letter the LMS man later sent to his old colleague. (*ET/DN*)

changes he had tried to implement during the war. It is impossible to say whether his work influenced BR in any way, but Edward Windle did play a part in this new programme as part of the Standard Locomotive Design Team led by Ernest Cox. So some latter-day LNER influence may have been exerted as BR's programme reached fruition.

By 1950, it seems that Thompson had decided to settle his affairs, possibly due to deteriorating health, but also a desire to help his sister Margaret. She had been widowed in 1944, when her husband, Henry, died whilst staying at the Cliffe Hotel in Cleveden, leaving an estate of barely £540. So his solicitor, Thomas Butler, drafted a new will in December 1949 to take account of Thompson's changing wishes. With this in place, he also took steps to give away, as gifts, much of his not insubstantial estate to those close to him, leaving himself minimal assets and a pension on which to live. To achieve this, he moved from 61 Westgate Bay Avenue to a rented apartment a few doors away at number 23. It was as if he was planning the end of his life so as to minimise the impact on others. In some ways, this reflected his experience as a soldier, where, in time of conflict when death was commonplace, it was usual for a dead comrade's kit to be packed up quickly with minimum fuss. He planned his funeral in the same way, 'I wish to have a Church of England service but I do not wish any friends or relatives to be present', he wrote in his will. He added no other details, but one assumes he may have expressed other preferences to his friends or relatives – cremation, no memorials and where to scatter his ashes. In this his approach was similar to his much admired father-in-law.

A cheerful and relaxed Edward Thompson returns to Doncaster to help celebrate Arthur Peppercorn's retirement in late 1949. It is thought that the lady in the centre, being plied with a drink by the CME, is Thompson's secretary, Ivy Shingler. She, it seems, remained in post until Peppercorn left the service. The second woman in the group is possibly Mrs Peppercorn (the CME's second wife). To her right is John Harrison, Assistant CME, and next in line is Luther Reeves, who Thompson appointed Mechanical Engineer Doncaster when Peppercorn became Assistant CME on a full time basis in 1945. (DN)

A Thompson B1 in repose awaiting a call for action, her fireman enjoying a short rest before the hard work begins. This engine appeared in April 1947 and lasted until February 1964, being cut up a month later at Doncaster Works. (*THG*)

As things turned out, his life still had a few more years to run and during this time his friendship with the Hall family deepened, and he spent more and more time at their home in North Wales. And it was here that he passed away during the night of 14 July 1954, having suffered from severe chest pains for some time.

In those days, treatment to counteract a coronary thrombosis was rudimentary to say the least, with rest being the only real option available. In such circumstances, the course of this illness is unlikely to be checked and have only one result. On his death certificate, the notes from the attending doctor, E.J.S. Evans, confirmed that he had had a massive heart attack. He added the words 'coronary atheroma', which denoted enlarged arteries caused by the build-up of plaque over a considerable period of time. So it is likely that Thompson had suffered from angina or chest pains for many years.

A day later, Maurice Hall registered his death in nearby Wrexham, notified the surviving members of Thompson's family and arranged the cremation for the 17th in the form Thompson had requested. He was survived by one sister, Katherine, Margaret having outlived her husband by only a few years, plus nephews and a niece. It was through them that a private notice appeared in *The Times*, plus a short obituary. Unlike Gresley and Stanier, he wasn't a public figure and was little known outside railway circles for that reason, so his death attracted little attention, which would probably have suited such a private man.

When probate was granted on his will in November 1954, leaving an estate valued at £721 after tax and expenses were subtracted, his success in distributing the bulk of his assets in advance was only too clear. All that remained would pass to his surviving sister, with some bequeaths to Maurice and Lillian Hall, in recognition of their friendship and help given so willingly over many years. With that, all signs of this singular man swiftly disappeared leaving barely a ripple.

The words written at his time of his death were respectful, praiseworthy and marked his not inconsiderable achievements. But as time passed, his reputation was slowly dismantled by a number of authors. In many cases, they appear not to have known him personally and scrutinised every aspect of his life and work, laying bare his apparent faults and transgressions without mercy. It was in many ways a one-sided debate, conducted unsympathetically and often without balance. By degrees, the demonization that would

In time, A1/1 *Great Northern* would be re-numbered 60113 by BR and remain in service until November 1962. (*THG*)

blight his memory became firmly established in the psyche of many. Later on, other views and opinions came to light and these allowed Peter Grafton to produce a much more balanced account of his life. But still there appeared to be gaps in his story that might help explain many things that have clung resolutely to his memory.

For example, his service in the Great War and the profound effect this had on his life and personality have barely been revealed. Yet for a whole generation this was the defining moment of their lives and often deepened or warped their personalities. Likewise, his work as a production engineer of great note is forgotten in the rush to debate locomotive design, as though this was the sole purpose of a Chief Mechanical Engineer in a railway company. Both roles are crucial to any organisation, but it was often the less glamorous engineering tasks that produced greater benefits for a business. As the Second World War proved, design and production are equally important and it was here that Thompson found his true calling, guiding his department through a time of unbelievable difficulty and change.

In some ways, he was his own worst enemy and, unknowingly perhaps, provided ammunition for his detractors to use. He didn't suffer fools gladly and could be blunt to the point of rudeness when a degree of diplomacy might have proved more beneficial. But equally, he gave his full support to those he trusted and those with true skill. He also gave praise where it was due and offered support to those in need with understanding and compassion. Equally, when the need to be ruthless arose, which is unavoidable at senior rank, he did so with a clear purpose in mind and without cruelty, despite what was later written. However, it is clear that he would never have won a popularity contest, but there again those who seek popularity rarely, if ever, lead effectively. Some, like Gresley, achieved a better balance but he was blessed with a more outward-going personality than Thompson, but even he could be ruthless and cutting when the need arose.

What of the perceived clash between the two CMEs? Much, probably too much, has been made of their differences, undoubtedly because it underpins later criticism of Thompson's actions. The long established argument would have us believe that the rebuilding of Gresley's A1 and P2s was an act of revenge carried out by a petty minded man out of spite! This fire was then stoked by layers of 'evidence' being added to prove the point.

Yet in Thompson's own words 'Gresley was the greatest British locomotive engineer since Churchward' and in such unequivocal praise of a supposed adversary the truth probably lies. He recognised only too well Gresley's strengths as a design engineer, but also recognised his singleness of mind which, at times, made him pursue one solution to the exclusion of other possibilities; in this case the conjugated valve gear. Thompson, or so it seems, found this frustrating, whether it be in carriage design or when the 2-to-1 gear began showing extreme signs of wear. But any attempt to suggest alternatives seem to have been rebuffed. For an engineer as highly qualified and as experienced as Thompson, this must have been wearisome, especially when it is the role of a good deputy to raise these issues and suggest alternative courses of action. In this situation it seems that it was only the diplomatic and skilled Bert Spencer who ever achieved this to any great extent with Gresley.

We will never know the complete truth about the relationship between Gresley and Thompson and in this void speculation and conjecture have taken root. If each man did harbour misgivings about the other, the true reasons for this are lost to time. It may simply have been that they were both strong, ambitious, ruthless men, who saw in each other some threat to their position, which led to resentment. If this is the case, Thompson still greatly admired Gresley and was prepared to praise him for his achievements. The feeling may have been reciprocated, as witnessed by Thompson's gradual promotion, but Gresley didn't live long enough to express a clearer view either way. But is there any justification for thinking that Thompson's acts, when becoming CME, were about anything other than a desire to improve the breed?

It seems to me that there were few CMEs who didn't take their predecessors' work, rebuild it and seek improvements with varying degrees of success. Stanier, Bulleid and Gresley, amongst others, were not averse to doing so and did it without apparent criticisms then or now. So why should Thompson suffer such vilification for following a similar path? Here you inevitably come back to his work on the A1 and P2 to find the reason. These were two of Gresley's finest designs, are revered to this day – faults and all – and Thompson had the temerity and arrogance to rebuild them into something that was inferior, or so it is believed. All well and good but this argument fails on many levels, not least of all the nature of business and the diverse, often complex

A P2 to A2/2 conversion under BR ownership in a scene that encapsulates Britain at that time. 60506 would survive in service until April 1961. (*DN*)

elements that come into play when any decision is made. Rarely, if ever, is one manager solely responsible for anything that happens, although collective guilt might soon be passed on to a scapegoat. Above and around Thompson were men of substance who wielded considerably more power than he did.

In the highly pressured situation created by war, Thompson was obliged to act on serious concerns raised by Charles Newton and his influential Regional General Managers about locomotive availability, safety, maintenance and suitability. If the motive power fleet couldn't be moulded and run effectively, then the LNER could not discharge its responsibilities at a critical time. And their particular concerns fell on the P2 and the tired, underpowered A1/A10s, plus the increasing problems experienced by Gresley's engines fitted with the 2-to-1 gear. No matter what Thompson may have said in their defence, and in the P2s' case there may have been a suggestion that they be moved south of the border where conditions might have suited them better, the running department's needs would come first. They wanted change and asserted their rights, no matter what the CME's feelings on the matter were. It is little

wonder that his temper could often be short and his manner eccentric. Such are the effects of severe stress, especially for someone for whom mental wellbeing had been sacrificed by service in the Great War.

Such was the quality of the man that he survived, brought in change and managed his department and company expectations in very difficult circumstances. At the same time, he still had the presence of mind to plan for the future. Bearing all this in mind, I think it true to say that few others might have managed so effectively. But this isn't to say that he was a design engineer of great skill, certainly nowhere near the calibre of Gresley. However, Gresley was not as good a production engineer as Thompson, hence the assertion that together they were an effective team.

Bert Spencer probably got closest to the truth when he wrote:

'He [Thompson] always had the good of the department at heart and could be ruthless in the execution of his duties when necessary. But there was another side to him which was considerate and accommodating. He appeared to think deeply about the future and

Thompson's A2/1 No.507, *Highland Chieftain*, picks up water from the troughs (possibly near Stevenage). She appears to be making light work of a long heavy train, judging by the lack of exhaust and her safety valves lifting. (*ET/DN*)

Another Gresley conversion – a K3 becomes a two-cylinder K5 in June 1945. (*PR/RH*)

introduced many changes to improve productivity and working conditions. These were aspects to which Sir Nigel and Bulleid gave little attention, preferring questions of locomotive design to the day to day tasks undertaken in the workshops. Thompson was a good forward-thinking manager and a good workshop manager. However, he was also an average, well intentioned engineer who relied upon Windle, in particular, for guidance when it came to locomotive design. The part played by Windle has been underestimated, as was his role in BR's standardisation plans.'

Spencer was probably right when it came to the relationship between Thompson and Windle, with the assumption it contains that the CME was the prime mover in the rebuilding programme, but not the architect. The truth may well be that Thompson outlined a programme and specification and his Chief Draughtsman did the rest. This was after all a fairly common practice then. For example, on the LMS, the CDs, Herbert Chambers and Tom Coleman, forged schemes which Stanier simply guided and approved, not being a noted designer himself. As head he took the credit and the criticism, but the true work probably lay in other hands.

In bringing this story to an end, I looked for words to sum up such a complex man and the way history has treated him. It is a difficult task and eventually I fell back on Richard Hardy's reminiscences. He was an educated man of honour and substance, but he also reached senior rank and this gave him greater insight into many matters. He was fair and honest in his assessments and had the judgement necessary to give them weight. It is true that Thompson and he clearly had a rapport, despite their differences in age and status at the time, but this didn't blind him to any faults. Towards the end

In assessing Thompson's career it is easy to forget the huge staff management task that fell on his shoulders at a time of great social upheaval. This was nowhere more apparent than in the employment of women, the ever increasing demand for improved employment rights and conditions, and better pay. Some found it hard to drop their staid Victorian values and embrace the future. They would try and hold an impossible line and found themselves in costly and tortuous disputes as a result. Thompson recognised that change was necessary and embraced it. And it was in his attitude to women industrial workers that this is most apparent. He welcomed them into the workplace and protected their rights. The two wars saw substantial numbers of women employed by the LNER, but with peace their numbers declined as men returned 'from the Front' to take up their old jobs. Nevertheless, Thompson ensured as many as possible were retained in his department and celebrated their massive contribution. This is one of a number of photos published at the end of the war to which Thompson added a brief commentary for publication. He ended with the words, which were taken from a memo he wrote, 'Goodbye to you ladies, and good luck go with you. You have done a good job of work and you leave the service of the LNER with the knowledge that you have been of invaluable assistance to the country's war effort and your work has been appreciated by the Company. Many of you have tackled jobs which only men did before the war, and you have succeeded splendidly. You will long be remembered.' (*LJ/RH*)

of his life, Richard pondered the life and career of his former leader and wrote in a letter:

'Choose to remember him as a man of dignity, charm and kindness. He was not petty-minded. He may have been obstinate at times but so was Gresley, for they were both powerful men who thought they were right and they were none the worse for that. He could fly into a rage, so they say, but so could many others and did.

'Thompson's engineering ability has been questioned; maybe he was a better administrator than an engineer, but so were many other great names of the past and there is no shame in this so long as you could pick good subordinates, which Thompson did.

'What of Thompson's engines? I can only speak as I find and if folk had confined themselves to this line of country, a different story may have been written. I did not have dealings with his "Pacifics" on the job but I did see No. 4470, when rebuilt, on one occasion

at Marylebone before she was inspected by the LNER board. Thompson was standing by the cab chatting to Driver Bill Andrews of Neasden who I accompanied for many miles when he was firing. Cheerful and forthright as ever, he proceeded to introduce me to the CME as "One of us". Not by a bat of the eyelid did Mr Thompson let on but the fact that I already knew the driver pleased him no end. I was invited into the cab and spent half an hour with the three men. Thompson was completely at ease and so were the rest of us. And that was the last time I saw him, although he wrote to me for several years.

'His engines were built in difficult circumstances. He had followed a great engineer who had been a legend, in a period in which the country was fighting for its very existence. His rebuild of the P2 was criticised much later, but folk tend to forget that the original engines left a lot to be desired, spending their war in Scotland when they ought to have been shouldering enormous loads on the East Coast.

This Gresley K4 became Thompson's two-cylinder K1/1 in 1945. When he was promoted to CME Peppercorn continued developing the concept and oversaw the production of 69 more. Engine No. 1997 became 61997 and remained in service until 1961. (*ET/DN*)

'The rebuilt B17s did not improve matters and if anything, the B2s became rougher than the original engines if that were possible. Then we come to the B1s, which when handled properly could match a Stanier Black 5 any day – they were lighter on coal and water, fast and free for steam and easier to maintain. The B1 was a remarkable engine, let us not forget.

'The L1s were far from perfect but we had no hesitation in putting one on a London "fast" from Ipswich on a Sunday when the regular engine was being washed out. They hauled nine or ten coaches to Liverpool Street on a tank of water, which was good work, but then they were driven properly with wide open regulator and short cut off.

'The K1s? They were marvellous little engines which did great work, even when they were rough. The J11 rebuild? A brilliant engine was the old "Pom" and the rebuild was that much better. When it came to the O4 to O1 rebuilds there was no greater admirer of the old GC O4 than me, but I have to say that the O1 ensured that the Annesley-Woodford "runners" became the fastest most punctual loose coupled freight service in the country. They were marvellous machines with a good turn of speed. The K5 was every bit as good as the K3 on the road and much more straightforward to maintain. We detested the 2-to-1 valve gear and the inaccessible middle valve but the K3s as built by Gresley did a great job on the road.

'Five hard years, hellish wartime conditions, a good understanding of what was required for the present and the future, some really good engines, some "also rans", a principled chief, a man of integrity and courage, remote perhaps but respected throughout his huge department, which covered so many facets of engineering. So now let Edward Thompson rest in peace, for he did his job.'

There is little doubt that Edward Thompson remains a controversial figure in railway history, yet at the time of his retirement, his work and contribution were respected by many. But at that stage few, if any, of 'his' locomotives had been tested and compared with other designs to any great extent. This would come when Peppercorn and then BR were in charge of these things.

A silk covered card Thompson sent to his wife in 1918. The motto was used by a number of regiments and has several translations, the most common being 'Evil be to him who evil thinks'. However, the Royal Engineers are better known for 'Everywhere and where right and glory lead'. Having observed Thompson's life in some detail it seems to me that these were words he aspired to, but like all of us being noble all the time is a very difficult proposition. On balance I believe he got very close and lived a life of substance and achievement. (*ET/DN*)

REFERENCES AND SOURCES

The National Railway Museum (Search Engine)
Records Consulted
Corr/LNER/1 to 6.
Calc/LNER/1.
Loco/LNER/1 to 9.
Spec/Don/7.
Spec/LNER/1 to 7.
Test/LNER/1 to 10.
The E.S. Cox Collection.
The R. Riddles Collection (donated by author).
The Immingham Collection (donated by author).
The E. Thompson Collection.

Other Collections
The Imperial War Museum library.
The Churchill Archive in Cambridge.
Museum of Science and Industry, Manchester.
Science Museum, London.
Institution of Mechanical Engineers, London.
R.A. Hillier.
D. Neal.
T.F. Coleman/M. Lemon.
B. Spencer.
R.A. Thom.
N. Newsome.
R.H.N. Hardy.
A. Ewer.
Paget Archive.

Books and Other Publications
Allen and Bursely, *Heat Engines,* McGraw-Hill 1941.
Bannister, E., *Trained By Sir Nigel Gresley,* Dalesman 1984.
Bond, R., *A Lifetime With Locomotives,* Goose and Son 1975.
Brown, E.A.S., *Nigel Gresley. Locomotive Engineer,* Ian Allan 1961.
Bulleid, H.A.V., *Bulleid of the Southern,* Littlehampton 1977.
Bulleid, H.A.V., *Master Builders of Steam,* Ian Allan 1963.
Bush, D.J., *The Streamlined Decade,* Brazillier 1975.

Cloete, Stuart, *A Victorian Son,* J. Day and Co 1972.
Coster, P., *Book of the A3 Pacifics,* Irwell 2003.
Coster, P., *Book of the A4 Pacifics,* Irwell 2005.
Coster, P., *Book of the V2 2-6-2s,* Irwell 2008.
Cox, E.S., *Chronicles of Locomotives,* Ian Allan 1967.
Cox, E.S., *Locomotive Panorama Vols 1 and 2,* Ian Allan 1965/66.
Cox, E.S., *Speaking of Steam,* Ian Allan 1971.
Culpin, M., *Psychoneurosis of War and Peace,* Cambridge 1920.
Dalby, W.E., *British Railways: Some Facts and A Few Problems,* IMechE 1910.
Dalby, W.E., *The Balancing of Engines,* Forgotten Books 1920.
Gazette various dates.
Gibbs, Philip, *Realities of War,* Heinemann 1920.
Grafton, P., *Edward Thompson of the LNER,* Kestrel/Oakwood 1971 & 2007.
Hardy, R.H.N., *Steam in the Blood,* Ian Allan 1971.
Haresnape, B., *Gresley's Locomotives,* Ian Allan 1981.
Holcroft, H., *Locomotive Adventure Vols 1 and 2,* Ian Allan 1962.
Hughes, Geoffrey, *Sir Nigel Gresley,* Oakwood 2001.
IMechE/ILocoE *Journals*
McManners, H., *The Scars of War,* London 1993.
Meccano Magazine
Nock, O.S., *Locomotives of Sir Nigel Gresley,* Railway Publishing Co 1945.
Pope, A., *Wind Tunnel Testing,* Wiley 1947.
RCTS *Locomotives of the LNER – Vols 2A & 6B,* RCTS 1973 & 1983.
Rogers, H.C.B., *The Last Steam Locomotive Engineer,* Allen and Unwin 1970.
Rogers, H.C.B., *Thompson & Peppercorn. Locomotive Engineers,* Ian Allan 1979.
Ross, T.A., *The Common Neuroses,* London 1923.
Sheppard, Ben, *A War of Nerves,* Jonathan Cape 2000.
Simmons, J., *The Victorian Railway,* Thames and Hudson 1995.
Steam World
The Engineer

Townend, P.N., *East Coast Pacifics at Work,* Littlehampton 1982.

Yeadon, W.B., *Yeadon's Registers – Nos 1,2,3,4,5,8,9,10 and 25,* BLR – various dates.

Photographic Sources/Credits

B. Spencer (BS), R. Hillier (RH), T. Coleman (TC/ML), Author (THG), H.A.V. Bulleid (HB), LNER *Journal* (LJ), LNER PR (PR), A. Ewer (AE), R. Thom (RT), D. Neal (DN), N. Newsome (NN), E. Thompson (ET) and BR PR (BR).

Copyright is a complex issue and often difficult to establish, especially when a photograph or document exists in a number of public and private collections. Strenuous efforts have been made to ensure each item is correctly attributed, but no process is flawless, especially when many of these items are more than 70 years old with photographers or authors long gone. If an error has been made, it was unintentional. If any reader wishes to affirm copyright, please contact the publishers and an acknowledgement will be included in any future edition of this book, should a claim be proven. We apologise in advance for any mistakes. A number of documents held by the NRM have been quoted in this book. My thanks to the museum for permission to do this.

INDEX